Aesthetics a

AESTHETICS AND MUSIC

ANDY HAMILTON

continuum

Continuum International Publishing Group

The Tower Building
11 York Road
London SE1 7NX

80 Maiden Lane
Suite 704
New York NY 10038

www.continuumbooks.com

British Library Cataloguing-in-Publication Data
A catalogue record for this book is available from the British Library.

ISBN 9780826485199 (Paperback)

Library of Congress Cataloguing-in-Publication Data
A catalogue record for this book is available from the Library of Congress.

Typeset by BookEns Ltd, Royston, Herts.
Printed and bound in Great Britain

CONTENTS

List of illustrations   vii

Introduction   1

1 Aesthetics and Music in Ancient Greece   10

   Music and *mousikē*, art and *technē*   11
   The Pythagorean and Platonic–Pythagorean   19
   mathematical conception
   The ethical conception, and Plato's more empirically-   26
   minded successors Aristotle and Aristoxenus
   The separation of the value spheres   29
   Medieval and Renaissance musical thought   32

2 The Concept of Music   40

   The possibility of non-musical aural or sound-art   40
   The concept of music   46
   Sounds, tones and sound-art   59

3 The Aesthetics of Form, the Aesthetics of Expression,   66
   and 'Absolute Music': aesthetics of music in the late
   eighteenth and nineteenth centuries

   The Romantic metaphysics of music   67
   Kant and formalism   70
   Hegel: historicism and truth-content   72
   Schopenhauer and Wagner: absolute music   76
   Nietzsche: the Apollonian and the Dionysian   78
   Hanslick and formalism   81
   Expression, form and absolute music   82

v

CONTENTS

4 The Sound of Music 95

The acousmatic experience of sound 96
Pythagoras and *musique concrète* 98
A broader definition of 'acousmatic' 101
Objections to the acousmatic thesis 103
The twofold thesis 108
A humanistic conception of music versus more 111
abstract conceptions

5 Rhythm and Time 119

Music as an art of time 120
The universality of rhythm 122
A Platonic, organic definition 127
Rhythm and metre 130
Rhythm and accent 137
Rhythm and movement 142

6 Adorno and Modernism: music as autonomous and 153
'social fact'

The advent of modernism 153
Adorno's aesthetics of modernism 158
Adorno and Kant: art as autonomous and purposeless 160
Adorno and Hegel: dialectic, historicism and 163
truth-content
Adorno and Marx: art as commodity or social fact 166
The culture industry 171
Music of the avant-garde: Adorno's limited grounds 174
for optimism
Dialectics and the autonomy of art 179

7 Improvisation and Composition 192

The aesthetics of perfection and imperfection 193
The concept of improvisation and 'improvised feel' 199
Spontaneity and the aesthetics of perfection 204
Free improvisers, interpreters and 'improvisation as a 207
compositional method'

Bibliography 218

Index 235

vi

ILLUSTRATIONS

1. *Kithara*, principal musical instrument of Ancient Greece. 12
2. *Aulos*, principal musical instrument of Ancient Greece. 12
3. *Kitharōdos* 14
4. Symposium scenes 15
5. Vibrating strings and the Pythagorean discovery. 22
6. Boethius discussing music with Pythagoras, Plato and 33
   Nichomachus.
7. 'Seed' by Eric Egan – a contemporary graphic score. 36
8. The American sloth singing the hexachord. 50
9. Birds and their songs. 51
10. Tropaire de Saint-Martial de Limoges. 123
11. Metre and rhythm. 131
12. 'Jig Piano' (2004–5) by Philip Clark. 132
13. 'Signal Failure' (1991–5) by Martyn Harry. 134
14. 'Thelonious Dreaming' (1990) by Philip Clark. 139
15. Rests that make a rhythmic contribution. 140
16. 'Composition's Finished?' (2006) by Philip Clark. 198
17. Steve Lacy's improvisation on Thelonious Monk's 208
    Misterioso.

To my mother, and in memory of my father

'One of two things is usually lacking in what we call philosophy of art: either the philosophy or the art'
(Schlegel)

INTRODUCTION

AESTHETICS

The most concise answer to the question 'what is aesthetics?' is that it is the philosophy of art and beauty – a subdivision of philosophy that deals with fundamental questions about the arts which the arts themselves are not able to answer, or are not entirely able to answer. (The definition needs developing to include the aesthetics of nature and everyday artefacts.) However, it is not quite right to say that aesthetics is simply a sub-discipline of philosophy, like ethics, metaphysics, epistemology, philosophy of mind and philosophy of science. I think that it has a broader remit, and that writers in aesthetics should bring to bear as much critical awareness and practical knowledge of the arts as possible.

At the same time, I believe, aesthetic experience is essentially democratic. 'Aesthetic' is a semi-technical term – like, for instance, 'self-consciousness' and even, perhaps, 'perception' – which has come to denote a philosophical sub-discipline. But although 'aesthetic' is a term of art in more than one sense, what it describes is ordinary and unmysterious: an attitude of intensified or enriched experience which Kant rightly described as disinterested, that is, devoid of practical interest. Thus the aesthetic is not the preserve of the 'aesthete' or 'connoisseur'. Aesthetic judgements are ubiquitous – that is, anything can be regarded aesthetically, and by anyone – and democratic.[1]

My approach to aesthetics is indebted to many writers but most of all to Kant and Adorno. Adorno is known for his highly original understanding of the social situation of art, discussed in Chapter 6, but it is also important to recognize that he

1

attempted to unify philosophical aesthetics and the analysis, criticism and history of art – a union also found in Hegel and which is, I believe, essential, though too rarely attempted. Hence my appropriating as an epigraph for this book the quotation from Schlegel which Adorno chose as the motto for *Aesthetic Theory*.[2] It is true that once we embark on the analysis of particular artworks, philosophical issues can be hard to keep in view – writers who manage this difficult task, such as Adorno, Richard Wollheim or Roger Scruton, are few. Even so, cross-fertilization between different artistic disciplines is essential to the practice of philosophical aesthetics which can become empty without it.

This issue is a vital one given the situation of philosophical aesthetics. This has greatly improved since Arthur Danto in 1964 referred to it as 'this least advanced field of philosophical inquiry and speculation'.[3] But because of its scientific bias and ahistorical approach which is particularly inappropriate in the case of aesthetics, there remains a puzzling philistinism at the heart of Analytic philosophy. Art is one of the most important of human activities, yet it is regarded by many Analytic philosophers as having peripheral philosophical significance – an astonishing and absurd state of affairs. I believe that the questions of aesthetics are as deep as any in philosophy, even if they are not always as abstract – hence its inherent need to draw together the artistic and philosophical in the way that I have mentioned. Indeed, I think that the most important questions in aesthetics are the relatively less abstract, less metaphysical ones – so here the metaphysics of music is neglected in favour of its human and social basis, found in issues such as the nature of rhythm or Western art music's autonomy or freedom from direct social function.

As important as the influence from Adorno, this book is based on a broadly Kantian conception of philosophical aesthetics. Kant is the founder of modern aesthetics, and Hegel only slightly exaggerated when he said that he spoke the first rational word on the subject. It is true that Kant could draw on a sophisticated recent tradition that included Hume, Shaftesbury, Baumgarten, Lessing and Hutcheson and that there had been philosophical work on the nature of beauty from ancient times. Plato took beauty to be a Form, allied to the Good, whose instances were objects of love. But the arts are subsidiary in his treatment, as we will see in Chapter 1; he regards them as possibly pernicious and wants them tightly controlled. Aristotle took a less exalted view of beauty but treated the arts more benignly. But for Kantians such as the present writer, the eighteenth century saw the true foundation of philosophical aesthetics, which brings together philosophy of art and philosophy of beauty and includes an aesthetic attitude to nature. Kant, to some extent anticipated by Hume, founded aesthetics as a branch of philosophical enquiry when he unified a class of judgements which had not previously been recognized as a unity. The domain of these judgements is one of understanding and experience that is distinct from ordinary cognitive judgement, from moral judgement, and from purely subjective likings and dislikings. As noted earlier, Kant was right to regard aesthetic judgement as disinterested, in the sense of being devoid of practical interest.

But though Kant understood it in a way that previous writers had not, the aesthetic attitude – to reiterate – is ubiquitous and has always existed. It is not an eighteenth-century invention, as philosophers sometimes suggest.[4] What did arise in the eighteenth century was what art historian Paul Oskar Kristeller termed the 'modern system of the fine arts'. On his view, Plato and the Greeks did not think of poetry and drama, music, painting, sculpture and architecture as species of the same genus, all practised by 'artists' in our current overarching sense of the term.[5] The modern system separated fine art from craft, and on a common view defined the crafts as aiming at a merely sensual pleasure or at bare utility, while the fine arts were the object of a higher, contemplative pleasure.[6] Also during the later eighteenth century there occurred other revolutionary developments in the world of the arts, notably the appearance of Romantic ideals of genius and self-expression, and the developing autonomy and associated commodification of art, linked with a developing bourgeois public sphere of taste. These are some of the issues discussed in relation to music in Chapters 3 and 6.

MUSIC

What kinds of music should an aesthetics of music consider? Surely all kinds. Yet until quite recently, Western aesthetics has focused on Western art music, commonly known as 'classical music'. The nineteenth century writer Eduard Hanslick, whose ideas are discussed in Chapter 3, described the music of South Sea islanders as an unintelligible 'wailing' accompanied by 'banging [on] bits of metal and wooden staves'.[7] Adorno shared his dismissive attitude to non-Western music and was concerned almost exclusively with the Austro-German classical tradition, though he wrote on the sociology of popular music, which he regarded as artistically servile. Their ethnocentrism aside, these attitudes are philistine – for the complexities of Balinese gamelan or Indian classical music rival those of Western art music. In this short treatment I have tried as far as possible to correct this imbalance of interest. The music of Ancient Greece is discussed in Chapter 1, and non-Western music in Chapters 2 and 5, while improvisation, which has a distinctive place outside Western art music, is the subject of Chapter 7. The contrast between popular and art music appears in the context of Adorno and modernism in Chapter 6, and if space had permitted would have been discussed at much greater length.

It is necessary at this point to say a few inadequate words about terminology. Most people know what is being referred to by the term 'classical music', but its drawbacks are obvious. In the other arts, the term 'classical' refers to a period of particular excellence or influence, but it has come to refer to the entire canon of Western art music. The more neutral description 'Western art music' is preferable. However, it is important to realize that there was no distinction between art and popular music until the later nineteenth century – one of the aims of aesthetics of music should be to show how what we take for granted is in fact historically conditioned. The concept of 'art music' is a deep one which could not be tackled in these pages in the depth which it deserves and must be left for a future occasion. I do, however, want to insist that the common view of so-called classical music as 'elitist' is culturally disastrous and should be rejected. The classics in all artforms are not 'the preferences of the elite', they are the common heritage of humankind. Over the course of history, these classics come to be the 'preferences' of a larger number than the local preferences of popular culture. Thinking in the crudest commercial terms, this year, Babyshambles sell more than Beethoven, Charlie Parker or Jimi Hendrix, and over fifty years Cliff Richard sells more than any of these, but over 200 years Beethoven, Parker or Hendrix will sell the most. In rejecting the Eurocentrism of earlier writers, it is important not to abandon the claims of aesthetic or artistic value which they upheld.

AESTHETICS AND MUSIC

I explained how this book's approach to aesthetics is indebted to Kant and Adorno, and that it casts the net as widely as possible in terms of music. Now I need to define more closely the standpoint which it defends in the aesthetics of music. As jazz improviser and composer Steve Lacy commented, music can be comprehended on many different levels:

> It can be regarded as excited speech, imitation of the sounds of nature, an abstract set of symbols, a baring of emotions, an illustration of interpersonal relationships, an intellectual game, a device for inducing reverie, a mating call, a series of dramatic events, an articulation of time and/or space, an athletic contest, or all of these things at once.[8]

Music can be any of these, but there is one thing which it is at all times: an art at least with lowercase 'a' – a practice involving skill or craft whose ends are essentially aesthetic, that is, the enrichment and intensification of experience.

This volume therefore takes seriously its title *Aesthetics and Music*. My topic is not just the aesthetics of music – I also wish to argue for an aesthetic *conception* of music as an art. To propose an aesthetic conception looks anodyne or even circular. Who could possibly deny it? In its defence, first, it should be insisted that the claim is not viciously circular. It would be circular only if 'artistic' and 'aesthetic' are equated, as too many writers are happy to do. But in fact the terms are not co-extensive. Something can have aesthetic value and not be an artwork, for instance. However – which is not quite the same thing – the concepts of art and the aesthetic do have a deep conceptual interdependence. I would argue that there could not be a society that appreciated sunsets aesthetically – that is, regarded them as beautiful – while failing to produce or at least recognize artworks, with lowercase 'a', where this includes craft products. Nor is the claim of an aesthetic conception an anodyne one. Even in the case of Western art music, an aesthetic conception of music has its critics, most of whom are sceptical about the very notion of the aesthetic. In contrast to these sceptics, as noted earlier, I regard the aesthetic as an everyday and unmysterious phenomenon. It is not just from the eighteenth century that music has been regarded aesthetically – an aesthetic conception of music applies throughout its history, as Chapters 1 and 2 argue.

Of the levels which Steve Lacy describes, the ideas that music is emotionally expressive and language-like – in particular that it is the language of feeling – and the assumption that it is an abstract art have been very influential at different times in its history. Music is called the language of feeling because it is not the language of anything else – but in fact, I believe, the artistic connection between music and the emotions has been overstated. These topics are not central to this book, though the place of emotion is covered in Chapter 3 under the heading of the aesthetics of feeling, while the idea of music as language-like is discussed in Chapters 3 and 6.

The claim that music is an abstract art is, however, of central concern. It has been much exaggerated and should be contrasted with the *humanistic conception of music* which I defend, according to which music is a human activity grounded in the body and bodily movement and interfused with human life. This conception is able to acknowledge music's language-like character as 'thinking in music, thinking with sounds, the way a writer thinks with words'.[9] 'Thinking in sound' suggests a form that thinking takes, not simply a beautiful pattern of sounds caused by thought. Music is a special kind of thinking that is able to bring together the sensuous and intellectual with unique intensity and sophistication.[10] At the same time, music is not a purely intellectual exercise; it is irreducibly physical, bodily and material. Music originates in singing and dancing, but making music with other objects is just as ancient. Its status as an exercise of the intellect, and its grounding in the human body and its movement, are affirmed throughout this book. These two dimensions reflect the nature of the aesthetic, which synthesizes the cognitive and the sensory, or thought and experience. This synthesis is particularly clear in the case of rhythm, the subject of Chapter 5.

Music's abstractness is qualified above all by its status as a performing art – by the human activity of producing sounds. Music is linked conceptually to dance, physical labour, ritual and other

6

human activities and, thus, with everyday life. The historical content of its material, stressed by Adorno, also goes against an abstract conception. For Adorno, musical material is the sediment of social relations; movements of classical symphonies such as minuet and scherzo originated in dance forms, while trumpet flourishes originate in military bands. My conclusion is that music is *abstract in form, but humane in utterance* – and utterance is essential. Platonic conceptions of the timeless work, reified in a score – what I term in Chapter 7 the 'aesthetics of perfection' – still persist, not least in their implications for improvisation, and should be resisted.

My humanistic standpoint has been greatly influenced by Roger Scruton's *The Aesthetics of Music*, which in its breadth and ambition shows that a philosophically profound aesthetics of music is possible. Written by a present-day Kantian who shares interesting affinities as well as antagonisms with Adorno – both are Kantians yet also elitists, though crucially Scruton is not a modernist – *The Aesthetics of Music* is a model for a comprehensive humanistic treatment. However, there is a tension between the humanistic inspiration for Scruton's work and the acousmatic thesis which he espouses, which says that when sounds are experienced as music, they are experienced as divorced from their causes. This is another sense of music's autonomy and abstraction: its autonomy from its physical sources. The acousmatic thesis is criticised in Chapter 4, which does however allow that this tension reflects a divide within our experience of music.

My project differs from Scruton's in its smaller and distinct range of topics. But the questions discussed here are, I believe, challenging and interesting, and many of them have not received their due in the literature. They are a selection, which is all that can be accomplished profitably in a book of this length. Since the aesthetics of music is essentially a creation of Ancient Greek and modern German writers, the opening chapter of this book examines Ancient Greek aesthetics of music, while Chapters 3 and 6 focus on the massive German contribution. Dividing these historical chapters are less directly historical discussions of the concept of music and its relation to contemporary sound-art (Chapter 2); the nature of musical experience (Chapter 4); rhythm (Chapter 5); and improvisation as contrasted with composition (Chapter 7). Although these chapters are not primarily historical, all contain a large amount of historical material. The aesthetics of music, like other areas of philosophy, has to be understood through its history.

ACKNOWLEDGEMENTS

There are four people in particular without whose help and inspiration this book would not have been possible. Jason Gaiger is a philosopher and art historian whose ability to synthesize those disciplines has been a model for my own endeavour in aesthetics of music. Roger Squires is a philosopher who recognizes that fundamental questions in philosophy arise in the arts. Both of these have, over the course of its production, read drafts of virtually the entire book and have greatly influenced its direction. I have also benefited from David Lloyd's technical knowledge of sound-recording and reproduction as well as his philosophical reflection; he produced many of the illustrations. Finally, Max Paddison over several years has provided inspiration in philosophical aesthetics and the benefit of his profound knowledge of Adorno and Kant.

I must also thank Derek Matravers, the editor of the series, for his advice and encouragement. He read through a late draft and made many helpful comments. Composers Philip Clark and Martyn Harry provided many insights, and with Eric Skytterholm Egan they provided some excellent and – they don't mind me saying – inexpensive musical examples. I am also grateful for comments from Keith Ansell-Pearson, Jacob Bard-Rosenberg, Paul Archbold, Andrew Barker, George Boys-Stones, Stewart Candlish, James Clarke, Michael Clarke, David Cooper, Christoph Cox, Stephen Davies, Raf De Clercq, Joanna Demers, Sophie Gibb, Bryn Harrison, Jonathan Harvey, John Hyman, Simon James, Peter Lamarque, Thijs Lijster, Justin London, Peter Manning, Brian Marley, Louise Richardson, Mark Rowe, Philip Samartzis, Roger Scruton, John Skorupski, Nick Southgate, Michael Spitzer, Chiyoko Szlavnics, Harold Tarrant, David Udolf, Emma Webb, Trevor Wishart and Nick Zangwill. Finally, my thanks to Abigail Heathcote for help in translating a passage in Schaeffer.

Chapters 2 and 7 are revised and extended versions of articles which have appeared in the *British Journal of Aesthetics*: Chapter 7 as 'The Art of Improvisation and the Aesthetics of Imperfection', *British Journal of Aesthetics* Special Issue, 40(1): January

2000, Chapter 2 as 'Music and the Aural Arts', *British Journal of Aesthetics*, 47(1): January 2007. Chapter 4 is a revised and abbreviated version of 'The Sound of Music', in *Sounds and Perception: New Philosophical Essays* edited by M. Nudds and C. O'Callaghan, Oxford: Oxford University Press, 2007.

NOTES

1 These ideas are stressed in the neglected writings of David Pole: 'An aesthetic response ... implies no more than a heightened present awareness of the qualities of an external ... object; and any object may be looked at this way ... [Though] clearly to say that all objects allow of our adopting this attitude is not to say that they equally reward it' (Pole (1983a), p. 33). The ubiquity of aesthetic judgement helps to undermine the claim that the aesthetic attitude is esoteric and elitist.
2 Adorno's motto in the 12th of Schlegel's *Kritische Fragmente*, in Schlegel (1958–).
3 Danto (2005), p. 18.
4 For instance Shiner (2001). The issue is discussed in Chapter 1.
5 Kristeller (1990), discussed in Chapter 1.
6 Shiner (2001), p. 141.
7 Hanslick (1986), pp. 69–70.
8 Weiss (2006), p. 14.
9 As Jules Combarieu comments, quoted in Dahlhaus (1989), p. 3.
10 The idea is developed in Johnson (2002).

CHAPTER 1

AESTHETICS AND MUSIC IN ANCIENT GREECE

Ancient Greek culture, in its own right and through its influence on Roman culture, was foundational to the musical development of the West. Its civilization lasted 500 years, from Classical Greece of the fourth and fifth centuries BCE, through the Hellenistic period from the death of Alexander in 323 BCE to the Roman conquest of Egypt in 30 BCE. My aim in discussing the place of music in this culture is philosophical in both an historical and a non-historical sense. It is important to show how enduring ideas in Western musical aesthetics have their origin in Ancient Greece and to cast light on the philosophical question of music in an alien culture using Greece as a case study. This project raises deep philosophical issues to do with understanding alien societies, for which many philosophers, who stress the importance of partici- pant or empathetic understanding, have used the German term *Verstehen*. One essential aim of this chapter is to show how things that are taken as given or natural are not in fact so. It is easy to overstate the extent to which all peoples and times have a basic concept of music in common, and if we go back even to what is the foundation of Western civilization in Ancient Greece, we find that this is an open question.

However, while there are fundamental differences across cultures, there are also fundamental affinities. As argued in the Introduction, in this volume I take seriously the title *Aesthetics and Music* and wish to defend an aesthetic conception of music which regards it as an art at least with a small 'a' – a practice involving skill or craft whose ends are essentially aesthetic and which is the necessary object of aesthetic attention, with sounds regarded as tones. To reiterate, no one would deny that music is an art with lowercase 'a', it is the interpretation of art as aesthetic which is contentious. It is true that many Ancient Greek theorists seem to neglect the auditory experience of music and do not regard it as an art in the sense in which we use the term. Hence it is argued – or even sometimes assumed – that the Greeks did not have an aesthetic conception of music but rather an ethical or a mathematical one. However, despite the apparently alien nature of the Greeks' mathematical and ethical conceptions of music, I believe that an aesthetic conception of music should be attributed here as in other cross-cultural instances. There are several reasons for making this claim. One is that those who neglect auditory experience are the theorists, not musicians, of whose views we know almost nothing. Another reason is the unduly dominant influence of Plato's rationalism, which, as we will see, has had an unbalancing effect on our conceptions of the arts in Ancient Greece.

MUSIC AND *MOUSIKĒ*, ART AND *TECHNĒ*

In the second book of his treatise *On Music* (*Perì musikēs*) Aristides Quintilianus writes:

> There is certainly no action among men that is carried out without music. Sacred hymns and offerings are adorned with music, specific feasts and the festal assemblies of cities exult in it, wars and marches are both aroused and composed through music. It makes sailing and rowing and the most difficult of the handicrafts not burdensome by providing an encouragement for the work. It has even been employed by some of the barbarians in their funeral rites to break off the extreme of passion by means of melody.[1]

Aristides is an important source for our understanding of music in Ancient Greece, though he wrote much later, during the Christian era around 300 CE. His remarks emphasize something on which all writers agree: music had a part in almost all important occasions of Greek life. Political and social systems were intertwined with music, which existed in the context of non-musical activities. Greek music embraced hymns, wedding songs, funeral laments, drinking songs, love songs, work songs and many other varieties.

Sources such as Aristides enable us to build up a fairly convincing picture of Ancient Greek music and musical life. It is not now known how Greek music sounded; only a few notated fragments have survived, with no clue for realizing them, and surviving texts on music are fragmentary and imprecise. The principal instruments were the *kithara*, an elaborate kind of lyre (see Figure 1); the *aulos*, a wind instrument commonly translated as 'flute' but in fact a pair of pipes with vibrating reeds in their mouthpieces (see Figure 2); and percussion. Male and female choirs, accompanied by the *kithara* or *aulos*, sang in the cult of the gods and at weddings and funerals. In the theatre, music had a central role in the dramas of Aeschylus, Sophocles, Euripides and Aristophanes. The great games of Ancient Greece involved much musical activity. As Landels comments, 'for the Greeks the sung word was almost as commonly heard, and certainly as important, as the spoken word' – not only in drama but also in poetry.[2]

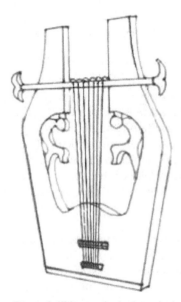
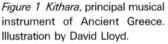

Figure 1 Kithara, principal musical instrument of Ancient Greece. Illustration by David Lloyd.

Figure 2 Aulos, principal musical instrument of Ancient Greece. Illustration by David Lloyd.

Nearly all Greek literature was sung, or accompanied by music and dance – though it is uncertain whether the *Iliad* and *Odyssey* were sung or merely recited – and purely instrumental music was also popular. The performance of a long narrative poem was likely to be in the form of a sing-song chant or kind of speech-singing. Notated compositions did exist, but most pieces were aurally transmitted. Instrumental music had a rather low status. Learning to play an instrument was part of a child's education, but performance as an adult was a lowly activity; it was slave girls and prostitutes who came to play at the symposium, a kind of intellectual party.

The integration of music in a seamless whole with other social activities raises important philosophical questions. There are in fact three intertwining or overlapping issues here, concerning the concepts of music or *mousikē*, of art in general or *technē*, and the domain of the beautiful or *kalos*. For the Greeks, music did not belong to anything like our modern system of the arts, which, as I will shortly explain, did not exist at that time; moreover, the sphere of aesthetic value was not distinguished from that of the ethical, religious, cognitive or practical in the way that it has been in the West since the eighteenth-century revolution in the arts (discussed in the Introduction). These issues are incredibly hard for us to grasp, and they make the challenge of explaining Greek conceptions of art and music a formidable one.

I will say something about how one might understand the relation of *mousikē* and music before moving on to the closely related question of *technē* and art. Although 'music' comes from the Greek word *mousikē*, classical Greece had no single word for what we call music; *mousikē* (Latin *musica*) was used in a much broader sense than we use 'music'. It literally means 'the business of the Muses', goddesses of poetic inspiration who sponsored every kind of intellectual or cultural activity. Perhaps the closest contemporary term would be 'humanities' – although the Greeks included science under that heading, their conception of science did not match ours and so the description 'humanities' may still be apt. The Greek educational system was divided into two components, *mousikē* and *gumnastikē*, the former referring to all cultural and intellectual studies, the latter to physical training; *mousikē* therefore refers to any art, craft or science practised under the aegis of the Muses, whether poetry, dance or music. The late

Figure 3 Kitharōdos (solo singer with *kithara*), from Attica, the region around Athens, about 480 BCE (from A. Barker: *Greek Musical Writings I: the Musician and His Art*, published by Cambridge University Press 2004. Reproduced by kind permission of Cambridge University Library).

Hellenistic and Roman division of liberal and vulgar arts included music among the liberal arts, but, as Shiner notes, this is music as a science (what became known as *musica universalis*); singing and playing at banquets for pay were part of the vulgar arts.[3] (As they still are, of course.)

Figure 4 Symposium scene. A young man plays the *auloi*, while a reclining guest sings. From Attica, around 480 BCE (from A. Barker: *Greek Musical Writings I: the Musician and His Art*, published by Cambridge University Press 2004. Reproduced by kind permission of Cambridge University Library).

The interpretative difficulties that result are shown in different translations of Plato's *Republic*. Jowett renders *mousikē* as 'music', while Waterfield variously has 'cultural studies', 'cultural education', 'musicology' or 'music'; Daryl Rice settles on 'arts and letters', while Jonathan Barnes refers to 'harmonics' (of which more shortly).[4] Not only is *mousikē* a general term for all cultural activities; even when the Greeks referred to music in the sense of singing and playing instruments, it was not clearly separated from poetry and dance – both Plato and Aristotle treat music and dance as elements of certain kinds of poetry, notably lyric and dramatic.[5] It may be argued that much later writers also conflated the different arts but could nonetheless talk intelligibly about them. Lessing contrasts poetry – which for him embraces literature, lyric poetry, epic – and painting, which includes sculpture. But he also has the terms to make the finer distinctions.[6] Surely the Greeks did also? I would argue that like the African peoples discussed in Chapter 2, they have no holistic term. They do not have a word for 'musician' in our sense, just as they do not have a word for 'artist' in our sense, meaning someone involved in an art in our modern system. Even so, reference will be clear in context; and there are terms for lyre-players and flute-players and singers. Also, as we will shortly see, the Greeks directed much speculation towards music in its more restricted present-day meaning and evolved an intricate scientific rationale embracing tuning, instruments, modes or scales and rhythms.

In the rest of this chapter I talk of 'music', but when the so-called music of the spheres is under discussion – the idea that the heavenly spheres operate in perfect mathematical ratio – 'harmony' (*harmonia*) is the fundamental concept. In this context, then, one should perhaps refer to 'harmony and number' rather than 'music and number'. *Harmonia* requires some explanation. Although Greek music until after the fourth century BCE was almost entirely monophonic, that is, unaccompanied melody, from the sixth century a new structural framework called *harmonia* had appeared. Its first meaning was 'tuning of an instrument', and thus 'dispositions of intervals within a scale', but it came to embrace features such as register, timbre and intensity, which characterize the musical discourse of a region – hence Aeolian, Dorian, Lydian, Phrygian, Ionian and so on. However, these names have come down to us as denoting different modes or scales. Playing just the white notes on the piano, the Ionian is now defined as C to C (the Western major scale), Dorian is D to D, Lydian is F to F and so on.[7]

To move from 'music' to 'art' in general. Just as *mousikē* is broader than our 'music', so *technē* is broader than our 'art'. Indeed, it is because the concept of art is underdeveloped in Ancient Greece that the concept of music (as an art) is underdeveloped, and vice versa – and I do believe that 'underdeveloped' is the right description. Again, though, one should bear in mind who the concept is being used by; another way of putting my claim is that music – in our present sense – was not thought amenable to theoretical, scientific or technical study by those thinkers such as Plato who were developing theoretical models. For such thinkers, art, craft and science were not readily distinguished, and all came under the heading of *technē*. The historian of ideas Paul Oskar Kristeller, in a famous article first published in 1950, argued that this conflation of art and craft constituted a more fundamental difference between the world of the arts in Ancient Greece and our post-Enlightenment era. For Kristeller, the Western system of the five major arts – painting, sculpture, architecture, music and poetry – did not assume definite shape until the eighteenth century, even though its ingredients went back to classical, medieval and Renaissance periods.[8] He concluded that 'classical antiquity left no systems of elaborate concepts of an aesthetic nature, but merely a number of scattered notions and suggestions that exercised a lasting influence down to modern times'.[9] Kristeller's thesis commands wide support, and it is now generally maintained that the Greek term *technē* (Latin *ars*) does not distinguish between art and craft, in the modern senses of these terms, but embraced all kinds of human activities which would now be called arts, crafts or sciences.

Kristeller's thesis poses a deep philosophical or aesthetic problem. One might feel that individual arts could exist without being collected together in a system, but Kristeller's point is that the term 'art' would not then be used in its present-day sense. However, many writers have argued against Kristeller that fine arts did exist in Ancient Greece, citing the treatment of painting, epic and tragedy as arts of imitation in writers such as Plato and Aristotle. (Though their concepts of imitation differ considerably, and they did not consider the possibility of non-mimetic art.)[10]

Eva Schaper takes Plato's distinction in the *Ion* between skill (*technē*) and inspiration (*poiesis*) as justification for talking about 'art'.[11] Nietzsche, in *The Birth of Tragedy*, claims that Socrates shows belated recognition that art has intrinsic value: 'the Platonic dialogues do not permit us to view him solely as a disintegrative, negative force [for art]'. Nietzsche suggests that when Plato portrays Socrates in his last days writing or reading poetry, he was concerned that poetry and music might be a neglected source of knowledge and value.[12] Nonetheless, Plato clearly maintains that the imitative arts are no more worthy of serious intellectual attention than someone waving a mirror around, doing magic tricks or imitating animal voices. Music, poetry, rhetoric, painting and so on must fall into the class of things which in the *Gorgias* he calls 'knacks' rather than 'skills', and as we might say, they are a matter of taste, not truth or falsity. Even Aristotle, who was more favourably disposed, held that what painting and tragedy have in common as imitations does not separate them in their procedures from arts like shoemaking or medicine.[13]

The thesis that the Greeks lacked a system of the arts has been taken to imply a deeper claim, that the value spheres of the aesthetic, the ethical and the cognitive, which we now take as separate, were not distinct. That is, judgements about the beautiful, the good and the true did not fall into clearly demarcated categories – in judging a person's beauty, for instance, the Greeks considered their moral qualities. Of this, more later. Here I simply note that nostalgia for the alleged unity of value spheres in Ancient Greece underlies the popular view that for the Greeks, the discipline of music was a synthesis of the arts and sciences, in laudable contrast to the present Western division between 'two cultures'.[14] This claim is connected with the view that the Greeks made no distinction between science and art – that there was a desirable unity or harmony in contrast to our divided culture. This idealization originates in German writers of the late eighteenth century, most notably Goethe, Hölderlin and Schiller, who looked back with yearning at the harmonious pre-modern world of the Greeks, which had not suffered the divisions of the modern era.[15] When we examine Ancient Greek theorizing about music, however, it becomes clear that Goethe's interpretation is anachronistic.

THE PYTHAGOREAN AND PLATONIC–PYTHAGOREAN MATHEMATICAL CONCEPTION

The substantial amount of surviving Greek music theory concerns, almost exclusively, acoustical and mathematical properties of music. It was not intended for practising musicians. My claim is that the musical theorizing which crystallized in the celebrated conception of the music of the spheres was a kind of proto-science; while for Greek thinkers, human music was an art or craft, in the present-day sense of those terms, and a lowly echo of cosmic harmony. So in fact there was a divide, not the unity imagined by Goethe and his successors. The idea of the music of the spheres originates in a very ancient mathematical conception of music which asserts its connections with number. This conception has had an enduring influence despite – or perhaps because of – its detachment from music-making as an auditory and human phenomenon. It is most strongly associated with the name of *Pythagoras*, who flourished about 550 BCE, nearly two centuries before Plato. Plato then uses the expression 'music of the spheres' as a conceit, a way of expressing the supposed fact that the heavenly spheres operate in perfect mathematic ratio, and through him it influenced later thinkers.

According to ancient tradition, Pythagoras was, after Thales, the originator of *philosophia* – the pursuit of wisdom, and precursor of both present-day science and philosophy. But the figure of Pythagoras is shrouded in historical mist, and scholarly opinion is divided on whether he really was a philosopher and mathematician or merely a magician and dogmatist. His status is more problematic than that of other pre-Socratic thinkers – the philosophers before Socrates. Although their work often does not survive as primary sources, there is direct quotation to it in the work of later writers. Pythagoras, in contrast, appears to have written nothing, and all we have are early and vague reports about his followers, and late and presumably forged works ascribed to them; there are no statements by Pythagoras which later authorities agree in attributing. Aristotle refers to 'so-called Pythagoreans', and only after Plato is he represented as the head of a philosophical school – so it is likely that Plato and his followers are the source of many so-called Pythagorean ideas. As Burkert puts it in his classic work *Lore and Science in Ancient Pythagoreanism*, 'a Platonizing interpretation of Pythagoreanism, which had a decisive influence on the later tradition, goes back to Plato's immediate disciples and differs sharply from the reports of Aristotle [which become] more important than ever; for he alone warns us to separate Pythagorean and pre-Platonic from Platonic material'.[16] The spell of Pythagoras' name – the fact that there was a continuing Pythagorean tradition – has made interpretation of his ideas even harder, Burkert argues:

> at the source of this continuously changing stream lay not a book, an authoritative text ... There is less, and there is more: a name ... Just as a city which was continuously inhabited over a period of time ... presents to the archaeological investigator far more complicated problems than a site destroyed by a single catastrophe ... the special difficulty in the study of Pythagoreanism comes from the fact that it was never so dead as, for example, the system of Anaxagoras or even that of Parmenides.[17]

(In Chapter 4, we see the influence of Pythagorean ideas in discussion of musical listening and the 'acousmatic'.)

With these reservations in mind, I will refer to the activities of the Pythagorean school, leaving open the question of how far it is the creation of Plato and later thinkers. The connection between music and mathematics was forged by the school's discovery of the relation between pitch and the length of a vibrating string – generally accepted as the first law of nature to be formulated mathematically.[18] The Pythagoreans discovered that the natural harmonics of vibrating strings divide into mathematical proportions; that is, there is a correspondence between the length of the string and the pitch of the resulting note. Nicomachus of Gerasa (late first to early second century CE) told in his *Manual of Harmonics* the famous but apocryphal story of how Pythagoras made his discovery after hearing the ringing sounds from a blacksmith's anvil. To explain what this discovery involved, and how it laid the foundations of Pythagoreanism and the mathematical conception, a short lesson on musical acoustics is required.

The Pythagoreans discovered that plucking two strings, one exactly half the length of the other, will produce notes in harmony. The sounds seem in concord and go together. Strings that are two-thirds or three-quarters the length of the first string produce the same effect. This is, when one thinks about it, a remarkable fact, and it forms the basis for the science of acoustics.[19] To put the matter more precisely, the first three overtones of the harmonic series – the main intervals of the musical scale, the octave, fifth and fourth – stand in the ratios 4:3, 3:2 and 2:1. To give an example: if a player bows the open E string of a violin and then places their finger on the string exactly midway between the neck and bridge, the resulting note will be the E an octave above. In the natural harmonic series, every note or tone is the fundamental or lowest tone of its own harmonic series or spectrum of overtones; the Pythagorean discovery is that the proportions between the overtones are constant, exhibiting the ratios just specified. One might assume that these ratios would be familiar to instrument-makers anyway, independent of theoretical discovery by the Pythagoreans, but Burkert argues that this is unlikely:

> The most common stringed instruments have strings of equal length and no finger board ... In the triangular harp the tension of the strings and their thickness played some role, but we do not know just what ... In a wind instrument with finger holes, that is, the *aulos*, the distances between the holes do not correspond directly or accurately to the ratios of the intervals; actually the holes were simply bored at equal distances.[20]

Only the monochord, an ancient single-string instrument with a moveable bridge, used mainly for teaching and tuning, could demonstrate Pythagorean theory with any exactness, and it is not known when such an instrument was invented.

Fundamental; 1st harmonic; unison; ratio 1:1

1st overtone; 2nd harmonic; octave; ratio 2:1

2nd overtone; 3rd harmonic; perfect 5th; ratio 3:2

3rd overtone; 4th harmonic; perfect 4th; ratio 4:3

Figure 5 Vibrating strings and the Pythagorean discovery. These diagrams illustrate the following acoustic facts: touching the vibrating string half-way along its length produces the first overtone, an octave higher than the fundamental tone which dominates; alternatively one could imagine what is in effect the same thing, taking a string that is half the length of the original string and vibrating it. Touching the string one-third of the way along produces the second overtone, a total of an octave and a fifth higher; touching it one-quarter of the way along produces the third overtone; and so on. Illustration by David Lloyd.

Tonality and tuning

The tonal system, developed in Western music from the seventeenth century onwards, is only an imperfect reflection of the Pythagorean vision. It uses the base of the harmonic spectrum – the first six overtones, to be precise, the fundamental, the octave, the fifth above it, the octave again, then the third and the fifth – a basis reflected in the scoring of the last chord in a Haydn or Mozart symphony, which to that extent is 'natural'. But the reflection is not exact. Tonality depends on an artificial system of equal temperament, dividing the octave into twelve equal semitones, which distorts the natural harmonic intervals a little to make changes of key possible. Bach's *48 Preludes and Fugues* for keyboard, Book I of which is known as *The Well-Tempered Clavier*, run through all twenty-four keys chromatically (C, C#, D, etc.), and was foundational to the development of tonality.[21] 'Well-tempered' does not refer to a specific tuning but simply to any tuning which allows one to play tolerably in all keys; 'equal temperament', in contrast, is a specific, exact tuning. The traditional view in musicology saw equal temperament as the logical goal of musical progress. But, as Ledbetter comments, with the rise in the 1970s of the authentic performance movement using original instruments, players experienced 'the purity and sonorousness of unequal temperament, [and] turned [from] the characterless, commonplace sound [that equal temperament] can give to an instrument'. The debate in the late seventeenth and early eighteenth centuries highlighted real advantages to each method, and, in the twentieth century, composers such as Harry Partch and Terry Riley have returned to experiment with unequal temperament, including its pure version of just intonation.[22]

The belief that music embodies numerical principles which underlie the laws of nature was common throughout ancient societies, including those of China, Babylonia and India.[23] Lippman describes this 'theory' as 'nothing less than a myth of Western civilization ... found in the poetry and literature of every age, in innumerable commentaries on Plato, and in astronomical tracts'.[24] Though it seems implausible that the belief in numerical ratios held by other ancient societies had no basis at all in an empirical knowledge of acoustics, the Pythagorean contribution was to make this hitherto mysterious relationship amenable to rational inquiry. As Mueller writes, 'everywhere in ... the Pythagorean tradition of Greek music, including Archytas, Plato, Euclid andPtolemy, the sense of the cosmic power of pure numbers and the willingness to indulge in meaningless numerical manipulation is always present'.[25] However, as noted earlier, Plato and his followers are the source of many so-called Pythagorean ideas. Plato appears to us as the first great and prototypical rationalist. That is, he maintains that reason provides the ultimate source of knowledge and, indeed, that our grasp of the physical world through the senses is not, properly speaking, knowledge at all; for him, empirical investigation is at best the prelude to the exercise of pure reason, and there can be no genuine science of the empirical.[26] It is likely, therefore, that it was Plato who first portrayed the Pythagoreans as exploring musical phenomena in order to deduce theoretical truths – as believing that the important truths about music consisted in its harmonious reflection of number. On his interpretation, the numerology of the Pythagoreans was speculative, not empirical, and applied to the cosmos as a whole; mathematics was a key to the abstract, essential nature of things.[27] Plato would have to concede that the ratios were discovered empirically by examining the properties of strings, but he would hold that it is fruitless to explore them empirically.

The Platonic–Pythagorean vision – that is, the Pythagorean vision as presented by Plato and his disciples – evolved into the celebrated doctrine of the harmony of the spheres, according to which the distances from the Earth to the visible planets and sun, as well as the velocities at which the celestial bodies circle the Earth, are in the same ratios as various musical intervals, especially those of the diatonic scale. These ratios were held to be present also in the compositions of substances and in the souls of good men. However, music was the only field in which these ratios had been discovered rather than merely postulated. The doctrine that music was essentially an abstract system of relationships expressible in a set of equations has haunted musical thought ever since Plato's time. It may seem bizarre that music was believed to extend to all of the cosmos, but it should be understood that this is music in the sense of 'harmonia' or harmony – the concept of harmony is even broader in its application beyond music than the concept of rhythm, which applies also to poetry, speech such as oratory, and bodily movement in dance, sport and elsewhere, as we will see in Chapter 5. While many writers talk of the music of the spheres, it would be preferable to refer to the harmony of the spheres.

Plato the rationalist, in addition to rejecting an empirical interpretation of Pythagorean theory, generally underplays the importance of the auditory in music. In *The Republic*, he presents an ethical vision of cosmic harmony in which music and astronomy are 'branches of knowledge [which] are allied to each other ... [as] the Pythagoreans claim'. Just as Plato's condemnation of physical as opposed to mathematical astronomy is not total – he holds that empirical investigation is necessary to give us the material for 'higher astronomy' – neither is his condemnation of empirical investigation of tunings.[28] But the role he envisages for it is strictly limited and subordinate. He is scathing about precursors of the Aristoxenians, who, as we will see, argued that tone is essentially an auditory phenomenon in which mathematical relationships are strictly subordinate. Such theorists, he writes, 'waste their time like the astronomers, measuring audible concords and sounds against one another' when they could be transcending the sensible world to gain exact knowledge through reason. He portrays Socrates as mocking the music theorists who subject the strings to a painful inquisition, stretching them on the rack in an effort to detect the smallest difference in pitch. Even the Pythagoreans are too wedded to the empirical, he believes, since they 'try to find the numerical properties hidden in these audible consonances, but they do not rise to the level of formulating problems and investigate which numbers are consonant and which not, and why'.[29]

In the *Timaeus*, Plato outlines this programme of pure number theory, in a cosmological vision which relates musical harmony to the harmony of the universe. There is no mention of human music. A scale without audible sound, comprising a series of numbers derived from ultimate principles, constitutes the basic harmonic structure of the world, the 'world-soul'; the Creator of the world-soul separates portions of the mixture of elements in the proportions of Pythagorean tuning. This conception of harmony is rationalistic, intellectual and supersensible. According to the Platonic vision, human music is the lowest form of music and merely echoes divine harmony, which is inaudible to us because with us since birth; rhythm and melody imitate the movements of heavenly bodies, reflecting the moral order of the universe. The

Roman writer Cicero restated Plato's mythical vision in his own *Republic*: 'Gifted men ... on stringed instruments and in singing, have gained for themselves a return to this [heavenly] region ... But the sound coming from the heavenly spheres revolving at very swift speeds is of course so great that human ears cannot catch it'.[30]

THE ETHICAL CONCEPTION AND PLATO'S MORE EMPIRICALLY MINDED SUCCESSORS, ARISTOTLE AND ARISTOXENUS

I have already mentioned that with Plato, mathematical and ethical conceptions of music are synthesized, and I will now turn to the latter. The idea that music possesses an ethical influence is just as ancient as the Pythagorean numerological vision, with which it is intimately connected through the concept of harmony of the soul and of the state. The ethical view is held by Confucius as well as by Plato and Aristotle. *Ethos theory* developed the ramifications of this ethical influence. A leading exponent was Damon of Athens in the fifth century BCE, who believed that a people's music expressed their character, arguing that the modes or scale systems expressed the personality types of the peoples who favoured them: the Dorians, Lydians, Phrygians and so on, mentioned earlier. Both Plato and Aristotle believed that music, in its human form, has a direct effect upon the soul and actions of humankind.

For Plato, as for Confucius, earthly music is suspect. In *The Republic*, Plato has Socrates argue that soft and plaintive modes, and complex rhythms, should be excluded from the education of the guardians and that innovations in music threaten the order of the state: 'One must be cautious about changing to a new type of music as this risks a change in the whole. The modes of music are never moved without movement of the greatest constitutional laws'.[31] In the *Laws*, Plato declared that rhythmic and melodic complexities should be avoided because they cause depression and disorder and prescribed that through musical and literary training 'the whole community may come to voice always one and the same sentiment in song, story and speech'.[32] These remarks show again that musical performance was less important to the Greek concept of *mousikē* than its embodiment of universal principles and higher truths. Later Hellenistic and Graeco-Roman writers

26

downplayed ethical concerns in favour of Plato's numerological vision.

Plato's great pupil and successor *Aristotle* agreed with him that music moulded human character, but, unlike Plato, he had a tolerant understanding of the value of music as part of the good life – he did not advocate banning any of the modes, for instance. This is because he is more inclined to view the cosmos as a commonwealth of individuals, rather than regarding individuals simply as elements of the cosmos. However, his philosophy of music is not as systematic or substantial as Plato's, and though it is more empirical – that is, based on perceptual knowledge or scientific investigation of things in the world, rather than the realm of thought or reason – there is dispute over the extent to which this is so. Lippman, for instance, argues that the mathematical conception of tone was common to the Pythagorean, Platonic and Aristotelian traditions: 'a fundamentally different approach to tone – an appeal to hearing and to an innate auditory and vocal sense of tonal relationships – is found only in the subordinate tradition of Aristoxenus and Theophrastus, which discards mathematics as irrelevant'.[33] This may be an overstatement, however, since Aristotle did question Platonic–Pythagorean number theory. He wrote in the *Metaphysics* that the Pythagoreans mistakenly 'supposed the elements of numbers to be the elements of all things, and the whole heaven to be a *harmonia* [harmony or musical scale] and a number', hence their 'charming' notion of the harmony of the spheres.[34]

Aristoxenus (*c.*300 BCE), a pupil of Aristotle, took the latter's more empirical approach further, stressing the role of the human listener and rejecting Pythagorean numerology and the related ethos theory. His treatise *On Harmonics*, the oldest work of Greek music theory to be substantially preserved, constructs a musical science based on Aristotelian principles, arguing that music is emotionally expressive and involves both the hearing and intellect of the listener. He was the first musical theorist to stress the value of ear training, and, in comparison to the authorities discussed so far, he emphasized the importance of the senses:

we endeavour to supply proofs that will be in agreement with the phenomena – in this unlike our predecessors. For some of these … rejecting the senses as inaccurate, fabricated rational principles, asserting that height and depth of pitch consist in certain numerical ratios and relative rates of vibration – a theory ... quite at variance with the phenomena.[35]

He anticipated the standpoint which assumed importance much later, from the eighteenth century onwards, that music is an autonomous discipline, entirely separate from arithmetic and astronomy and concerned with musical sound as distinct from noise or spoken language. For him, music is a self-referring phenomenal system, its significant form derived from the principles of its own organization; its audible constructions acquire ethical significance only by association, he maintains. Aristoxenus saw his position as mediating between rationalism and empiricism, but Ptolemy in the second century CE regarded his school and that of the Pythagoreans as the two extremes of musical theory. Burkert agrees that the two schools 'stood in a relation of hostility: the [Pythagoreans] accused Aristoxenus' followers of imprecision, and were accused, in their turn, of using arbitrary hypotheses and contradicting the clear testimony of the musical ear'.[36] The Epicurean and Stoic thinkers who came after Aristoxenus – such as Philodemus in the first century BCE – adopted a more naturalistic view of music, which they accepted as an adjunct to the good life.

As we have seen, the claim that on the Pythagorean vision, music was virtually a department of mathematics, requires qualification. The concern of the Pythagoreans, and of other thinkers in antiquity who elevated the status of *mousikē*, was not with audible music. So the cliché that there was a unity of arts and sciences in Ancient Greece, even assuming these concepts to have something like their current meaning, is false. Music had two senses. The practical art or craft – according to the theorists and philosophers – was a pale reflection of music in a second sense, the inaudible Pythagorean harmony underlying the universe. To reiterate, the authorities that are cited about Greek music tend to be theorists and philosophers, who were not interested in musical practice. By the same token, *aulos* players were probably not interested in the concept of the harmony of the spheres. Kristeller, for instance, is explicit that his primary resource is treatises on the arts, not actual artworks. In our own time, regrettably, there is still too much of a divide in aesthetics between concern with theory and with practice.

THE SEPARATION OF THE VALUE SPHERES

As noted earlier, Kristeller's thesis that the Greeks lacked a system of the arts has been interpreted as involving a deeper claim: that the value spheres of the aesthetic, the ethical and the cognitive, which we now take as separate, were not distinct. That is, judgements about the beautiful, the good and the true, which we assume to be made on separate bases, were somehow drawn together. Thus Martha Nussbaum writes that

> For the ancient Greeks ... Poetry, visual art and music were all taken to have an ethical role ... and a citizen's interest in them was understood to be an interest in pursuing questions about how best to live ... One sign of the thoroughgoing unity of the aesthetic with the ethical can be seen in the Greek word *kalon*. Usually translated as "beautiful" in some contexts, as "noble" or "fine" in others, it is in reality a univocal word, giving evidence of the Greek belief that only what is ethically fine is pleasing to behold and that visible beauty is a sign of excellence.

Shiner comments that 'The idea of beauty in the ancient world usually combined what our aesthetic theories have typically separated ... Both the Greek *kalon* and the Latin *pulchrum* were often used simply to mean "morally good"'. Kristeller himself writes that although the ancients were 'confronted with excellent works of art and quite susceptible to their charm, [they] were neither able nor eager to detach [their] aesthetic quality ... from their intellectual, moral, religious and practical functioning or context, or to use such an aesthetic quality for grouping the fine arts together'.[37]

Other authorities maintain that the value spheres were not, in fact, so unified in Ancient Greece – that the ethical did not absorb or eliminate the aesthetic but merely sought to appropriate it. The resulting position could be described as a *qualified separation of the value spheres*. What I have in mind is, for instance, the view that Janaway puts forward, that Plato was not blind to the realm of the aesthetic but had inhabited this realm, knew how seductive it is and declared his arguments a 'charm' to ward off the fine works of poetry.[38] Though familiar with an aesthetic conception of art, he wished to transcend it. For Janaway, Plato understands the basic premises of one kind of 'aesthetic' defence of the arts: 'He is aware that some people assign the arts autonomous value on the basis of the pleasure they provide to those who experience them ...'. So Plato holds that philosophy must be defended from the arts, which have at most instrumental value.[39] He would recognize that a *kithara*-player was skilful, a purely aesthetic assessment having nothing to do with morality or piety, and in various places, notably in *The Republic*, refers to 'lovers of sights and sounds' – but he believes that they fail to learn about beauty because they only look for individual beautiful things rather than by pure reason trying to divine beauty's essence. Plato wants to re-educate us to become finer connoisseurs of beauty led by our understanding of the good. The claim that only what is ethically fine is pleasing to behold – made in Nussbaum's quotation above – might be expressed better as the view that what is pleasing to behold is given positive ethical value. For Plato, the cosmos is the one definitively beautiful artefact and paradigm of phenomenal beauty; all other things can be considered beautiful just insofar as they contribute to its beauty.[40]

If the preceding arguments are correct, and the Greeks did to some extent recognize the separation of aesthetic and moral value, then Plato's position is comparable to that of later moralists about art. Thus when he objects to certain precise musical tunings, for instance of the interval of the major third, on the grounds of their malign ethical and educational import, he concedes that they sound better aesthetically. On this view, Plato was not alone among Ancient Greek thinkers in regarding music as morally dangerous, believing that it provoked sexual urges – a view which endures in the modern era as a challenge to aestheticism and art for art's sake, in the form of Adorno's criticism of jazz as 'loin music' and myriad moral panics directed at popular music in the past century, from early jazz to Elvis to punk.[41] The Greeks' ethical conception of *mousikē*, which as we have seen valued it primarily as part of moral education in the state, holds it to be of instrumental rather than intrinsic value – just as today, philistine attitudes to music education value it primarily because it helps to develop mathematical skills, for instance. So, proponents of this line of interpretation might conclude, it was aestheticism or 'art for art's sake', and not the aesthetic as such, which Plato and others failed to accept – the idea that aesthetic qualities should be appreciated in isolation from others. The Greeks might have felt that such qualities can be appreciated in isolation, but that they should not be.

I do not think this plausible line of interpretation is correct. The Greek attitude to the value spheres was not the qualified separation comprehensible to us. For what Janaway fails to acknowledge is that there were no 'arts' that formed a system, and which were recognized by some, if not Plato, as having autonomous value. Plato at least – though it is true that he is an extreme example – holds to a notion of beauty which is quite alien to us, divorced from the autonomy and subjectivity of aesthetic experience emphasized by Kant. Thus, underlying the dispute over the unity or separation of the value spheres are radically different conceptions of both the artistic and the aesthetic, which conceptions, I believe, are inextricably interlinked. The difference between the Ancient Greek and post-eighteenth-century positions lies in different conceptions of the possibilities of art, with their consequent or concomitant effect on the conception of the aesthetic – indeed, the claim that the value spheres are separated may just amount to the claim that there is a modern system of the arts.[42] Plato objects to the aesthetic conceived of as sensual – that is, he objects to hedonism or sensualism – because he has no conception of art as other than pleasurable or didactic. He does not regard the arts as having truth-content – where this is not the same as their being 'instructive' in the classical moralizing sense – and does not recognize that the aesthetic can be a synthesis of the sensory and the intellectual.

A defence of an aesthetic conception of music and other arts does not depend on the assumption, implausible in Ancient Greece, that music belongs to a system of fine arts, however. In Chapter 2, I will justify an aesthetic conception which regards music as an art with a small 'a', that is, a practice involving skill or craft whose ends are essentially aesthetic, which particularly rewards aesthetic attention and whose material is sounds regarded as tones. However, the unity of poetry, music and dance in Ancient Greece, and the absence of a system of fine arts, illustrates a more general problem concerning the presence of music in cultures radically divergent from our own. Despite differences in its conceptualization which this assimilation shows, writers consistently refer to music – in our sense – in Ancient Greece without doubting that the concept is instantiated. This indeed seems correct, but in the light of anthropological attitudes it is perhaps surprising. The consensus may arise because Ancient Greece is regarded as the basis of Western civilization and the lines of development to the modern Western concept of music can be traced from there; it is not a so-called primitive society wholly detached from our own. Anthropologists do not write about Ancient Greece; it is the preserve of more Eurocentric scholars. Even so, there is a real problem here, which I will return to in the next chapter.

MEDIEVAL AND RENAISSANCE MUSICAL THOUGHT

The Platonic–Pythagorean influence in musical thought was dominant at least until the Renaissance. The idea of music as an explanation of the divine universe was taken for granted by astronomers and astrologers, physicians, architects, humanist scholars and poets up to Isaac Newton. Medieval musical aesthetics, under the influence of Roman scholar and theorist Boethius (480–524 CE), continued the Platonic–Pythagorean tradition of thinking of music as a branch of mathematics, a framework which haunted musical thought for a millennium. Boethius solidified Plato's treatment into a threefold division. *Musica universalis* expressed the cosmic harmony of the spheres, determining the courses of the stars and planets, the seasons and the combinations of elements. It was reflected in *musica mundana*, which unified the healthy human body and soul. *Musica instrumentalis* or audible music, the lowliest of the three divisions, manifested in sound the mathematical proportions of the higher divisions. Thus, for medieval theorists, the true musician is a scholar who judges compositions and performances intellectually; the poet composes songs by instinct rather than knowledge; while the instrumentalist is essentially a skilled artisan. There emerged a dichotomy between a low, sensual, instrumental, secular music and an exalted, intellectual, vocal, sacred music.

Medieval theorists remained preoccupied with ways of calculating and representing musical ratios. But during the later Middle Ages, the Platonic–Pythagorean view of music as the branch of mathematics that pertains to sounds was gradually supplanted by the humanist view of music as a sonorous art, in which mathematics had the subservient role of calculating means to audible ends. Musical authorities debated whether, in tuning

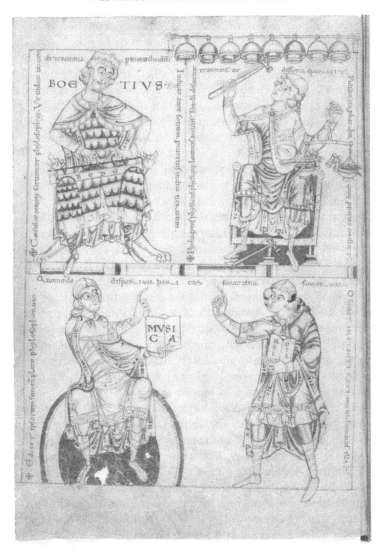

Figure 6 Boethius discussing music with Pythagoras, Plato and Nicomachus. From a twelfth-century drawing (from R. Hoppin, *Medieval Music*, published by Norton. Reproduced by kind permission of Cambridge University Library, MSIi.3.12 folio 61 verso).

systems, Pythagorean purity of numbers was paramount, or the judgement of the human ear. Thus Johannes de Grocheo argued around 1300 that the practical art of music was the application of mathematical theory to singing, rather than a branch of mathematics, while Tinctoris in the late fifteenth century regarded music as a practical human activity rather than a hermetic science or model of the cosmos. Zarlino in 1558 declared that the ear is judge. Instead of finding metaphysical reasons why each mode – Dorian or Ionian for instance – must reflect a different type of character or feeling, he appealed to the listener's experience.[43] Zarlino also argued that just as a poem has a subject, for instance the fall of Troy, so does a musical composition; but it is an audible subject or theme – music is not rhetoric. These were still advanced views, however; for most authorities, rhetoric was the basis of a courtly education, while musicians' music was for monks and artisans. The process by which music was liberated from literary or linguistic models was completed only with the rise of the ideology of absolute music during the nineteenth century, as we will see in Chapter 3. As music theorist Carl Dahlhaus put it, 'The older idea of music, against which the idea of absolute music had to prevail, was the concept, originating in antiquity and never doubted until the seventeenth century, that music, as Plato put it, consisted of *harmonia, rhythmos*, and *logos*' – 'logos' meaning language as the expression of human reason.[44]

The astronomer Johannes Kepler made the last important statement of the music of the spheres early in the seventeenth century – at the same time as the composer Praetorius wrote that 'God himself, as Plato says, has ordered all things in accordance with number, weight and measure'.[45] The complexity of tones, ignored by the mathematical conception, began to be recognized during the Renaissance, and in the seventeenth and eighteenth centuries the discovery of overtones reinforced the auditory conception. By the time that the tonal system became established, in the eighteenth century, the harmony of the spheres had become a fascinating historical curiosity, though the connection between music and mathematics endures.

In the next chapter, the aesthetic conception of music is developed further, in the context of developments in music during the twentieth century.

Musical notation

The introduction of a written notation in the twelfth or thirteenth centuries had momentous consequences for Western music. The drive towards polyphony and polyrhythm – music in more than one part, in which the various lines or parts move more or less independently, and in different rhythms – was one of the factors that led to the development of a graphic, mensural notation, without which such complex music could not be learned or transmitted. Originally, notation was probably a mnemonic device, to remind performers of music that was fairly fixed in advance; so when medieval notation did not specify pitch, this was not because it was at the performer's choice, but because performers knew the material and did not need reminding. But this is a matter of some controversy. Although notation began as a means of communicating music that had already been made, it became a driving force in the evolution of music. It liberated musical time from the tyranny of the syllable and, eventually, from expressiveness based on words; it finally led to the composer becoming a desk-worker rather than a performer and, finally, to the idea that a composition is defined by its score – what is known as the *work-concept*. The rise of the latter during the eighteenth to twentieth centuries, which involved increasing specificity in the score, increasingly limited the input of the performer to that of interpreter of an apparently fixed artefact. In the twentieth century, improvisation – in jazz and so-called free improvisation, discussed in Chapter 7 – provided an alternative to the increasing prescription of the score in classical music. At the same time, Western composers attempted to reintroduce performer freedom by deploying such devices as chance procedures and graphic notation (figures 7 and 16).

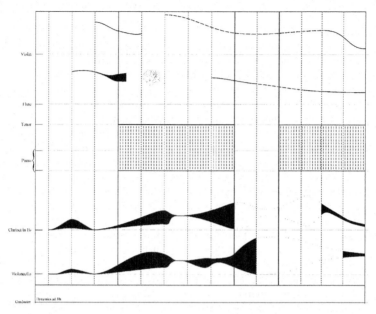

Figure 7 'Seed' by Eric Skytterholm Egan (2005) – a contemporary graphic score which attempts to make the performers' contributions equal to the composer's. Egan writes: 'This section is notated graphically because I believe it lends more freedom to the performer – the conductor can direct its course freely through a spontaneously created musical landscape. The musicians are not impeded by a set duration, musically represented through a given series of notes. The conductor controls the duration of the segments separated by the vertical lines, whilst the performers determine the pitch and duration of each individual musical gesture. Thus the composer can shape the section according to the image in the score and dynamically mould it to their own taste, whilst the performers control the harmonic/textural landscape. I aim to make every performance of the piece unique – a joint effort in which each party lends their own individual dimension.' Reproduced by kind permission of Eric Skytterholm Egan.

NOTES

1 Aristides Quintilianus (1983), p. 120. Barker comments: 'When Greek authors of Roman times wrote seriously about music, it is the music of a much earlier phase of their culture that they have in mind, usually that of the sixth and fifth centuries [BCE]' – this they rightly regarded as the golden age (Barker (2004), p. 2). An excellent selection of Greek texts is found in Barker (1984).
2 Landels (1999), p. 9. My descriptions of Greek music are indebted to this book, and to Comotti (1991).
3 Shiner (2001), p. 22.
4 Plato (1993), for instance 521d and 530d; Rice (1998); Barnes, entry on Plato in *Encyclopaedia Britannica*. The correctness of translation will depend on which part of *The Republic* is being translated. In Book 3, where Plato discusses early education, it is instrumental playing and listening to poetry that he means; in later stages of the curriculum it is harmonics.
5 Kristeller (1990), p. 169.
6 Lessing (1962). In the 'Preface', Lessing draws a single distinction between poetry and painting in their broadest senses; however, the central chapters of the book have detailed discussions of epic and lyric poetry, idyll, and so on, as well as of painting and sculpture.
7 A discussion of *harmonia* is found in Barker (1984), pp. 163–8, and most fully in Barker (2004).
8 Kristeller (1990).
9 Kristeller (1990), p. 172. By 'aesthetic', I believe he means 'artistic'.
10 In fact, poetry held a higher rank than the visual arts; this does not mean that it should be equated with a modern fine art, though Kristeller does comments that Plato and Aristotle were clinging to an older tradition that was disappearing due to the emancipation of instrumental music from poetry, indicating an incipient systematization of the arts (Kristeller (1990), p. 169).
11 Schaper (1968), p. 23.
12 Nietzsche (1999), section 14, pp. 70–1. Nietzsche's opposition between the Apollonian and the Dionysian is discussed in Chapter 3. Schaper comments that 'Plato's thought on the problems of creation, on the peculiar concreteness of the art work, on its moral implications, on the emotional involvement in it, on the sensuous character of the aesthetic experience, on art as play, and on art as belonging to the imagination, was the thought of a pioneer'. The elaboration of these concepts was left to Aristotle, whose views are in many respects completely opposed to Plato's, and who in his *Poetics* inaugurated aesthetics as a theoretical study (Schaper (1968), pp. 55, 13).

13 Shiner (2001), p. 21.
14 Famously analysed by Snow (1993).
15 See especially Trevelyan (1981).
16 Burkert (1972), p. 13.
17 Burkert (1972), pp. 11, 10. 'The renown of Pythagoras as the inventor of mathematics and mathematical natural science is explicable as a distortion of perspective; a pre-rational interpretation of the cosmos, along with arithmological speculation, is seen in hindsight as rational science' (p. 14).
18 Burkert (1972), p. 371.
19 A clear account of the discovery, and of how it led to the doctrine of the harmony of the spheres, is found in Armstrong (2005), Chapter 3. For a much more technical but still very engaging treatment, see Benson (2007), Chapters 4–5.
20 Burkert (1972), p. 374.
21 See for instance Ledbetter (2002), and the entries under 'Tonality', 'Temperament', 'Equal Temperament' in Sadie and Tyrrell (2004).
22 Ledbetter (2002), pp. 35–6.
23 Lippman (1994), p. 5; Burkert (1972), p. 356.
24 Lippman (1994), p. 8.
25 Mueller (1997). We will return later to Pythagoras' concept of the acousmatic.
26 In fact, he sees himself as offering a middle way between the extreme rationalism of Parmenides and the extreme empiricism of Heraclitus.
27 See Hussey (1997).
28 As Waterfield comments, in Plato (1993), p. 428, n.530b.
29 Plato (1993), 530d, 531c; see Burkert (1972), p. 371.
30 Cicero (1998), Book 6, Chapter 5.
31 Plato (1993), 398e–400c; 424b–c.
32 Plato (1970), ii, 664a.
33 Lippman (1977), p. 76.
34 Aristotle (1998), 985b32–986a2, 1090a20–23, 1093a28–b4; also Aristotle (1939), 290b21–3.
35 Quoted in Comotti (1991), p. 147.
36 Burkert (1972), pp. 370–1. See also Sadie and Tyrrell (2004), entry under 'Ethos Theory'. Barker comments that 'Aristoxenus is not by any means claiming that mathematics has no part to play in musical analysis: what he is insisting is that the mathematical tools must be applied to things recognizable as *heard*' (Barker (1978), p. 12).
37 Nussbaum (1996), Vol. 1, p. 175; Kristeller (1990), p. 174. 'Kalos' can mean anything from sexually exciting to beautiful to morally worthy. The separation of the value spheres is discussed further in Hamilton (in preparation).

38 Janaway (1995), p. 7.
39 Janaway (1995), p. 8.
40 As he argues in the *Timaeus* – Plato (1974), pp. 29–30.
41 Adorno's notorious views on jazz are discussed in Chapter 6; on aestheticism, see the box on pp. 85–6 of this volume.
42 These issues are discussed at greater length in Hamilton (in preparation).
43 Sadie and Tyrrell (2004), entry under 'Zarlino'.
44 Dahlhaus (1989), p. 8.
45 Quoted in entry under 'Plato' by Warren Anderson, in Sadie (1980).

CHAPTER 2

THE CONCEPT OF MUSIC

The development of musical thought into the modern era is taken up in Chapters 3 and 6. The present chapter looks directly at the concept of music, taking into account the musical developments of the past century. I defend the claim, presented in Chapter 1, that music is an art at least with a lower-case 'a' – a practice involving skill or craft whose ends are essentially aesthetic, that especially rewards aesthetic attention – whose material is sounds exhibiting tonal organization. Many people would argue that music is the universal or only art of sound. But in the modernist era, Western art music has incorporated unpitched sounds or 'noise', and the issue of non-musical aural arts has arisen – 'aural arts' is meant to parallel 'visual arts', which include painting, sculpture, photography, video and film. Perhaps there is an art phonography or art of recording, for instance, to parallel art photography? This question has an impact on the characterization of music itself, and here I contrast acoustic, aesthetic and acousmatic accounts. My conclusion in this chapter is that there is some truth in all of these. I will argue that acoustic and acousmatic accounts help to distinguish between music and non-musical sound-art, since tones – stable pitches – must predominate in its material.

THE POSSIBILITY OF NON-MUSICAL AURAL OR SOUND-ART

An aural art is one that is primarily addressed to the ear, and that uses sound as its primary material. To say that music is the universal or only aural art could seem almost tautological – what other 'aural arts' are there? In contrast to the visual arts of painting, drawing, sculpture, video-art and perhaps film, we rarely talk about 'the aural arts' or 'the arts of sound'. Poetry and radio drama are, in a sense, aural arts, but they are impure, in that they treat sounds mostly as having conventional or linguistic meaning. So it is at least true that music does not stand to the aural arts as painting stands to the visual arts but has a much more dominant role. Most of the visual arts are characterized with reference to a particular material medium – painting with reference to paint, whether oils, tempera, water-colour or household gloss, and similarly drawing, video-art and film. Sculpture, perhaps, is different – its traditional media of stone and bronze have been expanded in the past century to include many other materials. But on the received view, music, whose medium is sound, is the universal or only art of sound.

Given the developments of the past century, this view is no longer obviously correct. Clearly, music over the centuries of its development has been much concerned with sound, hence for instance the way that orchestras developed. However, the conscious or self-conscious *exploration* of sound, in a systematic way, occurred only in the twentieth century. During that time, Western art music experienced a revolution in its material basis; *the ideology of instrumental puritanism* has been supplanted by the concern with sound as sound.[1] This ideology dictated that only instrumental sounds, or sung vocal sounds of fairly determinate pitch, could be included within music. But with composers' growing interest in sound as sound, musical material has broadened to include non-tonal and noise elements. Although musical performance has always included non-musical noise which is inessential and even a distraction – for instance, the toneless scraping of the violin bow, or toneless breathing sounds on wind instruments – during the twentieth century, the boundary between music and noise acoustically defined was qualified. In the modernist era, beginning with the introduction of siren glissandos and other industrial noises by Varèse and Antheil, sounds which are unpitched or not discretely pitched were allowed into Western art music – though such unstable sounds had long been present in some kinds of traditional music.

Recording was the crucial technological advance which liberated a concern with sound as sound – never before could one analyse sounds and alter their envelope. Inspired by electro-

41

acoustic composition whether or not they directly participated in it, composers such as Stockhausen, Xenakis and Ligeti liberated timbre and texture as structural elements of musical composition through their use of sound-masses and other avant-garde techniques. Rock musicians have deployed feedback at least since the 1960s. Today, most theorists, if not ordinary listeners, assume that any sounds can be incorporated into music and that no intrinsic qualities are required. Smalley, for instance, comments that atonality, total serialism, the expansion of percussion instruments and the advent of electro-acoustic media, have all contributed to the recognition of the inherent musicality in all sounds.[2] And composer Chiyoko Szlavnics writes that 'attention to sound is crucial to contemporary music. [Contemporary music] which does not explore sound, in the way that electronic music, some American minimalism, and spectralism have done, simply sounds old-fashioned to me'.[3]

The twentieth-century concern with the properties of sound itself, as opposed to a traditional, more restricted concern with sound as tone, has shown itself in the development of sound-art that sees itself as non-musical, as well as in the attempt by music to embrace all sounds. This former development originated in the same attack on instrumental puritanism that liberated musical sound. Thus the Italian Futurist Luigi Russolo with his *The Art of Noises* (1913) and, more importantly, avant-garde composer Edgard Varèse in his mature work from the 1920s onwards, suggested a noise-based alternative to music as an art of sound. Varèse (1883–1965) used the term 'organized sound':

> In the twenties when I was ... giving concerts of modern music, I got sick of the stupid phrase "Interesting, but is it music?" After all, what is music but organized sound – all music! So, I said that my music was organized sound and that I was not a musician, but a worker in frequencies and intensities.

He added that with the advent of electronic music, people believe that this description applies only to manipulating electronic sounds – implying that his own non-electronic music, with its focus on acoustic qualities, was also 'organized sound' in this sense.[4] In the 1940s, partly bearing out Varèse's predictions about electronic music, a nascent sound-art appeared in the form of *musique concrète*, the school of composition founded by Pierre Schaeffer (1910–95). Schaeffer, in an incredibly labour-intensive process, used the primitive recording technology then available – disc-cutters and, later, tape-recorders – to create compositions based on a montage of everyday and natural sounds recorded on tape, such as doors slamming, steam trains puffing and people talking, as well as more traditional musical materials such as the piano and other instruments. Clearly, this sonic material transgressed the dictates of instrumental puritanism, which – to reiterate – said that only instrumental sounds, or sung vocal sounds of fairly determinate pitch, could be included within music.

Even the modernist avant-garde was unreceptive to *musique concrète*, criticizing it for the 'real world' distractions of its sonic material. Stockhausen, for instance, complained that the genre is replete with 'associations [which] divert the listener's comprehension from the self-evidence of the sound-world presented to him because he thinks of bells, organs, birds or faucets'. (By 'self-evidence' he presumably means hearing sounds as sounds or tones.) Pierre Boulez argued that when electronic composers use noise 'without any kind of hierarchic plan, this also leads, even involuntarily, to the "anecdotal", because of its reference to reality ... Any allusive element breaks up the dialectic of form and morphology'.[5] These composers perhaps looked only at earlier *musique concrète*, where the causal origins of the sounds were easily recognizable. (We will see in Chapter 4 the implications of this debate for the acousmatic nature of musical experience.) John Cage, however, took the opposite view, claiming that *musique concrète* was too conventionally musical – though for that iconoclast anything would be too conventionally musical.

Perhaps he was right, for certainly on some evidence Schaeffer aspired to create 'music'. He commented that 'From the moment you accumulate sounds and noises, deprived of their dramatic [literal] connotations, you cannot help but make music'.[6] Thus it seems that Schaeffer did not consider the possibility of creating a category of sound-art distinct from music, even though it could be argued that that was what he was doing. He increasingly felt that he had failed to deprive sounds of their literal connotations, declaring in despair that '*Musique concrète* in its work of assembling sound, produces sound-works, sound-structures, but not music'.[7]

Despite the pessimism of its founder, however, the influence of *musique concrète*, together with that of John Cage and the audio ecology researches of R. Murray Schaefer, has in the past two decades or so inspired a loosely defined movement known as sound-art or audio art.[8] ('Aural' parallels 'visual', but I continue with the more established term 'sound-art'.) Examples include Bill Fontana amplifying the tones produced by traffic crossing the Brooklyn Bridge, mixing them and sending the result by satellite round the world; David Dunn's concern with bioacoustics; and Alan Lamb's recordings of the 'Aeolian humming' of telegraph wires in Australia. Many of those who regard themselves as sound-artists have contested what they regard as the hegemony of music, hoping to liberate sound-art from its shackles, just as many art photographers wanted to liberate photography from painting. Thus, they deny that music is the only art of sound. For instance, sound-artist Francisco López explains how he is 'fighting against a dissipation of pure sound content into conceptual and referential elements ... trying to reach a transcendental level of profound listening that enforces the crude possibilities of the sound matter by itself'.[9] Not all of its proponents present sound-art in stridently non-musical terms, however; often they characterize it as having a concern with sonic space, or through a connection with the visual arts. Thus David Toop writes that sound-art, 'detaching itself from the organizing principles and performance conventions of music ... [has] explored issues of spatial and environmental articulation or the physics of sound using media that included sound sculptures, performance and site-specific installations'.[10] And LaBelle refers to 'the core of the very practice of sound art – the activation of the existing relation between sound and space'.[11] Certainly there are many intermediate cases where even proponents of non-musical sound-art will agree that there are musical elements, for instance, the audio-visual creations of Ryoji Ikeda.

In his recent book on sound-art, Brandon LaBelle cites the influence of the following developments in visual-art practice from the 1960s onwards: site-specific practice, performance art, installation art and land art. From the direction of sound, paralleling or expressing these influences, he discusses John Cage, La Monte Young, Alvin Lucier and Christof Migone (happenings and performance art); Iannis Xenakis, Max Neuhaus and Bernhard Leitner (installations); and Hildegard Westerkamp and

Bill Fontana (acoustic ecology).[12] Even those sceptical of the artistic value of such practices must allow that they challenge the popular logic that meaningful, organized sound must be either music or speech. This popular logic – what I term the *universalist* position that music is the only art of sound – traditionally goes with the assumption that music exploits as material a particular range of sounds, namely tones. However, we have seen how during the twentieth century universalism and the conception of music as the art of tones have become separated, as music has embraced more noise elements. I will argue that, paradoxically, the tonal basis of music has been clarified by the rejection of instrumental puritanism. Thus I reassert that music is the art of tones, while rejecting universalism and recognizing an emergent non-musical sound-art which takes non-tonal sounds as its material. To allow that any sounds can be *incorporated into* music is not, I argue, to say that any sounds can *constitute* music – thus, room is left for my conclusion that music makes predominant use of tonal sounds and that there is also a non-musical sound-art. Together with music, I will argue, sound-art exhausts the possibilities of high art among the pure aural arts.

The view that music is not the only art of sound finds support from a very different direction. Roger Scruton in *The Aesthetics of Music* writes that

> Music is a special kind of sound, and not any art of sound is music. For instance, there is an art, and an aesthetic intention, in designing a fountain, and the sound of the fountain is all-important in the aesthetic effect. But the art of fountains is not music. For one thing, the sound of the fountain must be heard in physical space, and should be part of the charm of a place.[13]

As we will see, Scruton holds that music exploits acousmatic experience – in which the listener spontaneously detaches sound from the circumstances of its production – while fountains do not. But the important consideration for present purposes is that fountain art cannot belong to the high arts. The art in constructing fountains is art with a lower-case 'a', and Scruton would probably maintain that among sound-arts, only music can aspire to high-art status. His position can be described as *sophisticated universalism*, that is, the view that music is the only or universal *high* art of sound – with a prestige status that links such arts as drama, painting, poetry and the novel. In contrast to this position, I believe that there is a potential high art of non-musical sound-art. However, I will argue that music turns out to be on a continuum with non-musical sound-arts, differing from them in the preponderance of tonal material. (This distinction is not in any way evaluative and is not intended to mark any great metaphysical divide.) What 'tonal' amounts to will be one task of this chapter to explain; within this argumentative context, I suggest materials for answering the more fundamental philosophical question 'what is music?'

THE CONCEPT OF MUSIC

The question of the nature and purpose of art – and of music as an art, and as a high art – is aesthetically more profound, but here I address philosophically basic issues concerning the characterization of music. My concern here is with the question 'what is music?', understood as on the level of 'what is language?' and 'what is depiction?' – though it is, I believe, inextricably linked with the question 'how do we conceive of music?' in a way not paralleled by the questions about language and depiction. I will argue that music possesses at least salient features and that these can be elucidated by looking at three different directions of characterization: acoustic, aesthetic and acousmatic. As will become clear, I am looking for salient features, not necessary and sufficient conditions; the characterization is tolerant of apparent counterexamples which are in fact parasitic on it, as will become clear from the case of muzak. The claim that music has salient features has been contested, if not by philosophers, then certainly by other thinkers. For John Cage, notoriously, there was no significant distinction between music and ambient sound, while Robin Maconie writes that 'for sound to be perceived as music is an act of individual determination ... what is music to one listener may be noise to another'.[14]

Slightly less subversive considerations arise from cultural relativism – from the fact that, like the concept of art itself, conceptualizations of music have changed historically and varied across cultures. As we saw in Chapter 1, the Western system of fine arts appeared in its modern form as late as the eighteenth century and does not apply universally either in historical or cross-cultural terms; therefore, one cannot appeal straightforwardly to the post-Enlightenment concept of art in characterizing music.[15] Recent ethnomusicological and anthropological studies have shown that many languages have terms which only partly cover what modern Europeans mean by the term 'music'. Inuit and most North American Indian languages do not have a general term for music; the Blackfoot language has 'saapup' as its principal word for music, but this means something like 'singing, dancing and ceremony'.[16] In Africa there is no term for music in Tiv, Yoruba, Igbo, Efik, Birom, Hausa, Idoma, Eggon, Luo or Jarawa. Even the German language distinguishes *Musik* and *Tonkunst*, though the latter term is now antiquated.[17] Indeed, R. Murray Schafer, the Canadian composer and writer on soundscape, brings the anthropological argument back home to Western music. He argues that before the musical sounds in our cities – church bells, the postman's horn – were replaced by mechanical noises and music moved into the concert hall, music and 'noise' were not distinct categories.[18] Ethnomusicologist Bruno Nettl allows that all cultures have something that sounds to Western ears like music and 'have a kind of sound communication that they distinguish from ordinary speech', but wonders whether 'the various things that are distinct from speech [are] really at all the same kind of thing?'[19]

In fact, it seems absurd to suggest that that non-Western cultures lack music. As Stephen Davies succinctly puts it, the term 'music' carries less conceptual baggage than 'art' – it is a less honorific title and so more readily applied.[20] Relativistic concerns raised in the previous paragraph are undermined first by noting that the existence of a continuum, and an area of vagueness, between speech and music, is not essentially problematic. Cultural concepts often exhibit such indeterminacy in their application. Speech is distinguished from music by its lack of fixed pitches, but football chants, religious chant and text-sound pieces such as Kurt Schwitters' *Ursonate* constitute interesting and genuinely intermediate cases.[21] It is not clear how one should take the suggestion, inspired by Murray Schafer, that before the Renaissance, speech and music were not divorced.[22]

Second, and more important, cultural differences do not make it impossible to isolate salient features of music. To say that would be to affirm the anthropologists' heresy – if anthropology, except in its Lévi-Straussian period, traditionally emphasizes difference, philosophy should recognize unity. A natural first response to this heresy is to argue that while not all societies conceptualize music in the same way as post-Enlightenment Western listeners, they do produce the same kind of aural phenomenon. This seems to be the response of Nettl when, in answer to his own earlier doubts, he argues sensibly that although many African societies do not have a conception of music matching that found in Western culture, 'the ease with which many African societies have adapted to the English or French conceptions of and terms for "music" suggests that the domain exists, integrally, even where no term is available'.[23] He comments on the widespread use of tones with consistent pitch, and of tonal systems using from five to seven tones; he adds that all societies have a type or kind of stylized vocal expression distinguished from ordinary speech – most readily called singing, but which might also be referred to as chanting, screaming, howling or keening.[24]

Thus the natural first response to the anthropological heresy assumes that it is the nature of these sounds, rather than producers' or listeners' experience or conceptualization of them, that constitutes music. A performance of Mozart could be experienced non-musically – as muzak perhaps – but it would be perverse to deny that it contained musical sounds, that is, organized tones, regardless of how a particular listener experienced or chose to experience them. So, one may conclude, what matters is not whether the sounds are experienced or conceptualized as this or as that, but what 'this' is when it is music – that sounds constitute music through their intrinsic nature and organization.

I believe that although the anthropologists' heresy must be avoided – the concept 'music' is certainly instantiated in all cultures – this natural first response is not the right way to do so. It tends to favour an *acoustic characterization* of music – a physical interpretation of the truism that music is organized sound. According to this characterization, musical sounds or tones consist of regular, stable, periodic vibrations; noise consists of irregular, unstable, non-periodic vibrations. Now there is, within the science of acoustics, a technical definition of noise as undifferentiated sound without definite pitch, or as material whose exact frequencies are not determined, but statistical.[25] However, this technical definition has no viable parallel in an acoustic characterization of 'music' as sound of periodic vibration, since acoustic organization is not a sufficient condition for music; both speech, and the hum of a finely tuned air-conditioning system at a definite pitch, would satisfy the acoustic characterization. Neither does that characterization yield a necessary condition for music. This is not just because after modernism, music has come to incorporate noise elements, since, as I will argue, a preponderance of tonal organization is still essential. Nor is the reason quite that in many kinds of non-Western music, non-tonal sounds may predominate; these cases will be included if the acoustic characterization of music is extended to include rhythm, defined in the first instance in terms of silences between tones.[26]

Mention of rhythm brings us to the fundamental reason why tones cannot be defined in wholly physical terms. Like 'noise', 'tone' has both a purely acoustic and an intentional definition. Musical tones certainly have physical parameters; they are determinate pitched sounds of a certain stability and duration, which as a result of their human production normally possess a degree of impurity, distinguishing them from pure sine tones.[27] However, for the purposes of characterizing music, the physical definition is too atomistic. 'Tone' in this less specialized, non-technical sense is a relational concept which refers not just to the nature of component sounds but also to how they are structured through rhythm, melody and harmony. This structure is evolving and meaningful, the kind that Webern despaired of listeners locating in his own music when he described one unsatisfactory performance as 'a high note, a low note, a note in the middle – like the music of a madman'.[28]

Another way of putting this point is that tones are not raw musical material, since they are already the product of human intentional action before they form music. There are tones in nature, such as birdsong and the song of the whale, but these are tones physically defined; with limited exceptions, tones not produced by human intentional action do not count as music. The wind-powered Aeolian harp produces tones without direct human agency – though the sound-producer itself is created intentionally – and it is doubtful whether the result is music.[29] Indeed, the form–matter distinction breaks down here, as it does elsewhere if pressed hard enough. As Lippman comments, 'all instances of [musical] material, tone itself not excepted, are forms as well, the outcome of some manifestation of human creativeness and intention'. As examples of such material he cites the tone of a violin, a major scale, a cadential progression of chords, waltz-rhythm, a melody taken for variations.[30] If musical tones are normally the product of intentional action and are apt for artistic organization, then the dichotomy between the intrinsic nature of sounds, and producers' and listeners' experience or conceptualization of them, breaks down. In describing the nature of the sounds, one will inevitably be referring to producers' and listeners' conceptualization of them – the phenomenon of music cannot be separated from its conceptualization.

Figure 8 The American sloth singing the hexachord, from Athanasius Kircher, *Musurgia Universalis*, vol. 1 (Rome: Francesco Corbelletti, 1650. Reproduced by kind permission of Cambridge University Library). *Musurgia Universalis* was one of the most influential music treatises of the Baroque period. Historian and music theorist Athanasius Kircher (1601–80) argued that human music has its origins in animal sounds. Perhaps impressed by the belief that South America was the site of the Garden of Eden, he took seriously the local folklore that the three-toed sloth is able to sing up and down a perfect musical scale – in fact the myth is likely to originate in the fact that a bird with the same habitat, the Common Potoo, sings a remarkably pure descending diatonic scale.

Figure 9 Birds and their songs, from Athanasius Kircher, *Musurgia Universalis*, vol. 1 (Rome: Francesco Corbelletti, 1650. Reproduced by kind permission of Cambridge University Library).

We must, therefore, turn to producer- and listener-centred accounts of music, which refer to the purposes for which musical sound is created and the kind of experience which it invites. To reiterate, the phenomenal thesis says that while a Mozart sonata could be experienced non-musically – perhaps as muzak – one could not deny that these were musical sounds, regardless of how a particular listener experienced them. What the phenomenal thesis fails to acknowledge is that while a listener on a particular occasion may experience Mozart non-musically, it is essential to the concept of music that there are many examples of sound regarded as music where listeners in general do not. So the phenomenal thesis should be rejected in favour of the plausible idea that 'organized sound' refers not just to purely acoustic properties but also to intentional organization by a human agent, whether composer, performer or listener. Hence the truism that music is organized sound is more plausibly interpreted by the *aesthetic characterization* of music presented earlier: music is an art with at least lower-case 'a' – a practice involving skill or craft whose ends are essentially aesthetic, and that especially rewards aesthetic attention – whose material is sounds exhibiting tonal organization. According to the aesthetic account, music in all societies is the object of an aesthetic attitude in that it falls under the heading of 'useless work'; that is, it involves the refining of skills which are not strictly necessary for any social purpose that the practice may have.[31] Musical sounds are those that are felt to be particularly rewarding as objects of aesthetic attention.

As noted in the Introduction, an aesthetic conception looks anodyne or even circular, only if 'artistic' and 'aesthetic' are equated in meaning. They should not be equated – something can have aesthetic value and not be an artwork, for instance – though these concepts do have a deep conceptual interdependence. There could not be a society that appreciated sunsets aesthetically, while failing to produce or at least recognize artworks, where this includes craft products. Nor is the claim of an aesthetic conception an anodyne one; it turns out to be surprisingly contentious. There exists in the literature a defence of something like the aesthetic characterization, though its author, Jerrold Levinson, rejects the label. He argues that music is sound organized by a person for the purpose of enriching or intensifying experience through active engagement – listening, dancing, performing – with the sounds regarded primarily, or in significant measure, as sounds. He contrasts regarding sounds as sounds with attending to them as 'symbols of discursive thought'; any verbal component, Levinson argues, must be combined with more purely sonorous material.[32] The two components of his characterization, namely, the purpose of enriching or intensifying experience and the regarding of sounds primarily as sounds, correspond to the two components of the aesthetic characterization just outlined: the aesthetic end and the tonal material through whose organization that end is achieved. I will now explore these components, which turn out to be closely connected, by developing Levinson's characterization.

To deal first with the purpose. Levinson's account concurs with my earlier claim that human intentional production is primary, and that birdsong and environmental sounds might at best be treated *as if* they were music. But is the purpose of intensifying or enriching experience – which, unlike Levinson, I believe *is* minimally an aesthetic purpose – too strong a condition? It may, for instance, imply that muzak is not music, which seems counterintuitive given its common label 'background music'. The issue turns out to have some depth.

Muzak

The term 'muzak' was coined in the USA in 1922 by George Owen Squier, who launched a company to pipe music, advertising and public-service announcements into homes and businesses; the word is a fusion of 'music' and 'Kodak'. His invention originated the modern concept of sound-design, integral to the concept of the modern selling space; research companies now exist which devote themselves entirely to it. The BBC programme 'Music While You Work', intended to increase productivity during the Second World War, could be regarded as an early example of muzak. Beginning in June 1940, it presented a non-stop medley of popular tunes. A BBC memo for the programme reads: 'Banned completely: numbers with predominant rhythm, insufficient melody or other unsuitable characteristics; numbers that are too lethargic and unsuited to any speeding up of tempo; all modern slow waltzes owing to their soporific tendencies'. 'Deep in the Heart of Texas' was also banned, as its clapping motif caused workers to beat hammers and other tools on the workbench, doing much

---

damage.[33] Today, sound-design is used to disturb inmates at Guantanamo Bay or to disperse youths in shopping centres. But its primary purpose was to make people spend money in shops, which it seems to do, as shown for instance by psychologists at Leicester University when they tested the effect of in-store music on customers' wine selections. On alternating days, French accordion music or German brass-band music were played; prices were similar, and national flags were attached to each display. When French music played, forty bottles of French wine and eight bottles of German were sold; when German music played, twenty-two bottles of German wine and twelve bottles of French wine were sold.[34] Perhaps muzak in lifts originated – like mirrors – in a desire to make using them less boring; in the original high-rises lifts were slow. Maybe muzak can enhance the aesthetic experience of shopping, by making shops and malls pleasant places to be, causing people to linger and buy more. But even if one accepts this rather trivial sense of enrichment, the primary purpose of muzak is surely to anaesthetize – literally, to deprive of feeling – by putting customers in a relaxed mood in which they are more likely to consume.

One does not have to accept Vance Packard's famous critique of consumerism to recognize crucial differences between the aims of muzak and the more positive relaxing effects of New Age, Ambient and techno, music therapy or traditional lullabies.[35] Related categories are background music such as Easy-listening, light music, Lounge music and eighteenth-century *Tafelmusik*; like muzak, chart pop music for FM radio play is treated to make it unintrusive to the listener.[36] While background music and commodified pop subordinate the aesthetic, muzak rejects it completely in favour of commercial or political imperatives. It has no aesthetic aim; it is not meant to be listened to but to elicit a subliminal, Pavlovian reaction. Odours or drugs would serve as well. Muzak is an evil because it is ubiquitous and so erodes people's aesthetic capacities – their ability to listen actively to anything – and degrades their response to music. Muzak, whether in lifts or restaurants or piped to telephone customers on hold, belongs under the heading of sound-design, and while sound design can have an aesthetic purpose, muzak does not. Sound-design can overlap with music, but its aesthetic aims are fused with more functional ones. The concept embraces such diverse phenomena as Native American or African talking drums and Morse code and is developed later in this chapter.

Muzak compilations certainly use, i.e., mention, music, and therefore aurally have many of its properties; they are engineered using processes such as compression, to make them bland and unintrusive. I am not sure whether to argue that muzak is not music. To show this, one would at least have to show that the author of Vivaldi-as-piped-down-the-phone-line is not just the eighteenth-century composer but also the Muzak Corporation. However, I am looking for salient features and not necessary and sufficient conditions for something to count as music. So the aesthetic characterization that I am defending requires only that the existence of quasi- or non-aesthetic genres such as muzak is parasitic on that of music, which does aim to enrich and intensify experience – that is, that not all music could be background music.

To sustain this claim, a further objection to the aesthetic characterization must be confronted, which says that genuinely aesthetic responses to music did not exist before the advent of autonomous art in the eighteenth century – art without direct social function whether for church, aristocracy or military. Considerations arising from anthropological relativism, presented earlier, questioned whether music is present in all societies; this new objection implies more plausibly that music, assumed to exist in all societies, need not always have aesthetic ends. Levinson – who, as we have seen, distinguishes the enrichment and intensification of experience from what he regards as more purely aesthetic aims – argues that music for the accompaniment of ritual, for the intensification of warlike spirit or for dancing does not call for aesthetic appreciation in the sense of requiring specific attention to beauty and other aesthetic properties. On this view, it is only since the Enlightenment that aesthetic responses have become purified; Neolithic peoples who gazed at a beautiful sunset were as much in awe of the Sun God as delighting in natural beauty, and in Ancient Greece the aesthetic and ethical were thoroughly interfused.

These claims rest, I believe, on an unacceptably rarefied interpretation of the aesthetic. Music has always on occasion been treated as background, though this tendency has become almost ubiquitous in the era of mechanical reproduction and muzak. But on the broader conception of the aesthetic which I subscribe to, Levinson's implication that music was not listened to aesthetically until the later eighteenth century is quite implausible. Bach, for instance, saw his keyboard music as a heightened intellectual and spiritual activity; though neglected after his lifetime, it was known by Mozart, Beethoven and Chopin. (Another way of presenting these issues is the topic of Chapter 3, on absolute and autonomous music.) So is that broader conception of the aesthetic correct? I believe that the enriching and intensifying of experience just is the aesthetic aim, and so the anti-aesthetic objection that Levinson makes is self-defeating. Underlying it is a key error – a purification of the aesthetic attitude that is also a rarefication. Levinson's characterization of the aesthetic response as 'contemplative and distanced apprehension of pure patterns of sound' may seem Kantian in its echoes of disinterested pleasure – though the reference to 'patterns of sound' is too static, and one should refer rather to an evolving syntax.[37] However, it implicitly equates aesthetic experience with the attitude of the so-called aesthete and is unduly restrictive.

As argued in the Introduction, the aesthetic is ordinary and ubiquitous; the eye or ear lingers on everyday objects, and 'pleasing to me' rapidly transforms into the genuinely aesthetic ascription 'pleasing'. 'Aesthetic purpose', I believe, is a description at least as informative as 'the purpose of intensifying or enriching experience through active engagement', while the consequences of direct social function – and of the imperfect separation of the ethical, aesthetic and cognitive value spheres before the eighteenth century – are overrated by Levinson and other writers.[38] In his discussion of universal features of music, ethnomusicologist Bruno Nettl mentions features of musical sound or style – singing, metre or pulse, a variety of pitches, use in ritual, for special events and in dance – and adds: 'Another universal is the use of music to provide some kind of fundamental change in an individual's consciousness or in the ambiance of a gathering'.[39] This, I would argue, is the aesthetic dimension, and it is universal.

The second element of the aesthetic account concerns the material of music. I have characterized musical material as tones – as we will see shortly, a benignly circular definition – while Levinson's proposal refers to regarding sounds primarily as sounds. Listening to music obviously does involve hearing sounds as sounds, where the implied contrast is with hearing sounds as non-naturally meaningful or perhaps – a possibility which Levinson does not mention – as naturally meaningful, that is, representing natural sounds. Music and speech both impose a structure on sounds, but the structure of speech is semantic while that of music is at most syntactic. (As we have seen, the existence of a kind of syntax gives music a language-like character.) Moreover, to describe music as an art is to say that unlike speech it particularly – and often richly or deeply – rewards aesthetic attention. But clearly this issue is a complex one. There is speech that is art – that is, drama and poetry, where one attends aesthetically to the actor's or poet's voice, to their delivery as well as the content of what they say. But music is essentially an art while speech is not. A sequence of sounds becomes speech if they are meaningful, and it is not essential, and indeed may be a distraction or barrier to understanding, to appreciate them 'as sounds'. With music, in contrast, it is essential to appreciate the sounds as sounds, in the sense that one does not attend to them for the information that they yield about the world, whether through their natural or non-natural meaning. This is a central feature of Scruton's treatment, as we will now see.

Having excluded such purely cognitive modes of listening, is it not possible that one could hear sounds as sounds in a way distinct from hearing them musically as tones – or indeed, that hearing sounds as tones is *not* hearing them as sounds? The traditional conception of music as the art of tones is somewhat overlooked by Levinson, but not by Scruton; at the same time, and logically independently, some avant-gardists argue that listening to sound-art involves hearing sounds as sounds in a distinct non-musical sense.[40] Scruton argues that musical listening does not involve hearing sounds as sounds, though he agrees with Levinson, and with modernists and postmodernists, that no intrinsic properties of sound – melody, rhythm, harmony – are required for something to count as music. However, he argues in opposition to modernist conceptions that melody, rhythm and harmony, though non-intrinsic, are still necessary, since these are defining properties of tones as opposed to sounds – and music is sound transformed into tones.

Scruton's claim is based on what I term an *acousmatic characterization* of music, according to which music is constituted by the listener's experience or response to sounds as abstracted from their worldly cause. Acousmatically, sounds are experienced as detached from the circumstances of their production; non-acousmatically, they are experienced as having a certain worldly cause. Scruton distinguishes acoustical experience of sounds from musical (acousmatic) experience of tones; for him, sound becomes tone when organized by pitch, rhythm, melody and harmony, and 'tone' is the intentional object of a necessarily imaginative and metaphorical musical perception. He, therefore, has a threefold classification – hearing sounds as sounds, as tones and as words – while Levinson assimilates the first two items under the heading 'hearing sounds as sounds'. For Scruton, the locution 'regarding sounds as sounds' implies that one is *not* having the central musical experience of acousmatic listening, while for sound-artists it suggests that one is listening to sound-art and not music – sound-artists would not agree that regarding sounds as sounds has to be non-acousmatic or merely informational.

Scruton's emphasis on the exploitation of the acousmatic experience of sound is highly suggestive, and it is taken up in Chapter 4; however, as I argue there, it is strictly incorrect. There is, I believe, a twofoldness to musical experience, which is both literal and metaphorical, non-acousmatic and acousmatic. Each aspect is a genuinely musical element of musical experience. Thus, listening to music involves experience in terms of causes of sounds, and experience which abstracts from those causes.[41] However, while the non-acousmatic is part of musical experience, the acousmatic is unique to it, so Scruton's stress on it is justified. Thus, as the discussion earlier in this chapter indicates, he is right to regard music as essentially an art of tones, conceived of in relational terms as structured rhythmically, harmonically and so on. It follows that in its reference to tones, the aesthetic characterization accommodates the truth in both acoustic and acousmatic treatments: music is an art with a lower-case 'a' – a practice involving skill or craft whose ends are essentially aesthetic, that especially rewards aesthetic attention – whose material is sounds regarded predominantly as tones.

In response to concerns that there is circularity in the characterization of music that makes reference to tones, I would say that the circularity is benign and reflects a conceptual and explanatory holism or interdependence of 'music' and 'tone'.

There is a relationship of mutual presupposition between the concepts 'music' and 'tone' – it is not possible to acquire one concept without also acquiring the other, nor can one show understanding of one without also showing understanding of the other. Underlying the aesthetic characterization is a deeper holism between art and the aesthetic. There seems to be an unwarranted suspicion of conceptual holisms which are surely an essential feature of language. Analytic conceptual holisms of an anodyne kind, such as that between 'monarch' and 'subject', which are true simply in virtue of the meanings of the terms involved, clearly do exist. The dictionary defines 'monarch' as 'sole or absolute ruler of a state'; when one asks what the state consists of, or who monarchs rule over, the answer must refer to subjects, while 'subject' is defined as one ruled by a monarch or other absolute authority. There may be a larger circle involving such concepts as 'sovereignty', 'authority' and 'state', but whatever this larger circle comprises, 'monarch' and 'subject' are members of it. The interdependence of this latter pair of concepts is undeniable because analytic, that is, true purely in virtue of meaning; it is therefore not philosophically interesting. Philosophically interesting holisms are those which are non-analytic, which have been denied or misconstrued in some way and from whose acceptance or denial important philosophical consequences follow. Examples include: self-consciousness and the first person; memory and personal identity; bodily awareness and bodily individuation; concepts of the body and concepts of external objects; and – to reiterate – art and the aesthetic. The general justification of such holisms is a deep question which cannot be pursued here.[42]

SOUNDS, TONES AND SOUND-ART

What are the implications of the preceding discussion for the concept of sound-art? I wish to advocate the position concerning the relation of music and sound-art which may be termed *non-universalism*. This position contrasts with conservative universalism and avant-garde universalism. *Conservative universalists* such as Roger Scruton argue that music is the universal (high) art of sound, and that it is essentially tonal – in the broad sense of tonal, of course, in which atonal music is tonal. Thus, they reject the possibility of any aural high art not based essentially on tones.

Conservative and *avant-garde universalists* agree in rejecting the concept of non-musical sound-art but differ in that for avant-gardists, 'non-musical sound-art' is a mis-labelling of an artistically valuable and genuinely musical enterprise, while for conservatives the enterprise itself is misconceived. Conservative universalism is no longer tenable, I believe; the real debate is between liberal or avant-garde universalism and non-universalism. Stockhausen advocates the former position. Taking electronic composers' discovery of the continuum between sound and noise – acoustically defined as unstable periodicity – as a vital development, he concludes that, 'Nowadays any noise is musical material'.[43] In similar vein, Marina Rosenfeld comments that 'instead of the notion of [avantgarde composer Morton] Feldman's work contributing to a history of "freeing sound from music" ... I experience the opposite: that in a great deal of groundbreaking twentieth-century music there was an attempt to radically reintegrate sound into music'.[44] Non-universalists, in contrast, claim that there is a genuinely non-musical sound-art which aims to 'free sound from music'. Thus Wiora assumes non-universalism when he writes: 'Music is a play of tones ... If [other sounds] are numerous, the result is only partially musical. If they predominate, it is no longer music'.[45] Non-universalism inherits the truth in conservative universalism that the central concept of music is tonal in the broad sense.

To develop a point made earlier about 'non-tonal' music, the claim that the central concept of music is tonal does not exclude borderline cases. A piece consisting of a pure, single sine-tone might not count as music because music characteristically uses impure tones, impurity being an inevitable consequence of human intentional production using the voice or traditional instruments. It might also be argued that a piece could involve no tones and yet be music – consider a piece for tam-tam with no pitched tone and maracas; or Australian Aboriginal music where glissandos and portamentos predominate.[46] In fact there is a continuum of universalist positions, from conservative to avant-garde, depending on the degree to which non-tonal material is allowed to enter into music. This is not simply a matter of contrasting a predominantly tonal composition into which elements of noise are incorporated, with one which predominantly comprises noise as material. For when the structural nature of tone is recognized, in a holistic account involving rhythm, melody and harmony as

THE CONCEPT OF MUSIC

opposed to an atomistic one, then it is possible to contrast *musical organization* of essentially non-tonal material – as found in some compositions by contemporary avantgarde composer Helmut Lachenmann, or in the Fiat advert in which car noises are organized in a rhythmic structure – with the physical or *non-tonal organization* of tonal material found in Varèse or Xenakis. This distinction is never clear-cut, though. For instance, Ligeti's early micro-polyphonic 'cloud pieces' from the 1960s and 1970s, such as 'Requiem', 'Atmosphères', 'Lontano' and 'Clocks and Clouds', are hard to place. They do not have a role for melody and rhythm in any conventional sense and so, it could be argued, have a tendency towards sound-art.

The arguments of avant-garde universalists tend to be empirical – they maintain that advocates of non-musical sound-art have rarely achieved anything significant.[47] However, I believe that there is a nascent category of genuinely non-musical sound-art, and the issue is how it should be separated from other categories and how its own internal distinctions can be captured. Sound-art should first be distinguished from sound-design, which itself falls into two categories. The first is what I will term *significant sound-design*, such as mobile telephone ring-tones, alarm-clock tones, car-horns, door-chimes, computer 'earcons' and airport announcement chimes.[48] The items in this category have a practical function and a non-natural meaning; they give explicit information. The second category of *non-significant sound-design* includes fountains, car or aeroplane engines and tones for synthesizers and other electronic instruments. There is also an interesting intermediate category of sound designed to convey subliminal meaning: the way, for instance, that the satisfying clunk of a car-door on an expensive model is crafted with the intention of conveying sumptuousness and quality.

Turning from sound-design to sound-art, two sub-categories can be distinguished. The first is *documentary sound-art*; although Cage's use of ambient sounds was not documentary, his influence on this genre is clear. Examples are found in work of the artists mentioned at the outset of this chapter.[49] The second category of sound-art, intermediate between music and documentary sound-art, is *non-documentary sonic composition*, which creates instead of merely documenting an environment. The successors of *musique concrète* in the *Group de Recherches*

61

Musicales, notably Bernard Parmegiani, provide examples of this category. Like music, non-documentary sonic composition invites twofold experience, both acousmatic and non-acousmatic, while documentary sound-art struggles to escape the non-acousmatic – even assuming its exponents wish to do so.[50] No example of so-called documentary sound-art could be merely documentary, however; any artistic creation, even if it only selects material, has a form. To set up a mini-disc player and microphone in an Underground station and record the sounds of passengers and trains for 77 minutes, then release it unedited on a 77-minute CD, still requires basic if mundane compositional decisions – when to start recording, the kind of microphone, its location and direction and so on.

As noted earlier in this chapter, the sound-art community has different views on the relation between sound-art and music. Philip Samartzis, for instance, though happy to call himself a sound-artist, is ambivalent about dividing avant-garde musical exploration from sound-art. He concedes that he thinks in musical terms and that sound-art's characteristic concern with spatialization – the choreographing of virtual space in a sound-system – comes out of musical modernism.[51] So it could be argued that the attempt at separation simply exhibits an unjustified 'genre anxiety' and that the issues here are purely sociological. However, I believe that I have offered convincing conceptual reasons, based partly on the concept of tone, why music and sound-art should be regarded as increasingly divergent tendencies, even though there is considerable overlap between them.

In the next chapter, we return to the historical approach of Chapter 1, and examine the fundamental aesthetic concept of absolute music, which has been so influential since the later eighteenth century.

NOTES

1 The term comes from Wishart (1996).
2 Smalley (1986).
3 Szlavnics (2006), p. 39.
4 Alcopley (1968), p. 194.
5 Stockhausen quoted in Kahn (1999), p. 112; Boulez (1971), pp. 22–3.
6 Quoted in Diliberto (1986), pp. 54–9, 72. In invoking the parallel of

solfege, Schaeffer was also emphasising the connections with traditional musical creation.

7   Cage quoted in Kahn (1999), p. 114; Schaeffer quoted in Kahn (1999), p. 110. Schaeffer explained that 'each time I was to experience the disappointment of not arriving at music ... In fact I don't consider myself a real musician ... A good researcher is what I am' (Schaeffer (1987)).

8   *Musique concrète* is discussed further in Hamilton (forthcoming 2007a).

9   López (accessed 2004). See also < http://www.sounddesign.unimelb.edu.au/site/index1.html >. Philip Samartzis, who admires López's work, comments: 'He uses microphones, tape-recorders and loudspeakers in a very orchestral manner, from the concerts I've attended – so it's all music! There's a formal element – it's in darkness, he loves the drama, it's very theatrical. This argument that he's trying to forge is part of the "bad boy" image' (telephone interview with the author, 9/11/06).

10 Entry under 'Environmental Music' in Sadie and Tyrrell (2004).

11 LaBelle (2006), p. ix.

12 LaBelle (2006).

13 Scruton (1997), p. 16. Scruton's general position is discussed in Hamilton (1999).

14 Cage's *4' 33"* exemplifies ambient sound, rather than representing or documenting it – the piece is a framing device; Maconie (1990), pp. 11–12.

15 The modern system of the fine arts is discussed by Kristeller (1990).

16 These examples come from Nettl (2001); see also Nettl (1989), and Robertson-De Carbo (1976).

17 'Musik' applies to all kinds of music, while 'Tonkunst' refers to Western art music, and was used in that sense by Hanslick; today it sounds pretentious or elitist.

18 'The string quartet and urban pandemonium are historically contemporaneous' (Schafer (1977), p. 103). See Van Leeuwen (1999), p. 1.

19 Nettl (2001), p. 466.

20 Davies (2001), p. 258.

21 The *Ursonate* consists of organized phonetics, notated in German. A recording by Schwitters himself from the 1930s was discovered many decades later and released on Wergo (Schwitters (1995)); other artists have also recorded it. The web page < http://www.ubu.com/sound/schwitters.html > is an excellent resource on this amazing piece. Jaap Blonk is a fine contemporary exponent of Dadaist sound poetry or text-sound – see for instance Blonk (2004).

22 'In The Middle Ages and the Renaissance the voice was still a musical instrument and music was embedded in every aspect of everyday life, just as many less developed cultures had and still have songs for grinding grains, songs for harvesting crops, songs for constructing houses ... But as clergical plainsong, the cries of night-watchmen, and the chanting of the ABC in schools were replaced by reading aloud, speech was divorced from music, and much flattened in the process' (van Leeuwen (1999), p. 1).

23 Nettl (2001), p. 466; entry under 'Music' in Sadie and Tyrrell (2004).

24 Nettl, in his entry under 'Music' in Sadie and Tyrrell (2004), cites several accounts in musical encyclopedias which assume a definition in terms of tones.

25 Grant (2001), p. 96.

26 A more developed definition of rhythm is presented in Chapter 5.

27 Hence Palombini's reference to the musical note or tone as 'a notable assortment of pitch, duration, and intensity, [which] has borne sway over European tradition and laid claim to universality' (Palombini (accessed 2004)). 'Tone' in this sense is not a musician's term; for most musicians, 'tone' refers to timbre. But Schoenberg objected to 'atonal' as a description of his music, on the grounds that all music uses tones.

28 Comment to Peter Stadlen after Otto Klemperer's performance of his Symphony Op. 21 in 1936, quoted in Moldenhauer (1979), p. 471.

29 An interesting discussion of the Aeolian harp is found in Hankins and Silverman (1995), Chapter 5.

30 Strangely, Lippman denies that violin tone is form. He continues: '[It] is restrictive to regard sound [that we produce] simply as material that is formed. Instead we are confronted with ... music as a social activity rather than an object that presents itself to consciousness ... more importantly, music contains something of this quality of activity in its very nature ... even apart from actual performance' (Lippman (1977), p. 45). The last sentence is close to Scruton's claim that music, in dynamic and other qualities such as movement, is the object of necessary metaphorical perception, to which we return later. Contrast Greene (1940), p. 46: 'The primary raw material of pure music is auditory sound with variations of pitch, timbre, intensity, and duration, plus silence, regarded as the mere absence of such sound ... [it is] entirely pre-artistic in character and constitutes the subject-matter of the physical science of acoustics'.

31 I am sympathetic to Denis Dutton's (2002) account of artistic skill; Pye develops the concept of 'useless work' in his (1978), for instance pp. 12–13, 34.

32 Levinson (1991), p. 272.

33 See <http://www.whirligig-tv.co.uk/radio/mwyw.htm>, accessed 2005.
34 North et al. (1999).
35 Packard (1960).
36 Kant had harsh words for *Tafelmusik*: 'an odd thing, which is supposed to sustain the mood of joyfulness merely as an agreeable noise, and to encourage the free conversation of one neighbour with another without anyone paying attention to its composition' (*Critique of Judgment*, section 44, Ak. 305).
37 Levinson (1991), p. 272.
38 As Young (2005) in effect argues. His claim is that music was the object of exclusively aesthetic attention even before the 'great divide' of 1800, when concert-going overtook the place of music in social, civic or religious ceremonies. He offers interesting empirical evidence to this conclusion.
39 Nettl (2001), p. 468.
40 Recall Francisco López's comment that he is 'fighting against a dissipation of pure sound content into conceptual and referential elements … trying to reach a transcendental level of profound listening that enforces the crude possibilities of the sound matter by itself' (López (accessed 2004)).
41 The issue is pursued in Chapter 4, and in more detail in Hamilton (forthcoming, 2007a).
42 A general account of conceptual holism is offered in Hamilton (forthcoming).
43 Stockhausen (1989), p. 109.
44 Cox (accessed 2004).
45 Wiora (1965), pp. 191–2; quotation translated in van Leeuwen (1999), p. 2.
46 I am indebted for these examples to Stephen Davies, including to his (2001), p. 49. His concern there is with the definition of a work as a sound structure or rhythmically articulated array of pitched tones; definition of a work is more open to objections from borderline cases than is the definition of music as such.
47 This seems to be Max Neuhaus's position in his introduction to P.S. 1's 'Volume: Bed of Sound' show in 2000, quoted in Cox (accessed 2004).
48 The tones played before announcements at Kuala Lumpur airport are particularly delightful.
49 An interesting recent example is Samartzis (2004), one of his best recordings in this genre.
50 See Chapter 4.
51 Telephone interview with the author, 9 November 2006.

CHAPTER 3

THE AESTHETICS OF FORM, THE AESTHETICS OF EXPRESSION AND 'ABSOLUTE MUSIC'

Aesthetics of music in the late eighteenth and nineteenth centuries

We now return to the directly historical perspective begun in Chapter 1, tracing the history of Western musical thought through the later eighteenth and nineteenth centuries, the era of the Enlightenment and the revolution of modernity. These developments were the most radical since ancient times. This period saw the emancipation of music from vocal models and the remarkable rise in the status of instrumental music, from the lowliest to one of the highest of the arts – contrast Kant's dismissive attitude in the *Critique of Judgment* from 1790 with Schopenhauer's grandiose evaluation less than thirty years later. It was also the era of Viennese classicism, of the music of Haydn, Mozart and Beethoven, which came to dominate – or create – the canon of Western art music. We examine the philosophical developments of the later eighteenth and nineteenth centuries that reflected and contributed to the elevation of music to its exalted status. Most of these developments occurred within German Idealism, the thought of Kant and his successors Hegel, Schopenhauer and Nietzsche, and they saw the appearance of certain key ideas of musical aesthetics – notably the concept of absolute music and the resulting idea of autonomy. When interpreted narrowly, these ideas resulted in formalism and the understanding of music as the most abstract art – misapprehensions which should be resisted, I will argue.

THE ROMANTIC METAPHYSICS OF MUSIC

From ancient times, vocal music was ranked above purely instrumental music, and the rhetorical or linguistic interpretation of instrumental music dated back to Ancient Greece. Since it now seems obvious that music is an aural phenomenon, and that a text – such as the lyrics of a song – is in some sense an extra-musical element, it is easy to overlook the fact that music, in almost all traditions, was once centrally vocal and dramatic. But the autonomy of music from text or rhetoric is an historically moulded assumption no more than two centuries old.[1] During the eighteenth and nineteenth centuries, Western art music became emancipated from an vocal and language model. For music theorist Carl Dahlhaus, the replacement of a literary with an autonomy model was a paradigm shift in music history: 'If instrumental music had been a "pleasant noise" *beneath* language to the common-sense estheticians of the eighteenth century, then the romantic metaphysics of art declared it a language *above* language'.[2] Call this the *language above language thesis*. According to the Romantic metaphysics of art, instrumental music was not a lower form of vocal music but the highest musical expression – the paradigm of absolute music.

Absolute music is pure, objective and self-contained – that is, not subordinated to words (song), to drama (opera), to a literary programme or even to emotional expression.[3] (It is important to stress that not all non-absolute music is music with or for a text – for instance, martial or ritual music.) The aspiration to absolute music and the increasing importance of instrumental music are related, though not the same process. The term 'absolute music' was first used by German Romantic writers, notably Herder, Jean Paul Richter and E. T. A. Hoffmann. The concept then appears in Hanslick's defence of *absolute Tonkunst* – literally, 'absolute art of tones' – against the music-drama of Wagner, and in the writings of twentieth-century theorists such as Heinrich Schenker. Partly through the famous review by E. T. A. Hoffman, Beethoven's Fifth Symphony became a template for absolute music, while Bach's *Art of Fugue* was appropriated from an earlier era.[4]

The opposed ideal of 'programme music' – 'paintings in sound' or 'tone-poems' with an extra-musical programme – took inspiration from Beethoven's Sixth Symphony, the 'Pastoral', with its evocations of birdsong and thunderstorms. In fact, the most popular forms in the nineteenth century were not absolute music. Pre-Wagnerian opera, oratorio, ballet and salon, romance and virtuoso display pieces, not symphonic and chamber music, were the main concerns of the music-going public; Beethoven's string quartets were recognized as a paradigm of absolute music only by the 1870s. The emergence of song as high art – often known by its German name *Lieder*, and clearly not absolute music – occurred only in the early nineteenth century.[5]

Absolute music was, therefore, a metaphysical aspiration and not a social fact; a part of composers' self-understanding, which presents a model of what they are trying to achieve.[6] Indeed, as Scruton puts it, 'The term "absolute music" denotes not so much an agreed idea as an aesthetic problem'.[7] It arose from a more general feature of art in the later eighteenth and nineteenth centuries, with which it is often run together: the growing *autonomy of music and art* – that is, its increasing freedom from direct social function. For Paddison, the autonomy character of music is the dominant idea of nineteenth-century aesthetics. *Heteronomous* – that is, non-autonomous – *music* has the function of serving the religious service, theatrical event or aristocratic banquet for which it was composed and performed. In this music and art, aesthetic aims were fused with or expressed through non-aesthetic ones – social, religious or ethical. Such art was produced for a personally known patron of a much higher social status than that of the artist, whose imagination was subordinated to the canons of taste of the patrons' social group – hence, the artwork had a weak individual and strong social character or style. This premodern or 'craftsmen's art', which is heteronomous, should be contrasted with modern or 'artist's art'.[8] The development of concert-life, from the late eighteenth century onwards, meant that musical performance no longer had a direct social function that subserved other practices, but became a practice in its own right. Music was now an art of modernity, produced for a market of buyers unknown to the artist at the time of production and addressed to a public of isolated individuals. The balance of power between artist and patron changed in favour of the former, and the artist gained greater independence from society's taste. The function of art could now become more purely aesthetic.

Absolute music is commonly equated with autonomous music.[9] However, there are two interrelated senses of autonomy: the autonomy of one art (in this case music) from other arts and the autonomy of art in general from non-art. Music's rise in status involved both, but the ideal of absolute music, I would argue, equates primarily with the first – though it is true that the two kinds of autonomy interact, since if one art is subordinate to another, it cannot be high art. When Romanticism inverted the ancient ranking of words above music, replacing a rhetorical or language model with an autonomy one, this was a case of 'music for music's sake' (the autonomy of one art) rather than 'art for art's sake' (the autonomy of art in general).[10] Programme music may be aesthetically autonomous in the sense of the autonomy of art in general and yet not autonomous in the sense of the autonomy of one art, because – according to its critics – it makes music subservient to a literary programme. Thus, at the same time that the arts in general were becoming autonomous, music became liberated from literary or linguistic models and became high art.

It is important to realize that the idea of autonomy as the defining feature of the modernization of art is itself a modernist idea – the quasi-political narrative of the emancipation of music is not a neutral history and arises from the work of a number of writers, most notably Adorno, as we will see in Chapter 6. Dahlhaus and Paddison are Adorno scholars – Dahlhaus was his student – and they sing from the same modernist hymn sheet. The hymns are uplifting, I believe, but we need to recognize their origins; cultural conservatives such as Scruton or Sharpe would tell the story a different way.[11] The eighteenth- and nineteenth-century writers discussed in this chapter were not familiar with the story of the growing autonomy of music, even though they were contemporary with it. Indeed, though increasingly they reflect the ideal of absolute music in their work, as pre-Marxists they never touch on the sociological issues highlighted by Adorno: music's emancipation from direct social function. Rather, they debate what may be characterized as the post-Romantic opposition of the *aesthetics of form* and the *aesthetics of expression*, which is therefore a central concern of this chapter.

Both within German Idealism and more widely, these two opposed tendencies followed the decline of Romanticism from the 1840s onwards. The aesthetics of expression was partly a more radical development of a 'feeling theory' which went back to C. P. E. Bach and arguably Monteverdi, but the aesthetics of form was genuinely new and a sign of music's rising status. The former aesthetic focuses on music's expressive power and the listener's emotional response to it; the latter locates value in the structure of the musical work. However, each rival aesthetic can be construed as a response to the challenge I have termed *the language-like character of music*. Music is like a language in having a syntactic structure but not actually a language because it has no semantics – no cognitive content can be pinned down. One persistent temptation, at least since the later eighteenth century, has been to regard it as a language of feeling. Another, and I think more justified temptation, has been to see its value as residing in its form or syntax. Kant is in some sense a precursor of the aesthetics of form, Hegel of the aesthetics of expression. Although associated with an aesthetics of expression, Schopenhauer was ambivalent on this opposition, while Nietzsche argued that the material of music is permeated with gestures redolent of meaning and thus fused the aesthetics of expression with that of form.[12] Hanslick has the reputation of an out-and-out formalist, though in fact matters are not so simple. Both the aesthetics of form and the aesthetics of expression contributed to the ideal of absolute music, as we will see.

KANT AND FORMALISM

Despite his apparently low estimation of music, Immanuel Kant (1724–1804) deserves a prominent place in this volume, since his highly influential aesthetics had a vital bearing on the course of the aesthetics of music. In contrast to his Idealist successor Hegel, Kant's discussion of individual arts is generally patchy and disappointing, and in the *Critique of Judgment* he apologizes – as one commentator says 'not without irony' – for this 'deficiency' in empirical matters.[13] The irony seems almost philistine. However, in the case of music, Kant's neglect at least in part reflects its lowlier status in the eighteenth century, and he seems able only to follow the consensus of his age in regarding wordless music as merely a beautiful play of sensations. He describes music as 'more a matter of enjoyment than of culture', and it does not fulfil what for him is the hallmark of valuable aesthetic experience, the free play of imagination with understanding, since it is inferior in the judgement of reason. It would be wrong to say that Kant regards music as a low form of art; his attitude to it seems more one of bemusement.[14] A key concept of Kant's aesthetics is his doctrine of *purposiveness without a purpose*, which, as we will see later, was the basis for Adorno's powerful treatment of artworks as functionless. Despite what is sometimes suggested, the latter was not Kant's own view, but it could be argued that he did in effect express the fundamental change in the concept of art towards something purposeless, without being consciously aware of it. For him, artworks mostly fall under the heading of *dependent beauty* as opposed to free beauty; the former makes essential reference to their perfection in terms of some concept or function. For instance, in aesthetic judgement of a painting, one must consider its lifelikeness – its function of creating lifelike representations. But Kant places purely instrumental music, together with designs *à la grecque* and foliage on the borders of wallpaper, under the contrasting heading of *free beauty*.[15] Free beauty – with its insistence on the possibility of autonomous aesthetic judgement – was the novel idea; dependent beauty is the traditional concept. Instrumental music, unlike dependent beauties such as vocal music, painting and literature, cannot express aesthetic ideas. These ideas 'body forth to sense' empirical notions like love, death and fame with 'a completeness of which nature affords no parallel' and rational notions such as freedom and God. The invention of aesthetic ideas belongs to genius. For Kant, instrumental music lacks the meaning and intellectual appeal of other arts; his view seems to be that it cannot be the product of genius.[16]

Kant regarded most of the arts as dependent beauties, therefore, and the ones that were not, notably instrumental music, he did not regard as fine or, as we say, 'high' arts. However, later writers took his view of free beauty – of autonomous aesthetic judgement – as the basis for the doctrine of *art for art's sake*.[17] An important element in this influence on later writers arose from the formalist strand in his thinking. *Formalism* says that form, as opposed to content, meaning, representation or extrinsic purpose, is the primary element of aesthetic value. Kant claimed that a pure judgement of taste attends exclusively to the form of the object or of its representation, while impure judgements of taste are affected by such factors as charm or emotion. He argues that colours, tones, textures and emotional content are mere 'charms' and believes that such elements 'deserve being considered beautiful only insofar as they are *pure*. And that is an attribute that already concerns *form*'.[18]

There has been much debate concerning whether formalism is a superficial or essential feature of Kant's aesthetic thought. In fact, Kant is an aesthetic formalist but mostly not an artistic one, since for him all products of the fine or high arts are dependent beauties.[19] His concept of dependent beauty, and his characterization of artistic genius as involving the expression of aesthetic ideas, makes him an *anti-formalist* about many artforms other than instrumental music. In fact, to reiterate, he seems perplexed about music; natural free beauty, on his account, promotes virtue, but Kant does not suggest that music is like nature in having a high moral affect. Kant is a formalist about music because he denigrates the art as a free artificial beauty which lacks aesthetic ideas; Hanslick, in contrast, who as we will see is usually regarded as a formalist, elevates music. Because of music's alleged abstractness, formalism has seemed attractive to philosophers of music. (These issues are pursued at length in the final section of this chapter.) Despite Kant's own denigration of music, his huge influence on nineteenth-century thought combined with that of Hegel, acting as a catalyst in the development of the romantic conception of autonomous music as a 'language above language' – a form of cognition on a par with philosophical speculation.

HEGEL: HISTORICISM AND TRUTH-CONTENT

Although he has a more positive evaluation of music as an art, G. W. F. Hegel (1770–1831) does not himself advocate the 'language above language' thesis. His aesthetics is profound and is grounded in his metaphysics; his vision of art history fits a grand historical plan. Hegel affirmed that art has an essential relation to philosophy and he elevated it within the sphere of systematic philosophical concerns. Unlike Kant, he has much of interest to say on the individual arts including music, his treatment of which is influenced by its burgeoning artistic status from the late eighteenth century – a development reflected in the interplay between the musical and the philosophical that is characteristic of early Romantic thought.

In the *Lectures on Fine Art* (1835), Hegel allows that 'the Kantian Criticism' found in the opening sections of the *Critique of Judgment* 'forms the starting-point for the true conception of artistic beauty'.[20] That is, he agrees with Kant that aesthetic judgement is disinterested, that beauty is the object of a universal and necessary delight and that it involves purposiveness without a purpose. But while Kant recognized that art has broader functions than the exercise of taste, Hegel argued emphatically that art's primary role is *the disclosure of truth*. He believes that art and religion are ways of discovering ourselves and the world, not merely ways of beautifying and sanctifying what has already been discovered. Thus, Hegel is a *cognitivist about art*: that is, he holds that its principal aim is not to give pleasure but to enhance understanding. The content of art is not abstract but is 'the sensuous appearance [*Scheinen*] of the Idea'; it appeals through the senses to the mind or spirit.[21] However, since Hegel's pervasive philosophical impulse is to elevate purely conceptual modes of expression above sensory ones and art embodies metaphysical truth through a sensory medium, he is deeply ambivalent towards it. Nonetheless, he does allow that as well as being understood conceptually, truth must be felt and loved through religion and experienced sensuously through art: 'for in inwardness as such, in pure thought, in the world of laws and their universality man cannot endure; he also needs sensuous existence, feeling, the heart, emotion'.[22]

Hegel's treatment of art, like the rest of his philosophy, differs most profoundly from Kant's in its pervasive historicism. The fundamental claim of historicism is that concepts and norms are historically conditioned. Hegel's historicism is not relativist, however – he does not hold that all historical systems of thought are equally valid – and he maintains that modern philosophy represents an advance over ancient philosophy in our understanding of ourselves and the universe. He holds, against Kant, that philosophical doctrines are not simply the product of pure reason, but are also the result of historical conditions; our concepts, including those of art and the aesthetic, are always developing. Philosophers up to his own time, Hegel believed, had failed to realize that what is held to be 'natural', such as classical artistic ideals, is often culturally determined.

Hegel is responsible for the influential idea that each artform has a dynamic of development – a grand historical narrative of autonomy. Influenced by Hegel, art theorist Heinrich Wölfflin recognized that in art, 'not everything is possible at all times' – an insight into the historical nature of the making and appreciation of art and an affirmation central to the modernist project which we return to in Chapter 6.[23] For Hegel, the history of art reflects the movement of *Geist* or Spirit in its transition from the sensuous (architecture, sculpture and, finally, painting) to the non-sensuous (music and poetry). The framework for this transition is three-fold: Symbolic (pre-Greek), Classical and Romantic – by 'Romantic' Hegel means not the artistic and intellectual movement of the later eighteenth and early nineteenth centuries, but all post-classical or post-Greek art. The Symbolic arts are represented by architecture, the Classical arts by sculpture. The Romantic arts – painting, music and poetry – are the summit of artistic achievement in their expression of the 'inwardness of self-consciousness', whose content is 'not tied to sensuous presentation': 'In this way Romantic art is the self-transcendence of art but within its own sphere and in the form of art itself'.[24] However, in Hegel's terms, Romantic art is inherently paradoxical, since while art is defined as the reconciliation of form and content, in Romantic art these are again separated and opposed. This is what he means by the self-transcendence of art – Romantic art, like all art, exists in sensuous form, but its content of spiritual inwardness marks a turning away from sensuous form.[25] In its ability to represent sensuous forms, sculpture is the most aesthetic art, while music is the most inward art – meaning that it is not dependent on sensuous appearance but is closer to thinking and conceptuality.

His pervasive historicism, and bias towards cognitivism and suspicion of sensuous experience of art, means that Hegel's re-evaluation of music is equivocal. He holds that art in general, and within the latter's overall development, each individual art in turn, flourishes and declines in accord with the progression from sensuous to non-sensuous – thus, the arts yield overlapping patterns of historical development. Romanticism – the era after Greek classicism – signals the *end of art*, that is, the end of art's progressive development. For Hegel, 'the keynote of Romantic art is *musical*', since music is emancipated from external reference. Because music mediates the spatial sensuality of painting and the abstract spirituality of poetry, it has an important place within

Hegel's system. Music exists solely in time, and its proper element 'is the inner life as such, explicitly shapeless feeling ... music's *content* is constituted by spiritual subjectivity in its immediate subjective inherent unity, the human heart, feeling as such'.[26] For Hegel, music is the art of the soul, directly addressed to the soul, because it shares the property of self-negation through time – musical sound is perpetually dying away and vanishing. Its penetration of the self is the reason for its elemental might.[27]

Unlike Kant, Hegel is resolutely anti-formalist and argues that music rises to the level of a true art only when it has spiritual content and expression. At the same time, however, Hegel believes that of all the arts music has the greatest potential freedom from specific content: 'Whilst ... the painter or sculptor should be recommended to study the forms of nature, the musician has no parallel field of study at his disposal, save for the forms that have already been developed which would have to be adhered to'. Hence the claim that music is emancipated from external reference.[28] Holding that music is non-spatial, Hegel accords it a high value; but he believes that it represents the world of feeling and so cannot have the spiritual profundity of poetry.[29] Such claims place Hegel as a precursor of the aesthetics of expression.

Though he was not a cultural conservative, and his critical standpoint towards society was developed explosively by Marx, by the standards of his time Hegel had conservative musical tastes. He valued vocal over instrumental music, and the language-centred nature of his thought precluded any real understanding of purely instrumental music, and especially the comparatively abstract music of contemporary Viennese classicists Haydn, Mozart and Beethoven.[30] Hegel seems unaware of the growing autonomy of art and makes no mention of his exact contemporary Beethoven, who was greatly celebrated in his time.[31] However, it may have been Beethoven's music, and certainly that of C. P. E. Bach, Mozart and Haydn, which he had in mind when he wrote: 'Today's dramatic music often looks for its effect in violent contrasts by forcing into one and the same musical movement opposite passions which are artistically at variance ... [the results are] opposed to the harmony of beauty the more sharply characterized are the opposites'.[32] It is ironic that Hegel criticizes 'today's dramatic music' – that is, Viennese classicism – when later writers such as Adorno drew comparisons between his dialectics and those of Beethoven.

SCHOPENHAUER AND WAGNER: ABSOLUTE MUSIC

At last a philosopher – Arthur Schopenhauer (1788–1860) – was able to recognize music without qualification as a cardinal human activity, even though his bravura philosophical treatment of it must be considered untenable. *The World as Will and Representation*, published in 1818, though it did not become influential until the second half of the nineteenth century, is the classic statement of the Romantic metaphysics of music and of the 'language above language' thesis. It is unique among philosophical writings in the central systematic role it gives to music and in its effect on the history of music. Wagner regarded reading it as a decisive moment in his intellectual and musical development, since it made him reverse the priority of drama over music in his operas, synthesizing symphonic and operatic traditions. As Paddison puts it, Schopenhauer 'sends Wagner some way back in the direction of absolute music'.[33] The compliment was not returned, however. After attending a performance of *The Flying Dutchman*, Schopenhauer commented that Wagner did not know what music was.[34]

Despite his gifts as writer and polemicist, Schopenhauer's aesthetics of music is not immediately persuasive. Like Hegel's, it rests directly on his metaphysics, which is in brief an amalgam of Kant and Plato, influenced by reading of the Hindu Upanishads, and laced with a pessimism reinforced by then dominant interpretations of Buddhist writings. Schopenhauer holds with Plato that the world of sense-experience has only 'relative being'. Drawing on Kant's claim that the subject knows itself in itself because it knows that its will is free, Schopenhauer argues that all things have willing as their essential nature. This 'willing' is a blind and mostly unconscious striving, resulting in a state of constant lack of fulfilment from which aesthetic experience provides a temporary escape. Schopenhauer radically reinterprets Kant's account of aesthetic judgement as disinterested, seeing it as transcending ordinary forms of perception and, therefore, possessing special value. Like Hegel, his great rival, Schopenhauer regards art as a form of knowledge. He holds that while ordinary perception is focused on particular material objects, aesthetic perception attends to the permanent ideas behind them; the artistic genius's abnormal gift for objective, will-less perception allows others a concentrated glimpse of the world of Ideas.[35] The subject's whole consciousness is filled with quiet contemplation of the natural object actually present; one 'ceases to consider the where, the when, the why, and the whither of things, and looks simply and solely at the *what*'. Art, he argues, leads us to 'perfect resignation, which is the innermost spirit of Christianity as of Indian wisdom, the giving up of all willing'.[36]

For Schopenhauer, music is the highest of the arts, because it least represents the world of appearance; its relationship as a representation 'lies hidden very deep'. While other arts attempt to gain knowledge of ideas, music is an immediate copy or manifestation of Will itself and, at the same time, is the artform most capable of freeing us from the baneful force of the will. It is totally independent of the phenomenal world; it simply ignores the world, and it could in some sense continue to exist even if the world did not. Schopenhauer's metaphysics of music is the most florid expression of the 'language above language' thesis:

> In a language intelligible with absolute directness, yet not capable of translation into that of our faculty of reason, [music] expresses the innermost nature of all life and existence ... the composer reveals the innermost nature of the world, and expresses the profoundest wisdom in a language that his reasoning faculty does not understand.

Schopenhauer believes that music allows us to apprehend the world in a manner akin to philosophical contemplation: music is 'an unconscious exercise in metaphysics in which the mind does not know it is philosophising'. Music attempts to do 'intuitively' and 'unconsciously' what philosophy does in a fully rational form.[37]

Schopenhauer espoused the Romantic aesthetics of expression rather than the aesthetics of form, though as noted earlier, when qualified these aesthetics are interrelated in supporting the ideal of absolute music. Acknowledging that music has been regarded as the language of feeling, just as words are the language of reason, Schopenhauer denies that it can express particular emotions, arguing that subordination to listeners' feelings, association with words or programmatic imitation will degrade it to the level of the phenomenal world.[38] What music expresses, he argues, is 'not this or that individual and specific joy, this or that grief, or pain ... but rather joy, grief, pain ... *themselves*, in the abstract to some extent'. It follows that here the will has no object and there is nothing for it to strive for, and so peaceful contemplation is possible: 'music reproduces all the movements of our innermost being but quite divorced from phenomenal life and remote from its misery'. Paddison argues that this extreme version of the theory of expression 'becomes what is sometimes mistakenly regarded as its opposite: formalism'.[39] Schopenhauer's view that emotions are expressed in music 'only in their form' became a nineteenth-century aesthetic commonplace. Through his highly abstract interpretation of the aesthetics of expression, he stands as one of the foremost proponents of absolute music.

Schopenhauer's commitment to absolute music implied an ambivalent attitude towards opera. Describing it as 'an unmusical invention for the benefit of unmusical minds', he condemns then-popular French grand opera with its colourful pageantry, and fanciful pictures and plot; while the truly musical mind desires only the pure language of tones.[40] Wagner agreed, and in place of the 'set piece' opera of Rossini and Meyerbeer, he conceived what critics and scholars termed *music-drama* – the composer himself never used the term. This was intended as a return to Greek drama, the symbolic expression of national aspirations through racial myth. Writing his own libretto, Wagner set a poetic drama to a continuous vocal-symphonic texture. Basic thematic ideas or *leitmotifs* marked dramatic highpoints and were developed by the orchestra as 'reminiscences' in accord with the psychological needs of the action. This new conception was fully embodied in the *Ring* cycle of four operas first performed in 1876. Given its symphonic unity, it is absolute music despite the presence of voices.

NIETZSCHE: THE APOLLONIAN AND THE DIONYSIAN

The philosopher-prophet Friedrich Nietzsche (1844–1900), who was also a minor composer, became a disciple both of Schopenhauer and of Schopenhauer's disciple Wagner. Having heard *Tristan and Isolde*, at the age of twenty-four in 1868, he was introduced to Wagner and became his friend and, as he afterwards wrote, 'one of the corruptest Wagnerians'. *The Birth of Tragedy Out of the Spirit of Music*, Nietzsche's first book published in 1872, was Wagnerian propaganda, advocating music-drama as a modern rebirth of tragedy. Its account of the ritual origins of Greek tragedy became widely influential.

The thesis of *The Birth of Tragedy* is that art develops according to a fruitful dialectic or opposition between the *Apollonian*, reflecting Classical order and self-control, and the *Dionysian*, expressing Romantic ecstasy. Nietzsche's account of Greek culture is speculative and infuriated contemporary scholars, but his main aim was to make us see our own culture in the 'polished mirror' of that of the Greeks – a continuation of Goethe's fascination with Greek culture discussed in Chapter 1.[41] Nietzsche argued that the Ancient Greek cults of Apollo and Dionysus prefigured the Classical–Romantic polarity of Western art, and he associates them with 'art of the image-maker or sculptor' and the 'imageless art of music' respectively.[42] For Nietzsche, the Apollonians advocated objectivity of expression, simplicity and clarity, and their favoured instrument was the *kithara*. The Dionysians, on the other hand, preferred the *aulos* – the double-piped reed instrument expressed subjectivity, sensuality and emotional abandon. Nietzsche hopes for a 'fraternal union' in which the Dionysian predominates, while 'Dionysus speaks the language of Apollo, but finally it is Apollo who speaks that of Dionysus' – when this happens, 'the supreme goal of tragedy, and indeed of all art, is attained'.[43] Greek tragedy synthesized these opposed elements and declined when Euripides replaced the Dionysian with the Socratic – 'the death of tragedy through the spirit of reason', in Danto's neat inversion.[44] In our day, Nietzsche believes, the Dionysian can be regenerated through Wagner's music-drama.

For Nietzsche, music is the Dionysian art par excellence – though great art need not literally be musical, it must be generated out of 'musical mood', that is, Dionysian consciousness. *The Birth of Tragedy* echoes Schopenhauer's position that music, in its highest function, is quite distinct from all other arts because, unlike them, 'it is not a copy of the phenomenon but an immediate copy of the will itself, and therefore complements *everything physical in the world* and every phenomenon by representing what is *metaphysical*, the thing in itself'. Nietzsche argues that music does not need images and concepts but merely tolerates them as an accompaniment: 'it is impossible for language to exhaust the meaning of music's world-symbolism'.[45] However, he also seems to argue the opposite view that 'music at its highest stages must seek to obtain its highest objectification in images'. Perhaps the conflict is resolved in the 'birth-of-tragedy' thesis that music originates in a union with poetry, and that great art is a synthesis of Dionysian and Apollonian.[46] Nietzsche's predominant view is an intriguing synthesis of the aesthetics of expression and the aesthetics of form. In *Human, All Too Humans*, from 1878, he argued that

> Music is, of and in itself, not so significant for our inner world, not so profoundly exciting, that it can be said to count as the *immediate* language of feeling; but its primeval union with poetry has deposited so much symbolism into rhythmic movement, into the varying strength and volume of musical sounds, that now we *suppose* it to speak directly *to* the inner world and to come *from* the inner world.[47]

That is, the initial and early dominance of vocal music – the union of music and poetry – means that we associate certain sounds with certain feelings.

Nietzsche maintains that absolute music is

> either form in itself, at a primitive stage of music in which sounds made in tempo and at varying volume gave pleasure as such, or symbolism of form speaking to the understanding without poetry after both arts had finally been united over a long course of evolution and the musical form had finally become enmeshed in threads of feeling and concepts ... In itself, no music is profound or significant, it does not speak of the "will" or of the "thing in itself".[48]

By 1876, however, as Nietzsche later put it, he had renounced his two youthful enthusiasms, the pessimistic philosophy of Schopenhauer and the decadent music of Wagner. Like impoverished souls who yearn for voluptuous intoxication, 'They deny and revile life, and are, therefore, my antipodes'.[49] Nietzsche came to feel that in Wagner he had mistaken a sickly, neurotic Romantic for a healthy, life-giving Dionysian; the Christian symbolism of Wagner's late masterpiece *Parsifal* revolted him, and in *The Wagner Case* of 1888, he proclaimed Bizet's *Carmen* as the Dionysian ideal.[50]

HANSLICK AND FORMALISM

Viennese critic and music theorist Eduard Hanslick (1825–1904) went further than Nietzsche in rejecting the 'feeling' aesthetic that had been dominant for the previous century. Hanslick is known as the advocate of Brahms' 'absolute music' against Wagner's music-drama. He dismissed opera as 'a constant compromise between dramatic realism and musical beauty, and rejected the 'programme music' of Berlioz, Liszt and Wagner. In fact, as we have seen, it is wrong to limit the 'absolute' ideal to instrumental music.[51] Although Hanslick is associated with the aesthetic of absolute music, it was Wagner who first coined the term. But because Hanslick appropriated the concept into a theory of the 'specifically musical', Wagner failed to recognize that the 'orchestral melody' of his own mature operas, which drew directly on Beethoven's symphonies, could also be regarded as absolute music.[52] So both Hanslick and Wagner, for different reasons, commit the same critical error.

Hanslick's *Vom Musikalisch-Schonen* (1854) has been translated misleadingly as *On The Beautiful in Music*; more accurately it is *On the Musically Beautiful*, since for Hanslick the beauty of music is 'specifically musical'. Rejecting composer Robert Schumann's claim that 'the aesthetics of one art is that of the others, only the material is different', he argued that the beauty of an art is inseparable from its specific techniques.[53] (It is interesting, in light of the received interpretation of Hanslick as a formalist, that he rejects this characteristic claim of formalism.) Thus, music has intrinsic value, but only instrumental music (absolute music) has true musical value. For Hanslick, music is fully autonomous and self-referential and cannot express feelings such as joy or grief even indefinitely or in the abstract, as Schopenhauer suggested: 'The function of art consists in *individualising*, in evolving the definite out of the indefinite, the particular out of the general. The theory respecting "indefinite feelings" would reverse this process'.[54] For Hanslick, music conveys the dynamic aspect of feelings only – their waxing and waning. Bujic argues that both Hanslick and Nietzsche agree on 'the basic inability of music to refer to a definite meaning, it is only that Nietzsche found it necessary to acknowledge borrowings from poetry as a means of overcoming the deficiency, whereas [Hanslick] acknowledged [it] as a unique form of communication'.[55]

With Hanslick, the concepts of form and theme moved to the centre of musical aesthetics.[56] For him, the content and value of music resides in the play of sounds, artistically combined as 'tonally moving forms', or as an early translation put it, 'The essence of music is sound and motion'. Hanslick writes that a completely realized musical idea 'is already self-subsistent beauty; it is an end in itself, and is in no way primarily a medium for the representation of feelings or conceptions'. He regards its form or structure as the real substance of music; feeling is simply the effect produced.[57] Musical material – harmony, rhythm and melody – expresses musical ideas which unlike feelings are determinate and are 'their own purpose'. 'Music demands once and for all to be grasped as music ... Music has sense and logic. It is a kind of language which we speak and understand yet cannot translate' – here Hanslick also endorses the Romantic idea of music as expressing non-conceptual knowledge, as language-like but not language.[58]

Hanslick's approach, like Hegel's, is broadly cognitivist, but it is not historicist. He maintained that, in aesthetics, the beautiful object and not the feeling subject should first be investigated. But he argues that Hegel 'insensibly confounded his predominantly art-historical viewpoint with a purely aesthetic one', though also hints that the material of music is not natural or raw, but historical, a claim developed to full effect, as we will see, by Adorno.[59] However, Hanslick's misconceived aspiration to set up a 'scientific' musical aesthetics is opposed to both Hegel and Kant. Despite his reputation as a formalist – a position that we will examine shortly – Hanslick criticizes the Idealists' undervaluation of the sensuous. For him, musical beauty is concrete, sensuous and immediate. Hanslick's standpoint was widely influential. Twentieth-century musicologists treated formal analysis as essential to the understanding of music, while his treatment of emotion and expression has been widely influential in Analytic aesthetics.

EXPRESSION, FORM AND ABSOLUTE MUSIC

Hanslick, I believe, offers the first modern treatment of the aesthetics of music, and much of his account remains viable – in contrast to the conservatism of Hegel, the metaphysical excesses of Schopenhauer and the intellectual opportunism of Nietzsche. Since this is an essay in philosophy, and not just history of ideas, we need to ask what is the truth in the aesthetics of form, the aesthetics of expression and the ideal of absolute music to which they contributed? The aesthetics of expression, I believe, is misconceived. This is not because some music is not emotionally expressive, or because music as such is, strictly speaking, not capable of expressing emotion, as Hanslick insisted. Emotion-ascriptions are secondary or metaphorical but may be objective nonetheless. (This point is developed in Chapter 5.) Adorno rejected both the aesthetics of expression and – in strict terms – that of form, but even he allows that no music exists without expressive elements: 'in music even expressionlessness becomes an expression'.[60] The interpretation and understanding of music certainly does involve careful attention to its expressive qualities; a decision about whether the mood of Brahms' late 'Intermezzo', Op. 117 No. 2, is one of tranquil nostalgia or bleak despair has a crucial impact on the performer's interpretation.[61]

It would perhaps be overstating the case to object that expression of emotion is not unique or special to music compared to the other arts and is not a special source of value in any of them. Aristotle, or one of his followers, believed that it does have a special relation to music:

> Why do rhythms and melodies, which are composed of sound, resemble the feelings, while this is not the case for tastes, colours and smells? Can it be because they are motions, as actions are also motions? Energy itself belongs to feeling and creates feeling. But tastes and colours do not act in the same way.[62]

This claim is convincing, but to pursue it one needs to examine the more fundamental question of the conceptualization of music as motion. This, in general, the aesthetics of music has not done, and it is the topic of Chapter 5.

It is an interesting question how the aesthetics of expression arose, and why it has been so prominent in post-Romantic aesthetics of music. One factor is the language-like nature of music. Because no cognitive content can be assigned, the temptation has been to regard music as a language of feeling.[63] Now one could ask why architecture, design and other abstract arts have not been regarded as expressive in the same way. (Perhaps, in the case of abstract painting, they have.) In any case, the aesthetics of expression does not seem a very plausible response to the puzzle of the language-like character of music. Another possible reason for the persistence of an aesthetics of expression lies in evolutionary explanations of music. Darwin was genuinely puzzled by music's apparent evolutionary redundancy: 'As neither the enjoyment nor the capacity of producing musical notes are faculties of the least use to man in reference to his daily habits of life, they must be ranked amongst the most mysterious with which he is endowed'. His suggestion is that music originated in the mating calls of our half-human ancestors, which now 'call up vaguely and indefinitely the strong emotions of a long-past age'. Evolutionary and linguistic considerations come together in Darwin's hypothesis that musical sounds formed a basis for the development of language.[64] These suggestions are intriguing, but the implications that evolutionary explanation holds for aesthetics is a large issue which I cannot pursue further here.[65]

The aesthetics of form is more plausible, I believe, and is more obviously linked to the ideal of absolute music. The latter concept is essentially contested – recall Scruton's caution that the term denotes an aesthetic problem rather than an agreed idea – and Spitzer has some justification in regarding the debate between absolute music and the extramusical as exhausted.[66] A heterogeneous set of features have been collected under the heading of absolute music. Spitzer, like many writers, runs it together with autonomy when he cites non-absolute aspects of early music – pre-Bach, maybe, or pre-Monteverdi: 'its dependence on social context, its design as a functional practice rather than an aesthetic object of quasi-religious contemplation, its symbiosis of compositional process with performance practice, and the rule-bound generativity of its musical language'.[67] However, it is important to reiterate two senses of autonomy:

1. Autonomy from the non-artistic, including from emotional expression, and social autonomy.
2. Autonomy from other arts.

When Hanslick asserted music's aesthetic autonomy, he was asserting both 1 and 2, but they can be separated. Adorno provides the deepest treatment of the first sense of autonomy, and it is discussed in Chapter 6. The second sense is the core ideal of absolute music discussed in this chapter, which asserts the aesthetic autonomy of music from literary and rhetorical models and its equality with the other arts – 'the autonomy of one art' as opposed to the autonomy of art in general.

In its multifarious aspects, the ideal of absolute music is central to musical modernism, the topic of Chapter 6; Schoenberg, for instance, was a resolute advocate. With the rise of modernism in the late nineteenth century, the ideal became generalized into a set of attitudes and tendencies across the arts, for which music became a paradigm as a result of its own struggle during that century to become abstract or 'absolute'. That at least is how modernists saw it, and painters took music's struggle as the model for their own. Such attitudes are associated with formalism, and, thus, with *aestheticism*, or *art for art's sake*, a cultural movement that reacted to the ills of modern industrial society by withdrawing from social engagement to inwardness. This development constituted a hardening of the aesthetics of form. The ideal of absolute music is an affirmation of this growing abstraction of music, but it is a theme of this volume that music is not essentially abstract; even the works of absolute music are related to human gesture and performance.

Aestheticism, or art for art's sake
' "But jazz is decadent bourgeois music," I was told, for that is what the Soviet press had hammered into Russian heads. "It's my music," I said, "and I wouldn't give up jazz for a world revolution" '. Langston Hughes's moving affirmation, which appeared as a motto to Josef Skvorecky's *The Bass Saxophone*, assumes aestheticism in a salutary, moderate form. This says that art has intrinsic value and is not subservient to other values, notably political ones.[68] Hughes is asking: what kind of revolution is it that compels the destruction of something as artistically valuable as jazz?

Aestheticism is a comparatively modern attitude, however. Historian Eric Hobsbawm comments that before the revolutions of 1848, 'art for art's sake', though already formulated, mostly by conservatives or dilettantes, could not yet compete with art for humanity's sake, or for the nations' or the proletariats' sake: 'Not until the 1848 revolutions destroyed the Romantic hopes of the great rebirth of man, did self-contained aestheticism come into its own'.[69] At its most extreme, art for art's sake holds that art is of no use whatsoever – notably that it has no moral use, not aiming to be didactic or edifying – and is quite divorced from life. Paddison writes: 'The *l'art pour l'art* position, especially as expressed by the French Symbolists, emphasized both the separation of art from life and the process of progressive control over "material" ... which further encouraged the intensive development of the art work as a "closed world"'.[70] The development of this ideology is central to the development of a modernist aesthetic, he believes. Thus the later nineteenth and early twentieth centuries may be regarded as the era of aestheticism and 'art for art's sake'. Through Wagner's influence on Baudelaire and the symbolists, literature retreated from referentiality, while the musical influence on abstraction in the visual arts is illustrated in the friendship between Schoenberg and Kandinsky.

In ordinary language, art for art's sake or aestheticism means the elevation of aesthetic above moral qualities (though the *OED* definition does not carry this implication, defining aestheticism as simply a concern with the aesthetic). Here are some more precise definitions:

1 *moderate aestheticism* or *separatism*: there is a concept of aesthetic value separate from moral and other values. This is the thesis of the separation of the value spheres discussed in Chapter 1, and in one sense, art for art's sake;

2 *radical aestheticism*: (a) aesthetic value is superior to moral and other values (Nietzsche, Oscar Wilde); (b) *formalism*: moral qualities are irrelevant to the evaluation of an artwork as an artwork, but so also are non-moral qualities such as representational content or meaning;

3 the claim that the aesthetic is the domain of disinterested, distanced contemplation, involving a special attitude, the preserve of experts or 'aesthetes';

4 art is or ought to be divorced from life. Wilde asserts that art 'has an independent life, just as Thought has, and develops purely on its own lines'.[71]

One possible implication is that the history of art is separate from social and political history, and has its own laws of development – a view which contradicts the social stance of much current art history, with its focus on patronage.

What then should we make of the aesthetics of form, in its late incarnation as *formalism*? We have noted how proto-modernist proponents of art for art's sake regarded music as the paradigm artform because of its non-referentiality and abstraction. 'Formalism' was a pejorative label for their ideal, or at least a particular way of stating it, expressed in Walter Pater's dictum: 'All art constantly aspires to the condition of music'.[72] Oscar Wilde wrote in similar vein in the preface to *The Portrait of Dorian Gray* in 1891: 'From the point of view of form, the type of all the arts is the art of the musician ... All art is quite useless'. And according to pioneer abstract painter Wassily Kandinsky: 'Music ... is completely emancipated from nature ... Painting today is still almost entirely dependent upon ... forms borrowed from nature. And its task today is to examine its forces and its materials ... as music has long since done'.[73]

Formalism is a loose association of doctrines, as Mothersill sensibly notes, and there is no well-formulated definition that applies across the arts. However, she argues, its core idea is that in assessing a work of art, elements which suggest or establish a link between the artwork and the world should be disregarded.[74] But what exactly is this 'form' that formalists refer to? 'Form' is often held to refer to the perceptual elements of an artwork and the relationships holding between them, as opposed to its meaning, reference or utility.[75] Formalism has ontological and evaluative versions, which say respectively that an artwork is constituted by its form or structure, and that its value lies in its form or structure. Paradoxically, however – and this reflects the elusiveness of the position – formalism can also stress elements that may not be perceptibly present. *Narrow formalism* holds that only the inter-relations between individual sensual qualities – colours, lines, shapes, sounds and so on – are formal elements, and not those qualities as such. *Broad formalism*, in contrast, does describe such qualities as formal, when by 'form' is meant 'those things that are directly and sensually perceived in the work'.[76] Boretz defends narrow formalism: 'Sounds are not part of music, however essential they are to its transmission. Neither are paint, pigment and canvas parts of paintings, nor masses of bronze parts of sculptures'.[77] This position denies that music is an art of sound, on the grounds that medium-specific features of an art are not essential to it, and has the implausible consequence that two works with different elements and even belonging to a different artform can share the same form. (Recall Schumann's claim rejected by Hanslick.)

In fact, like many philosophical positions, formalism turns out to be unoccupied – except perhaps by dilettantes and ideologues, if that is a fair description of later nineteenth- and early twentieth-century figures Pater, Wilde, Bell and Fry. As we have seen, Kant was not a formalist about all the arts and neither, arguably, was Hanslick. Thus I disagree with Zangwill, who, in advocating 'moderate formalism', offers a partial defence of what he regards as Hanslick's ontological and evaluative formalism. He construes the distinction between absolute and non-absolute music as one between the freely and the dependently beautiful, in Kant's terms discussed earlier: 'Contrary to Hanslick's formalist evangelism ... [non-absolute music] may be aesthetically valuable because of the *way* it serves [such] non-musical purposes [as marching, dancing, telling a story, meditating, or praying]'. (This interpretation presages the suggestion in Chapter 6 that the distinction between autonomous and heteronomous art rests on that between free and dependent beauty.) Arguing that some artworks have only formal properties while others have only non-formal properties and yet others have both, Zangwill maintains that some music gains by being mixed with the non-musical, while other music must be understood formally, in its own terms.[78]

This is a sane response to the debate concerning absolute music, but is it a correct interpretation of Hanslick? The latter's position seems close to those who criticize formalism for attempting to separate form and content. As we have seen, Hanslick rejects the aesthetics of feeling, and makes 'forms moved in sounding' the content of music; form is a content appearing in tonal material, and it is 'inner form', not outward appearance, an essence or 'musical idea'.[79] Thus he seems to equate form and content, rather than treating them as opposites in the way that formalists are meant to. Hanslick maintains that in the case of music, form and content mutually determine and complement each other:

> This peculiarity of music, that it possesses form and content inseparably, opposes it absolutely to the literary and visual arts, which can represent the aforementioned thoughts and events in a variety of forms ... In music there is no content as opposed to form, because music has no form other than the content.

Tones themselves are content, but they are already formed; they are form, but forms already fulfilled; the themes of a piece of music are its essential content, and the composer thinks and works directly in tones rather than translating some kind of conceptual content into them: 'In music there is sense and consequence ... There is a profound meaning in the fact that one speaks of "ideas" in musical works, and, just as in speech, a practised judge can easily distinguish true ideas from mere clichés'.[80] This is an 'intramusical' logic. It might be argued that Hanslick offers a more sophisticated kind of formalism. But it is odd for a formalist to say that form and content are inseparable; that reads more like a traditional *criticism* of formalism. Scruton argues that Hanslick's formalism is undermined by his metaphor of music as 'forms moved through tones', for the attribution of motion to music is just as metaphorical as ascriptions of emotion; nothing relevant in the music actually moves. The point is well taken, as we will see in Chapter 5, but Scruton puts the matter better when he says that since Hanslick tacitly accepts that music is the object of a metaphorical perception, he is not a formalist at all.

There is no doubt that formalist criticism had a benign influence on the reception of modernist art. Hanslick, by stressing the value of music independent of text, dance or scenic action, and formalist art critics, by stressing the purely visual values of the visual arts, helped to defend artistic autonomy. But as an antidote to impure as opposed to aestheticist conceptions of art – in the sense in which I have defined aestheticism as separation of the value spheres – formalism is excessive. The fundamental objection to formalism is the interpenetration of form and content argued for in Chapter 2. Modernist art critic Clement Greenberg, for instance, comments that he is not a formalist because the doctrine assumes that 'form' and 'content' in art can be adequately distinguished.[81] The aesthetic is the fusion of the sensual and the intellectual, and form cannot epitomize that meeting point without reference to content.

Throughout this volume, I am concerned to question the assumption that music is the most abstract of the arts. Abstraction is qualified most importantly by music's status as a performing art that involves the human activity of producing sounds and by the historical content of its material. The next chapter develops the resulting standpoint by considering the acousmatic thesis, which says that musical experience involves abstracting from the causes of the sounds. The acousmatic thesis tends to separate music from the world, and I will argue that it should be qualified by a humanistic standpoint which links music to dance, movement and gesture.

NOTES

1 As discussed in Dahlhaus (1989), Chapter 1.
2 Dahlhaus (1989), p. 8. Paddison echoes his comment, arguing that instrumental music was transformed from 'an art form regarded as a pleasant but meaningless entertainment without cognitive value … [to] the vehicle of ineffable truths beyond conceptualisation' (Paddison (2002), p. 318).
3 Not to be confused with Absolute Music at Main Street, Fairborn, Ohio – <http://www.absolutemusic.com> – which claims to be 'your complete music shop'. They also sell autonomous music.
4 Rumph (2004), for instance, describes Hoffman as Beethoven's first great critic and champion, and as 'one of the original proponents of "absolute music"' (p. 6).
5 'In the period between the death of Beethoven and about 1860, the symphony without a programme might have been considered moribund, and the [future] could have been perceived to belong to music that was explicitly poetic' (Rushton (2001), pp. 155, 172).
6 Paddison (2002), p. 320; see also Dahlhaus (1989), p. 3.
7 Entry under 'Absolute Music' in Sadie and Tyrrell (2004). Treitler comments: 'the slogan "absolute music" took on its own power, like a political banner that is seized by persons of quite divergent persuasions … Yet there is a core of belief that the slogan signified throughout … the conception of an autonomous instrumental music that is essentially musical because it is not determined by any ideas, contents, or purposes that are not musical' (Treitler (1989), p. 177).
8 Elias (1993); see also Berger (1997).
9 For instance by Pauly (1959), and Spitzer (2004), p. 131.
10 Classical theorist Heinrich Koch assumed the language model when he wrote in 1802 that instrumental music was an 'abstraction' of vocal music (quoted in Dahlhaus (1989), p. 11). But in the late eighteenth century both the Romantic poet Heine and the writer Wackenroder claimed that music speaks a language which we do not recognize in our everyday life. The language model still has adherents. Sharpe (2000), for instance, argues that the cognitive elements in music – the recognition of a theme on its return, the identification of a canon, the realization that a movement is approaching its peroration – originate in an imitation of rhetoric.
11 Scruton (1997), Sharpe (2000). See also Berger (1997), whose views are discussed in Chapter 6.
12 As argued by Paddison (2002).
13 Kant (1987), p. 7.
14 Kant (1987), p. 198. Understanding Kant's precise attitude towards

music calls for close attention to section 53 of the *Critique of Judgment*.

15 Early French neoclassicism, from around 1750, was fascinated by classical Greek taste, and ornamental and architectural designs parodied classical features such as Vitruvian scrolls and geometrical garlands.
16 A good discussion of free and dependent beauty is found in Kirwan (2004), Chapters 2, 7 and 8.
17 See textbox 'Aestheticism' at end of chapter, pp. 85–6.
18 Kant (1987), sections 13 and 14.
19 Mothersill (1984) p. 226, Dziemidok (1993), p. 188 and Zangwill (2001), p. 60, point this out.
20 Hegel (1993), p. 64. For the limited material which it presents, Bosanquet's more elegant translation is preferable to Knox's.
21 Hegel (1975), Vol. I, pp. 111 and 71.
22 Hegel (1975), Vol. I, pp. 97–8. For a clear outline of Hegel's aesthetics, see Wicks (1993). Houlgate (2004), Chapter 9, provides a clear interpretation but its anti-modernism should be treated with caution.
23 In the introduction of his *Principles of Art History* (1986) (first published 1915), Wölfflin states that each artist has their own individual style; beyond this there is a national style, and finally a period style, all of which rise and fall cyclically.
24 Hegel (1975), Vol. I, p. 80.
25 See Johnson (1991).
26 Hegel (1975), Vol. II, p. 626.
27 Hegel (1975), Vol. II, p. 908; see Johnson (1991).
28 Hegel (1975), Vol. I, pp. 228, 229, 232.
29 Johnson (1991), p. 152.
30 As Johnson (1991) argues, p. 152.
31 See Paddison (2004), p. 207.
32 Hegel (1975), Vol. II, p. 947.
33 Paddison (2002), p. 331; see also for instance Stein (1960).
34 Gardiner (1963), p. 234. Gardiner's book provides an excellent account of Schopenhauer's aesthetics.
35 Schopenhauer (1969), Vol. I, sections 34, 36, 37, 50.
36 Schopenhauer (1969), Vol. I, section 48, p. 233.
37 Schopenhauer (1969), Vol. I, section 52, pp. 260, 264.
38 Schopenhauer (1969), Vol. I, section 52.
39 Paddison (2002), p. 331.
40 'On Aesthetics', in Schopenhauer (1970), p. 163. *Grand opéra* is French opera of the Romantic period, dominant from the 1830s onwards and represented by Rossini, Auber, Halévy and, above all, Meyerbeer. It

was sung throughout, required enormous forces and made for a great spectacle – provoking Wagner's reputed dismissal of Meyerbeer's 'effects without causes'.

41 'Assorted Opinions and Maxims', in Nietzsche (1986), p. 218.

42 Nietzsche (1999), p. 14.

43 Nietzsche (1999), p. 104, section 21, see also section 24. The question is discussed in Young (1992), p. 31.

44 Danto (2005), p. 39.

45 Nietzsche (1999), p. 36, section 6 – see also sections 5 and 16. This last claim is echoed in his fragment 'On Music and Words': 'The highest revelations of music make us perceive ... the crudity of all imagery, and of every affect chosen for analogy; e.g., as the last Beethoven quartets put every perception, and ... the entire realm of empirical reality, to shame ... ' (Nietzsche (1973), p. 25).

46 Nietzsche (1999), section 17. See also Young (1992), p. 38.

47 Nietzsche (1986), para. 215.

48 Nietzsche (1986), para. 215; see also *The Wanderer* ... 149–69.

49 Nietzsche (1958), 'Nietzsche Contra Wagner', 'We Antipodes'.

50 Liébert (2004) offers an excellent discussion of Nietzsche and music.

51 Kierkegaard in *Either/Or* regarded Mozart's *Don Giovanni* as so unified in form and content that it could also be regarded as absolute music: 'its idea is altogether musical in such a way that the music does not help along as accompaniment but discloses its own innermost nature as it discloses the idea' (Kierkegaard (1987), p. 56).

52 Dahlhaus (1989), pp. 26, 41; Chapter 2 addresses the complexities of the issue of Wagner and absolute music. The clash between the rival aesthetics had one curious illustration. Brahms' only formal engagement with fellow Viennese composer and Wagner supporter Anton Bruckner was lunch at his favourite Red Hedgehog: 'Both turned up with entourage. Everybody crowded around a table, waiting for one of the famous men to say something on this momentous occasion ... There was a long, excruciating silence. Finally Brahms picked up a menu and declared, for history: "Oh, dumplings with smoked meat! That's my favourite!". Immediately Bruckner's peasant voice chimed in, "I say, Doktor Brahms, dumplings and smoked meat! That's where we two agree!"' (Swafford (1998), pp. 562–3).

53 Hanslick (1986), p. 8.

54 Hanslick (1986), p. 21. Hanslick talks of the representation of emotions rather than their expression.

55 Bujic (1997).

56 As Dahlhaus (1989) notes, pp. 73, 109.

57   Hanslick (1986), pp. 28–9.
58   Hanslick (1986), Hanslick criticizes an overliteral comparison between music and language on p. 30.
59   Hanslick (1986), p. 39; Chapter 6.
60   He cites Schoenberg's use of 'extraterritorial chords that had not yet been occupied by music-linguistic intentions' – an inverted ninth chord with the ninth in the bass, used repeatedly in *Verklaerte Nacht*, and the fourth chord motif in the Chamber Symphony (Adorno (1998)).
61   This question is provoked by Radu Lupu's magisterial interpretation (1987). The issue is a very large one of course; an interesting discussion, focusing on the interpretation of Mozart, is found in Hildesheimer (1983), pp. 199–202.
62   Aristotle (1952), 920a 3–7.
63   An extreme example of this tendency is Cooke's philosophically naive (1960).
64   Darwin (2004), Chapter 19, pp. 636, 639. As was his wont, Darwin presents reports from fellow investigators of varying credibility, citing spiders and seals that are attracted by music and a mouse that is apparently able to sing up and down the tempered scale in semitones! (pp. 634–5).
65   For those who wish to pursue the question of music and emotion, Budd (1985), Matravers (2001), Levinson (2006) and Davies (1994) are recommended.
66   Spitzer (2004), p. 131.
67   Spitzer (2004), p. 131.
68   Skvorecky (1980), which includes Skvorecky's poignant essay 'Red Music', an impassioned dissection of totalitarian philistinism in Czecholovakia under the Nazi and Soviet dictatorships.
69   Hobsbawn (1962), p. 325.
70   Paddison (1993), p. 69.
71   Wilde (1909), p. 54.
72   He continues: 'That the mere matter of a poem . . . its subject matter, namely, its given incidents or situation – [or] the mere matter of a picture [viz.] the actual circumstances of an event, the actual topography of a landscape – should be nothing without the form, the spirit, of the handling, that this form . . . should become an end in itself, should penetrate every part of the matter: this is what all art constantly strives after, and achieves in different degrees' (Pater (1948) (first published 1877), pp. 271, 273).
73   Wilde (1994); Kandinsky, *On the Spiritual in Art*, in his (1982), Vol. I, pp. 154–5. The issue is interestingly discussed by Morgan (1984).
74   Mothersill (1984), p. 222.

75   See, for instance, the entry under 'Formalism' in Kelly (1998), Vol. II, p. 213.

76   See, for instance, Dziemidok (1993), p. 186.

77   Boretz (1970), p. 543.

78   Zangwill (2001), pp. 73–4. See also Zangwill (2004).

79   Dahlhaus (1982), p.54.

80   Hanslick (1986), pp. 80, 82, 78.

81   'Problems of Art Criticism: Complaints of an Art Critic' (1967), quoted in Curtin (1982), p. 326. Malcolm Budd sensibly comments that 'Formalists are motivated by a concern to preserve the autonomy of artistic value, but mistakenly believe that the only way to achieve this is by insulating artistic value from any aspect of a work – function, subject, emotion, thought – that has extra-aesthetic reference' (entry under 'Formalism' in Craig (2000)).

CHAPTER 4

THE SOUND OF MUSIC

Conductor Sir Thomas Beecham's delightful quip that 'The English people may not understand music, but they absolutely love the noise that it makes' trades on the fact that music *is* the sound.[1] But what is it to hear sounds as music? This chapter explores the *acousmatic thesis* that to hear sounds as music involves divorcing them from the worldly source or cause of their production. The concept of the acousmatic was developed in the 1940s and 1950s by *musique concrète* composers such as Pierre Schaeffer. *Musique concrète*, we saw in Chapter 2, is early electronic music, which has no performers and so no visual element to engage audiences or listeners. Its exponents believed that 'listening without seeing' allowed sounds to be more easily appreciated for themselves. When traditional, non-electronic music is performed, in contrast, the circumstances of its production are fully visible. But it could be argued that listening without seeing – acousmatic listening – captures something essential to truly musical experience.

The acousmatic thesis is associated with the enduring abstractionist position illustrated in the previous chapter under the heading of formalism. This position detaches music from the world, making it the most abstract of the arts – a pure 'art of tones'. However, the acousmatic thesis does not strictly imply the latter position. As advocated by Scruton, for instance, commitment to a pure art of tones is qualified by a humanistic understanding that the concepts of music, dance and human gesture are interlinked. My argument is that, even so, the acousmatic thesis neglects the importance of the human production of musical sounds to which appreciation of music makes essential reference, and which therefore limits music's abstract nature. It also neglects the way that our experience of music also refers to the nature of sound-producers – the instruments – as physical objects and the physical phenomena of sound-production. It is not true that music is the object only of metaphorical perception, therefore, as Scruton maintains; attending to sounds as part of the human and material worlds is a genuinely musical part of musical experience.

THE ACOUSMATIC EXPERIENCE OF SOUND

Scruton, in *The Aesthetics of Music*, develops what I term the acousmatic thesis as follows. In musical experience, he writes

> we spontaneously detach the sound from the circumstances of its production, and attend to it as it is in itself ... The acousmatic experience of sound is precisely what is exploited by the art of music ... The history of music illustrates the attempt to find a way of describing, notating, and therefore identifying sounds, without specifying a cause of them.[2]

Later, he writes that

> The person who listens to sounds, and hears them as music, is not seeking in them for information about their cause, or for clues as to what is happening. On the contrary, he is hearing the sounds *apart* from the material world. They are detached in his perception, and understood in terms of their experienced order: this is ... the acousmatic character of musical experience ... the notes in music float free from their causes ... What we understand, in understanding music, is not the material world, but the intentional object: the organization that can be heard *in* the experience.[3]

Zuckerkandl, quoted by Scruton, in some ways anticipates this general position: 'Tone ... does not lead us to the thing, to the cause, to which it owes its existence; it has detached itself from that; it is not a property but an entity'.[4] Other writers also adopt this position, for instance, Edward Lippman:

Hearing is satisfied with its own objects, and has no need to relate them to further objects and events of the outside world. This is especially evident in the case of tone and tonal configurations ... [Sonority's] ontological status is clearly that of an object peculiar to hearing; it can not be located at all in environmental space.[5]

The key thought behind the acousmatic thesis may, I think, be presented as follows: an economy of meaningful sound appears to liberate sounds from the need to have a worldly source, and so music escapes the gravitational pull of its causal origin. What remains in musical experience is its non-worldly or musical cause or rationale.[6]

We saw in Chapter 2 how Scruton, agreeing that no intrinsic properties of sound are required, argues in opposition to modernist conceptions that melody, rhythm and harmony are necessary yet non-intrinsic. For him, these qualities are properties not of sound, but of tones, that is, pitched sounds, and sound becomes musical tone when organized by pitch, rhythm, melody and harmony. Scruton develops his account of tones through traditional defining features of pitch, rhythm, melody and harmony. Timbral and spatial aspects of music, which seem to relate sounds to the circumstances of their production, are interpreted by him in a manner which he believes is compatible with the acousmatic thesis. He makes various distinctions between the acousmatic and non-acousmatic realms, distinguishing acoustical experience of sounds (non-acousmatic) from musical experience of tones (acousmatic); the real causality of sounds from virtual causality between tones; the sequence of sounds from the movement of tones that we hear in them.

Scruton links the acousmatic thesis with the claim that tone is the intentional object of intrinsically metaphorical musical perception. Thus, the objective but phenomenal acousmatic realm exhibits a 'virtual causality' between tones, in contrast to the real causality between sound-producers – musical instruments included – and sounds. Virtual causality is found in melody, where we hear not just change, but movement – a rising and falling in pitch, and tension and resolution. It is also found in rhythm: 'To hear rhythm is to hear a kind of animation ... Beats do not follow one another; they bring each other into being ... and breathe with a common life'.[7] Talk of movement is metaphorical – only the performer's body and limbs, the instrument and air molecules, literally move – but essential to the experience of music.[8] This important and persuasive thesis of the *necessary metaphorical perception* of music is discussed later in this chapter, in its relation to the acousmatic thesis, and in Chapter 5.

It is essential to recognize that the acousmatic thesis is a claim about how musical sound is *experienced* – with or without reference to its physical cause – not about how it is *known* to have that cause. In acousmatic experience, the thesis says, the listener knows that the sound has a physical cause, but it is not that which they attend to. Rather, they attend to the imagined or virtual causality present in the musical foreground, and which is 'heard in' the medium. What motivates the acousmatic thesis – I would argue – is this process of 'hearing-in', which shows interesting parallels, and contrasts, with the concept of 'seeing-in', the twofold experience of painting and picturing developed by Richard Wollheim. While the latter phenomenon is much discussed, its aural equivalent is almost entirely neglected, and it is a valuable feature of the acousmatic thesis that it corrects that neglect. The problem with it is that aesthetic experience embraces the non-acousmatic, just as it embraces the non-representational element in painting, and so ultimately I reject it. Nonetheless, I show that the thesis yields significant insights into the nature of musical experience and expresses an important dichotomy in terms of which the experience of music can be understood. I conclude this chapter by proposing a twofold account of musical experience involving both acousmatic and non-acousmatic – a duality apparent in other sound-arts and sound-design, and in any aesthetic experience of sound.

PYTHAGORAS AND *MUSIQUE CONCRÈTE*

Composers in the tradition of *musique concrète* did not espouse the acousmatic thesis in the form that Scruton presents it. As we saw in Chapter 2, *musique concrète* was among the earliest uses of electronic means to extend the composer's resources to non-tonal sounds. (Non-tonal in the sense of 'not based on tones' – as opposed to atonal, 'not based on the tonal system of major and minor keys'.) Unlike traditional composition, it did not depend on performers to interpret or realize a notated score. As we saw in Chapter 2, when Pierre Schaeffer founded the school of *musique concrète* in the 1940s, he used the primitive recording technology of disc-cutters and tape-recorders to create compositions from a montage of everyday and natural sounds – mechanical and human noise, as well as more traditional musical materials such as the piano and other instruments. These sounds were modified in various ways – played backwards, cut short or extended, subjected to echo-chamber effects, filtering out or reinforcing of certain frequencies, or varied in intensity – which in later *musique concrète* had the effect of destroying clues about the source of the sounds.[9] The term *concrète* is meant to convey the idea of working directly or concretely with sound material, in contrast to the composer of traditional music who – according to exponents of *musique concrète* – works indirectly or abstractly through a system of notation which represents the sounds to be made concrete. *Concrète* also conveys the genre's concern with natural, real-world source-sounds, though in theory recorded electronic sounds were not forbidden.

While *musique concrète* typically treats and often transforms 'worldly' sounds from everyday life such as footsteps, trains and doors slamming, pure electronic music from the Stockhausen tradition – initially known by its German designation *elektronische Musik* and sometimes referred to as sound synthesis – is produced at least in part by computer synthesis. However, despite the ideological divide between *musique concrète* and pure electronic music, most practitioners were not purists. In *Hymnen* from 1966–7, Stockhausen used recorded sounds of national anthems, which are recognizable though they are also transformed; in the early 'Gesang der Jünglinge', which uses recordings of a child singing, there is an even closer affinity to *musique concrète*. Today, while the French and German traditions have come together, distinct tendencies are still apparent.[10] But the historic divide between *musique concrète* and *elektronische Musik* now concerns how the composition is realized in the performance-space as much as the kind of material exploited – hence the contrast between sound *diffusion* of acousmatic music and sound *reproduction* of taped music.[11]

For Schaeffer, a composition is experienced acousmatically when a curtain has been lowered between its constituent sounds and their previous worldly existence. In this situation, which the medium of recording privileges, sounds are treated as objects divorced from their sources or causes. Schaeffer took the term 'acousmatic' from Pythagoras' alleged practice of lecturing to students from behind a screen so that they would attend to the words and not the speaker; the esoteric or religious sect of Pythagoreans were called *akousmatikoi*, 'those willing to hear'. Thus, Schaeffer wrote, 'We can, without anachronism, return to an ancient tradition which radio and recording follow in the same way today, restoring to hearing alone the entire responsibility of hearing a perception ordinarily leaning on other sensory evidence'.[12] The *musique concrète* tradition took up the term 'acousmatic', and later exponents often described their work as 'acousmatic music'.[13] They tend to describe 'acousmatic listening' as 'listening without seeing' – though Schaeffer is concerned not just with how listeners should perceive sounds but also how composers should treat their material. In both cases, he maintains, one should ignore the physical origin of the sounds employed and appreciate them for their abstract properties. Schaeffer also termed the process 'reduced listening', arguing that recording encourages it through the possibilities of listening without seeing and indefinite repetition. Sound reproduction has a double role: 'to retransmit in a certain manner what we used to see or hear directly and to express in a certain manner what we used not to see or hear'.[14] In this way, Schaeffer seeks to reconcile technology with nature, treating the medium of analogue recording like the curtain which concealed Pythagoras from the *akousmatikoi* – excluding visual experience while enhancing experience of the sonorous object.

Strictly, reduced listening should not be equated with listening without seeing; rather, it is listening that is enhanced by not seeing. The object of acousmatic or reduced listening is what Schaeffer calls a sound-object (*objet sonore*), apparently discounting the common-sense assumption that sounds are temporal processes rather than things: 'When [sound recognition] is effected without the aid of sight, musical conditioning is shaken up. Often surprised, sometimes uncertain, we discover that much of what we believed was only in fact seen, and explained, by the context'.[15] Schaeffer recognized that a Pythagorean curtain will not discourage our curiosity about causes, to which we are instinctively drawn. But he maintained that reduced listening counteracts this tendency.[16] (Compare the constant repetition of a word – its meaning is forgotten as one is drawn to the sound itself.) At first, where we are ignorant of what is causing the sound, we want to know what it is; with practice, however, the desire dissipates.[17] It should also be noted that one can desire to *know* the origin of the sound, while at the same time *experiencing* it acousmatically.

A BROADER DEFINITION OF 'ACOUSMATIC'

The concept of the acousmatic is not restricted to what, for most listeners, is the rather specialized domain of electro-acoustic composition. It has a broader application, as Scruton's work shows – and it is his thesis which is my main concern. In fact, Scruton and exponents of *musique concrète* differ concerning both the definition of the acousmatic and its application. First, the definition. To reiterate, in describing their work as 'acousmatic music', those in the *musique concrète* tradition cite the Pythagorean definition of 'acousmatic' as 'listening without seeing'.[18] Compare this definition with Scruton's broader and subtler characterization of acousmatic listening as excluding both thought and awareness of the source or cause of the sound. On his account, such listening could occur while the cause of the sound is visible; so while both Schaeffer's and Scruton's senses of acousmatic involve detaching the sound from its circumstances of production, they should not be equated. (A third possibility is listening without knowing the cause – 'awareness' conflates the second and third possibilities.) Recall Scruton's description of the acousmatic character of musical experience: 'The notes in music float free from their causes ... What we understand, in understanding music, is not the material world, but the intentional object: the organization that can be heard *in* the experience'.[19] Clearly, when someone hears musical sounds, they may gain information about their cause, but Scruton's claim is that in musical listening we spontaneously detach such information. This descriptive claim contrasts with the more prescriptive claim of the Schaefferians. According to Scruton, we do not have to choose to listen to musical sounds acousmatically but do so quite naturally and spontaneously; Schaefferians – thinking in terms of 'listening without seeing' – believe that the listener has to make an effort to forget the origins of the sounds. As my later arguments show, I believe that the Schaefferians are nearer to the truth here.

Scruton and Schaeffer also differ fundamentally over the application of the acousmatic. Schaeffer focused on experience of non-tonal sounds or noise, which before his time music had hardly embraced, while Scruton applies his concept to what *musique concrète* composers regard as traditional music. For Scruton, indeed, typical cases of *musique concrète* would not qualify as music. However, Schaeffer's followers, at least on occasion, have allowed that acousmatic experience can apply to traditional music. Luke Windsor, for instance, allows that there is 'both *intentionally* acousmatic music and music that is more *coincidentally* acousmatic' – presumably he means *musique concrète* and traditional music respectively.[20] Moreover, *musique concrète* compositions are indeed compositions – that is, while reduced listening involves a concern with sound itself, in which one develops a heightened attention to the nature of individual sounds, one returns to the whole, incorporating that new attention into the complex totality. While *musique concrète* is sound-art or a precursor of sound-art, it shares many of the traditional concerns of music.

I need to say more about the contrast between acousmatic and non-acousmatic. Sound experienced in terms of its cause – as the sound of some event such as a door slamming, a dog barking or a clarinet being played – has been or might be described as: significant, anecdotal, associative or dramatic sound; or, conceived explicitly as a kind of experience, the purely acoustic, the practical, the literal, the documentary, the non-aesthetic. The description 'purely acoustic experience' could apply just as well to the acousmatic as to the non-acousmatic case, and so is best avoided – I will return later to the suggestion that the acousmatic is simply the aesthetic as applied to sound. 'Literal', 'practical' and 'documentary' have the right connotations.[21] Say I am walking in the woods and hear a creaking sound above me. An acousmatic response would be, 'That's a very interesting high-pitched sound, intermittent and rising in intensity' – perhaps it could be located in Schaeffer's taxonomy of sound-objects. A non-acousmatic response, in contrast, might simply be (looking up) 'Is that a branch about to topple onto me?' – hearing is subservient to sight in information-gathering.[22] The acousmatic experience of sound excludes its literal qualities – as in the case of music, the listener detaches the sound from its worldly source or cause. In contrast, literal experience of sound involves a practical or technical interest. Rescuers listening for the cries of survivors buried by an earthquake treat those sounds practically and not acousmatically; a sound engineer's concern with a recording may be literal in contrast to a musician's. Medical students are taught to listen for certain rhythmic patterns in a heartbeat, and their listening must be non-acousmatic; they are searching for information – for symptoms of a disorder – not for musical properties.[23]

Is it really possible to experience non-musical sounds acousmatically, as I have just assumed? The rationale of *musique concrète* is that it is possible, while the impression given in Scruton's *The Aesthetics of Music* is that it is not. However, elsewhere Scruton writes that 'our language for characterizing sounds tends to describe them in terms of their normal source – dripping, croaking, creaking, barking. But reference to a source is not essential to the identification of the sound, even when it is compelled by the attempt to describe it'. He continues: 'music is an extreme case of something that we witness throughout the sound world, which is the internal organization of sounds as pure events [detached from a cause]'.[24] Such a position opens the way to a genuinely non-musical sound-art with elements describable by Schaeffer's taxonomy of non-musical sounds. Certainly it is the case that sound phenomena which are not music or sound-art have acousmatic – one might say musical – aspects, such as the rhythm of a train engine or the melody of speech patterns. A heartbeat is a natural rhythm, birdsong is melodic; nature can be musical, even if is not music. Music, as argued in Chapter 2, has to be an intentional production.

OBJECTIONS TO THE ACOUSMATIC THESIS

The acousmatic thesis faces some strong objections, which in my conclusion, result in its defeat – both the acousmatic and the non-acousmatic are essential aspects of musical experience. The issue is a subtle one, however, and needs careful handling. The question is not whether ordinary musical listening involves attention to both cause – instrumental or vocal medium – and melody, rhythm and so on, but whether these are both fully musical aspects of musical experience. I do not say that Scruton denies these two aspects of listening; my argument is rather that he wrongly denies that the non-acousmatic aspect has a genuinely musical status.

The most important objections to the acousmatic thesis are now considered in turn.

Timbre
In its everyday sense, timbre is, precisely, the quality or tone colour of a musical note which distinguishes different types of musical

instrument, or the individual qualities of different vocalists. Timbre comprises those qualities of a musical sound which relate it most directly to its source, even if pitch, rhythm and harmony also do so to some extent – a high pitch is unlikely to be produced by a tuba, though when it is, it has a special timbral quality. Experience of timbre must therefore be regarded as non-acousmatic; if it is an essential part of musical experience, as it surely must be, then the acousmatic thesis is undermined. When listening to a piano concerto or a jazz pianist, one cannot help thinking 'piano', and so it is essential to the musical experience that one attends to its causal origin. Timbral qualities include resonance – in the case of voiced sounds, for instance, the quality imparted by the action of the resonating chambers of the throat and mouth and nasal cavities – harshness, roughness, mellowness, nasality, reverberance, shrillness and stridency. Acoustically, these qualities are 'impure'. Pure tones – those lacking other than a fundamental frequency – can occur in music, but most musical tones are composites of partial vibrations of the vibrating body as well as vibrations of the whole mass. A typical violin tone is relatively rich in overtones, while the flute and tuning fork are closer to a pure tone – though even these have noise elements, such as the breathy sounds of the flute.[25]

Space

Acousmatic experience cannot involve awareness of the spatial origin or movement of sounds, which clearly concerns their cause or source. Therefore, acousmatic experience is not sufficient for the appreciation of those kinds of music which aim to achieve spatial effects through placement of groups of performers or sound-producers – where it is important that one attends to the direction of the sounds. Despite the examples of Baroque antiphonal music and nineteenth-century compositions with off-stage musicians, such a purpose was not prominent before the twentieth century. But it is central to contemporary compositions beginning with Stockhausen's *Gruppen* and *Carré*, though prefigured in some ways by the work of Charles Ives. Almost from the start of his career, Stockhausen wished to undermine traditional concert-hall stereo listening. Describing *Gruppen* rather grandiosely as the first example of 'spatial music', he demands specially designed halls with moveable seating to allow his music's 'theatrical polyphony' to be realized:

Musical space has been fixed in the western tradition ... [its] function has been neutralized ... we are not birds, ... and would rather sit in one spot ... most of the audience can't even stand, let alone move during a concert, so our perspective on musical space is utterly frozen ... If I have a sound of constant spectrum, and the sound moves in a curve, then the movement gives the sound a particular character compared to another sound which moves just in a straight line. Whether a sound moves clockwise or counter-clockwise, is at the left back or at the front ... [are] configurations in space which are as meaningful as intervals in melody or harmony.[26]

Virtuosity

Acousmatic experience cannot involve awareness of virtuosity in performance, so it will not allow for appreciation of music where this is a significant element in the listening experience. It is part of one's experience of Liszt's *Transcendental Studies*, or Paganini's *Caprices*, or Louis Armstrong's 'Swing that Music', that these are technically extraordinarily difficult; a recording of Liszt's pieces where the right-hand part was over-dubbed using two hands would lose the elements of devilry, risk, excitement and relief. This point applies to other expressive qualities too: the sense of strain generated by the first violin part in the 'Cavatina' of Beethoven's Op. 130 string quartet – which calls for very high positions on the lower strings of the instrument which are very taxing for the performer – is an intrinsic part of that quartet's expressive power. These qualities are apparent audibly, but also visually, hence the final objection to the acousmatic thesis:

Non-auditory experience of music

We feel as well as hear sounds. Some music seems to emphasize this fact, for instance, Edgard Varèse's, where a sense of sound as vibration is integral. As we saw earlier, Schaeffer's concept of the acousmatic was built on the assumption that where sight is involved, it is difficult and perhaps impossible to experience sounds while abstracting from their causal origin. When we witness a musical performance, experiencing musical sounds as humanly produced seems inescapable. We see, as a direct causal process, how the music is energized by the actions of performers.

The visual aspect of performance creates tension, as when we see the percussionist raise the hammer to beat the drum or a pianist perform a daring leap. The gyrations of the conductor and pianist are vital to the audience's comprehension, and an accent accompanied by an outflung arm seems to become more intense. Many of these effects arise through music's primitive connection with bodily gesture, and especially dance.[27] But electronic music creates its own kind of tension, since listeners cannot prepare themselves mentally for the sounds that will occur. What is seen – or not seen – affects what is heard.

All of the preceding objections to the acousmatic thesis arise from the fundamental fact that music is an art of performance. We do not attend musical events simply for the auditory realism or perfection unattainable through recordings; rather, we want to see as well as hear the creation of musical sounds.[28] So the acousmatic thesis seems obviously false. This reaction is premature, however. There is a further defence of the thesis, one which involves a broadening of the concept of the acousmatic. Consider again the timbral objection. According to this further defence, in listening to a piano concerto one abstracts from the particular but not the general cause – one experiences the sounds as those of a piano, but not necessarily of *that* piano, the particular instrument causing the sound. To experience the sounds as those of a particular instrument is to adopt the attitude of a piano-tuner, piano salesperson, piano-maker or pianist in professional mode, looking for the best instrument to use – an aesthetic concern, certainly, but only indirectly an aesthetic concern with the improvisation or work being performed. (In the case of the salesperson, aesthetic judgement is totally at the service of getting information about the quality and market value of the piano.) Acousmatic experience can be disrupted by such experience of the particular cause – thus we say that an out-of-tune piano spoils one's pleasure in the music. The fundamental aesthetic concern with a particular piano is that it allows the performer to make good music.

The result of this line of argument is a *qualified acousmatic thesis*: to hear sounds as music is to abstract from their particular cause but not necessarily from their general cause. As it stands, however, this qualification is not sufficient. The experience of a general cause – 'piano' but not 'that piano' – can occur with improvised music as well as composition; but in instrumental and especially vocal improvised music, the particular and not the general cause seems essential to musical experience. When I am listening to the singing of Billie Holiday, Mose Allison or Bob Dylan, it is part of my musical experience and enjoyment that I do not abstract from the particular cause and do not abstract from its production by a particular individual. I do not, for instance, experience the sounds as just having some generic cause, for instance, 'African-American jazz singer'. It may well be that particular features of vocal sound emphasize the non-acousmatic.[29]

There is a further development of the acousmatic thesis which, though elusive, offers a response even to this seemingly decisive objection. It is based on the claim of a necessary metaphorical perception of music – which in one form is central to Scruton's treatment – and argues that the perception of 'piano' is metaphorical not literal and that the content of perception is culturally mediated. This consideration applies to experience of general and particular causes alike. A vivid example is the experience of piano sound. Keyboard music of the Classical and Romantic eras – from Haydn up to Bartók in fact – which has so shaped our perception of the piano, is so concerned with the projection of a legato sound that it makes us forget that true legato is impossible on the instrument. It is possible with strings, brass and woodwind, where the envelope of sound is extinguished as the player moves from one note to the next, without overlap and, if they wish, without any gap.

Listeners ignore the decay of the piano's sound and accept the aspiration to a perfect legato as real. The gestures of the pianist help to sustain this illusion – and so the visual experience of an illusory cause supports rather than opposes the acousmatic thesis. Charles Rosen comments that

we hear the sounds in a Beethoven piano sonata as if they were sustained by string instruments or voices ... More than any other composer before him, Beethoven understood the pathos of the gap between idea and realization, and the sense of strain put on the listener's imagination is essential here.

A piano of Beethoven's time is ideal because of its greater inadequacy for conveying such an effect, he continues, but adds wryly that the modern piano is sufficiently inadequate to convey Beethoven's intentions.[30] The sound of the piano is perceived metaphorically, as akin to a legato string sound, even though, on reflection, listeners recognize that the instrument cannot really produce this sound. The phenomenon is one of the profound mysteries of Western art music.

Another illustration of metaphorical perception which, strictly speaking, does not involve illusion, is the experience of declamatory French horns, for instance in a Bruckner symphony. Here one immediately perceives a horn-call, with its connotations of hunting and the chase; the sounds are heard as organized into a distinctive musical phrase, with conventional or cultural connotations. Yet, of course, this is not literally a horn-call, but a cultural construct whose effect partly derives from the historical practice of horn-calls. Even sounds which appear to call particular attention to their causes, such as 'dirty' sounds – the bottle-slide technique of the blues guitarist or the growling or squeaking noises produced by a free jazz saxophonist – are objects of metaphorical perception. Dirty sounds tend to be stylized imitations of the human voice by an instrumentalist. It is perhaps no coincidence that Western art music, with its profound structural concerns, has a preference for pure over dirty sounds – hence the subversive impact of John Cage's prepared piano sounds.[31] But still, to say that dirty sounds are stylized is to regard them as possessing a cultural overlay – to regard them as objects of a metaphorical perception.

THE TWOFOLD THESIS

The preceding responses, I believe, are not sufficient to save the acousmatic thesis. There is a literal as well as metaphorical dimension to musical experience; but since the claim of necessary metaphorical perception does not strictly imply that all aspects of musical perception are metaphorical, the latter thesis is both weaker and more plausible than the acousmatic thesis. (Though it is questioned in connection with rhythmic movement in Chapter 5.) The acousmatic thesis is too prescriptive about what musical experience involves. Part of the pleasure in listening to music is a sensuous pleasure in sounds, which may not involve acousmatic experience. And there is a further issue. Attempts to broaden the acousmatic – such as the qualified acousmatic thesis described earlier, which admitted experience of causes in a general sense – may succeed simply in equating 'acousmatic' with 'aesthetic (as relating to sound)'. On this view, musical experience is not experience of sound divorced from its cause; rather, it is experience which involves an aesthetic attitude towards its cause. A Kantian conception of the aesthetic holds that aesthetic experience of sounds divorces them from their original context and does not treat them as providing information. If the acousmatic is interpreted as 'not involving an interest in information about the cause of the sound', it simply becomes the Kantian aesthetic as applied to sound. This is a definition towards which Scruton himself sometimes inclines.[32] But although it may well be that the genuinely musical experience is essentially aesthetic, the upshot is that the acousmatic ceases to be distinctive.[33]

In place of the acousmatic thesis, I propose a *twofold thesis*, which says that listening to music involves both non-acousmatic and acousmatic experience and that both are genuinely musical aspects. (In the case of singing which involves a text, the experience becomes threefold; one can listen non-acousmatically to the voice, attend to its musicality acousmatically, or focus on the meaning of the words.) This thesis is implicit in the work of various writers. For instance, William E. Thomson comments that

> Tone differs from noise mainly in that it possesses features that enable it to be regarded as autonomous. Noises are most readily identified, not by their character but by their sources; e.g., the noise of the dripping faucet, the grating chalk, or the squeaking gate. Although tones too are commonly linked with their sources (violin tone, flute tone, etc.), they more readily achieve autonomy because they possess controlled pitch, loudness, timbre, and duration, attributes that make them amenable to musical organization.[34]

And composer Jonathan Harvey writes: 'One is constantly alternating as a listener between delight in the sound and delight in the structure, depending on the composer's emphasis (and the player's)'.[35] Even those sympathetic to Pierre Schaeffer have recognized that musical experience is twofold in this sense. In his investigation of *musique concrète*, Luke Windsor holds that 'for the listener at least, attempts to break through the acousmatic "screen" in order to ascribe causation to sounds are an important facet of musical interpretation'.[36]

The analogy with Richard Wollheim's twofold thesis of 'seeing-in', concerning the experience of pictorial representation, is deliberate. Wollheim's claim is that one experiences a picture non-representationally and atomistically, as a set of marks on a surface, and also representationally. For Wollheim,

seeing-in permits unlimited simultaneous attention to what is seen and to the features of the medium ... if I look at a representation as a representation, then it is not just permitted to, but required of, me that I attend simultaneously to [pictured] object and medium ... though of course [my attention] need not be equally distributed between them'.[37]

The analogy with musical experience is that just as looking at a painting involves experiencing or being involved in both the represented scene (the Nativity or the peasant's boots) and the means of representation (paint-marks on canvas), so listening to a piece of music involves experiencing the sound as part of a musical world of tones and as having physical properties and origin. This twofoldness may reflect the contrast between atomistic and holistic experience – the acousmatic is holistic experience of musical structure, while the non-acousmatic is atomistic experience of individual, merely causally related and meaningless sounds.

Now as noted earlier, the question is not whether ordinary listening involves attention to both cause or medium and tonal aspects, but, rather, whether each is a fully musical aspect of musical experience. My objection is not that Scruton rejects twofoldness, but that he wrongly denies the genuinely musical status of the non-acousmatic aspect. He does indeed seem to hold with Wollheim that there is a single act of attention. Thus, while Wollheim argues that I must be able to see the cornfield in the picture in the same act of attention that reveals to me that it was produced by means of a palette knife working on chrome yellow paste, Scruton argues that I must be able to hear the phrase that opens the second movement of Brahms' Symphony No. 4 as a melodic unity, at the same time as hearing that it is sounded on the horns. According to this concept of 'double intentionality', acousmatic experience is available in one and the same act of attention that embraces the real-life causality of the musical medium; we focus on something real while attending to something that is imagined in and through it.[38]

Perhaps Scruton is right to suggest that one should not or cannot pick out aspects like spatial properties and timbre and treat them as non-acousmatic, as if they could be the object of a distinct act of attention. The issue is not clear. However, double intentionality does not, as he seems to assume, offer a kind of proof of the acousmatic thesis, for the reason that, as I have been arguing, 'real-life causality' is a genuinely musical part of musical experience. For 'genuinely musical' here, one could substitute 'genuinely aesthetic'. The genuinely musical is not entirely imagined, entirely the product of metaphorical perception or essentially acousmatic. Nonetheless, it seems to be a consequence of the nature of sound that mediation through the concept of causality has a particular significance in musical experience that it does not have in arts such as painting and literature.

It is undoubtedly the case, however, that a more developed musical understanding tends towards the acousmatic. We say that the playing of a novice musician is beginning to make musical sense, that it is becoming less mechanical – we can experience it more acousmatically, though the mechanics of sound-production may later be exploited intentionally, as effects. (For instance, contemporary avant-gardist Helmut Lachenmann's extended instrumental techniques draw attention to the means of their production – one of his primary reasons for exploiting them.[39]) Likewise, a novice's appreciation of music is less acousmatic than a more developed understanding. The novice in a particular genre – Western listeners confronted with Tibetan throat-singing, for instance – will want to know how the sounds are produced. If someone cannot recognize what is the instrument being played, to that extent their musical experience is impoverished, even though they may be able to give a quite detailed description of the kind of sound – reedy, nasal or whatever. However, one might still appreciate the music without knowing the kind of instrument that is producing it.

A HUMANISTIC CONCEPTION OF MUSIC VERSUS MORE ABSTRACT CONCEPTIONS

In his persuasive account of music as the object of metaphorical perception, Scruton assumes what I have been calling a humanistic conception, stressing the origins of music in dance, ritual and gesture, and its connection with human life and activity. Here I will try to develop what I mean by a humanistic account, contrasting it with more abstract conceptions. *Philosophical humanism* certainly has a meaning in other areas of philosophy. In philosophy of mind, as I understand it, it involves the rejection of materialist standpoints and asserts the personal as opposed to subpersonal or neuro-physiological nature of psychological ascription. Thus humanism counters dominant trends in this area of philosophy arising from physicalist or mind–brain identity theories and from cognitive science.[40] Perhaps a humanistic standpoint in aesthetics is harder to distinguish, since this area of philosophy is difficult to conceive non-humanistically. But even here some writers have tried to do so, and the cliché that music is the most abstract of the arts suggests an *anti-humanistic conception.* The cliché is pervasive, yet it is never really argued for convincingly – like formalism, as we saw in the previous chapter, to which it is related. Arising from many different directions, it amounts to a slogan more than a philosophical standpoint.

'Abstraction' proves an elusive target, in part because the opposition between abstract and humanly concrete is dialectical in Adorno's sense. That is, it belongs with those debates in aesthetics and philosophy where, as we will see in Chapter 6, standpoints that are apparently opposed turn out to be interpenetrating. That is, the opposites are not diametrical but overlapping. Thus, what at first sight appears abstract in fact has concrete, sensuous or meaningful elements. The autonomy of musical sound from its causes, which tends to separate music from the world, is one of several reasons why music is held to be the most abstract of the arts. But although Scruton's humanistic conception appears to be in tension with his advocacy of the acousmatic thesis, the concept of musical form that arises from the acousmatic does not need to be abstract.

Consider the totally synthesized electronic music which constitutes the limiting case of acousmatic abstraction considered in this chapter. While *musique concrète* drew music and life together by using everyday sounds as its material, Stockhausen's early studies were constructed from sine-tones and so were totally abstract – though as we saw, he later used non-synthesized sound-sources. However, even electro-acoustic composers apparently most committed to abstraction have adopted a humanistic standpoint and questioned whether such abstraction is possible or desirable. Jonathan Harvey, for instance, observes that sounds in electronic music often have only vestigial traces of human instrumental performance – no one can be envisaged blowing, hitting or scraping anything. However, he maintains that this process of abstraction has necessary limits. Citing music's relation to rhythms of heartbeat and breathing and to our sense of gesticulating, walking, running and dancing, he declares it 'onomatopoeic through and through'.[41] It follows that acousmatic listening, which abstracts from causes, constitutes an idealized approach even to electroacoustic music. Music's autonomy from its causes is an incomplete one.

The acousmatic is not the only dimension of musical abstraction. Abstraction dates back to the ancient Pythagorean concept of music as number discussed in Chapter 1. But the most important impetus towards an abstract conception of music is the rise of the work-concept in the later eighteenth and nineteenth centuries, and the resulting assumption that the musical artwork resides in the score. Brahms' fairly innocuous comment, 'No one can do [Mozart's] *Don Giovanni* right for me. I enjoy it much better from the score', is taken to extremes by musical Platonism, according to which performance becomes secondary or even inessential.[42] The musical work is regarded as an eternal structure whose expression in sound is inessential. Glenn Gould, in his words if not the recorded performances he continued to make, advocated this metaphysical position. Platonism is an extreme expression of what I term the *aesthetics of perfection*, which emphasizes the timelessness of the work and the authority of the composer. In Chapter 7, this standpoint is contrasted with a humanistic *aesthetics of imperfection*, which values the event or process of performance, especially when this involves spontaneity and improvisation – though, again, these opposites turn out to be dialectically interpenetrating.

Modernist composer Arnold Schoenberg was an aesthetic perfectionist in this sense. He objected to the expression of the performer's personality when this obscured the truth of the work. This attitude had more justification in his time, which suffered from such Romantic excesses as Bach with huge string sections. But imperfectionists are right to reject Schoenberg's idea of performers as anonymous interpreters of a sacrosanct text – mere reproducers rather than interpreters, with no individual viewpoint. A distinct complaint about Schoenberg's music is one that also arises from his attitude to the score – that it gives rise to the phenomenon of 'eye music', where structural determinants of form can be experienced only on the page, and not in performance. Schoenbergian serialism, especially in its extreme post-Second World War manifestation of total or integral serialism, is the paradigm of 'eye music'. The tone-row and its manipulation, and in total serialism the rows governing other parameters such as rhythm and timbre, is legible in the score but not audible in performance. To refer to a piece as 'eye music' is rightly taken to be a damaging artistic criticism, and it is a consequence of privileging the score above performance.

The post-eighteenth-century reification of the score suggests that the idea of music as the most abstract of the arts largely dates from that era. This historical claim is also supported by music's adherence before that time to a language model, which is non-abstract. The contrasting model of music as non-representational and without semantic content – language-like in having a syntax, yet apparently not saying anything – is also a powerful motive for an abstract conception. The concept of abstract painting, which arose with modernism, and which was realized most purely after the Second World War in Abstract Expressionism, is the clearest common use of abstraction in this sense – 'non-depicting' and perhaps 'non-representational'. Such art, to reiterate, took autonomous or absolute music as its model.

Adorno's assertion that musical material is historical – and so non-abstract – is considered in Chapter 6. Although his claim seems to undermine the idea of absolute music, in fact Adorno is an heir to its tradition – as also, in its unassuming way, is this book. In questioning the assumption that music is an abstract art, the essential role of form must still be acknowledged. It could be said that music is *abstract in form, but humane in utterance* – and utterance is essential. Bach's music is often regarded as the most abstract sound structure, but it had meanings in its time and is realized through performance interpretation. Indeed, although form reaches its high points of complexity in the classics of Western art music, all music has a form. Again, the issue turns out to involve a nest of interpenetrating dialectical oppositions. Musical modernism, in reacting against programme music, conceives structure or form through the post-Romantic metaphor of organic unity. This is a biological and not an abstract conceit;

form is a regarded as a living thing. Therefore something that at first seemed abstract in fact turns out to be concrete and humanistic. There is an echo here of the conclusion of Chapter 3, that there never really have been any true formalists – Hanslick is regarded as favouring an abstract conception, yet he defines music as sound in motion or tonally moving forms. His position also ties music to human life and gesture, therefore.

The peculiar language-like character of music is captured in Jules Combarieu's attractive formulation quoted earlier that musical composition and improvisation consist in 'thinking with sounds, as a writer thinks with words'.[43] As Hanslick rightly insisted, the idea externalized by the composer in music is 'a tonal idea, not a conceptual idea which has been translated into tones'.[44] (There are 'conceptual composers' like Cage and Wolff whose works perhaps form an exception.) The idea of music as 'thinking in sound' gives no support to an abstract conception – it is a form that thinking takes, not an abstract pattern of sounds caused by thought. When it transcends the most commodified genres, music is able to synthesize the sensuous and intellectual in a uniquely intense and compelling way. It then embodies what Julian Johnson refers to as 'the basic categories of thought: the differentiation of its materials and their discursive development within a logical sequence. It presents specifically musical ideas through specifically musical forms, elaborated in a way that engages us intellectually, emotionally and spiritually'.[45] Music displays a cognitive and a bodily dimension, reflecting the nature of the aesthetic itself in its synthesis of thought and experience.

The most fundamental reasons for rejecting the claim of musical abstraction lie in the facts of sound-production and performance – we hear in and through musical sounds the actions that go into their making. As Stephen Davies argues, musical instruments are not a dispensable means of making the right-sounding noises – the idea of music as the auditory bodying forth of human action is deeply ingrained. The voice, and other instruments held intimately against the body, mean that embodiment melds indissolubly with the music that is sounded: '[this] in its turn implicates the human body and organic processes through the ebb and flow of its pulse and rhythm, of its gestures and sighs, of its tensions and resolutions'.[46] Such considerations are elusive, and discussion of rhythm makes them clearer. This is the topic of the next chapter, and it provides further evidence of the interfusion of music and human life, and thus for the humanistic standpoint. Discussion of these issues also casts further doubt on how 'metaphorical' the experience of music has to be.

NOTES

1 Watson (1991), p. 331.
2 Scruton (1997), pp. 2–3.
3 Scruton (1997), p. 221. In fact, Scruton sometimes speaks of the acousmatic thesis as ideal rather than actual: 'in day-to-day matters, we leap rapidly in thought from the sound to its cause, and speak quite accurately of hearing the car, just as we speak of seeing it. But the phenomenal distinctness of sounds makes it possible to imagine a situation in which a sound is separated entirely from its cause, and heard acousmatically, as a pure process' ((1997), pp. 11–12).
4 Zuckerkandl (1969), p. 273.
5 Lippman (1977), pp. 46–7, 50.
6 The acousmatic thesis does not yield a criterion that separates music from speech; it seems equally plausible to claim that to experience sounds as meaningful speech involves divorcing them from the source of their production.
7 Scruton (1997), p. 35.
8 Scruton (1997), p. 92. These claims concerning rhythm are discussed in Chapter 5.
9 See for instance Wishart (1986), p. 45.
10 On the history of electronic music, see Holmes (2003).
11 Diffusion of a stereo source over a multi-channel loudspeaker system is the norm in *musique concrète* and implies live control during performance, and interaction with the performance space. In the electronic-music tradition, in contrast, each channel on the tape is mapped onto a single loudspeaker, implying an attempt to replicate the composer's conceived space within the performance space – intervention in performance is concerned solely with balance, not with exploiting the individuality of the space. See Harrison (1999).
12 Schaeffer (1966), p. 91, my translation.
13 According to Dhomont (accessed 2002), the term 'acousmatic music' was introduced by *musique concrète* composer François Bayle in 1974.
14 Quoted Palombini (accessed 2004).
15 Schaeffer (1966), pp. 93, 97, translation by Abigail Heathcote.
16 He writes: 'the repetition of the physical signal, which recording makes

possible ... by exhausting this curiosity ... gradually brings the sonorous object to the fore, [and] progressively reveals to us the richness of this perception' (quoted in Cox and Warner (2004), p. 78).

17 Chion (1994), p. 32.

18 Dack, for instance, writes that '[the] acousmatic situation must be extended to all those listening environments in which sounds are heard without any visual confirmation of their sources'; Michel Chion quotes Schaeffer's definition of acousmatic sound as 'sounds one hears without seeing their originating cause', adding '[The opposite of] visualised sound ... The acousmatic truly allows sound to reveal itself in all its dimensions' (Dack (1994), p. 5; Chion (1994), pp. 71–2, 32; Schaeffer (1966), pp. 91–9).

19 Scruton (1997), p. 221.

20 Windsor (2000), p. 9.

21 The term 'literal' is used by electronic composer Trevor Wishart (1996). Schaeffer writes that 'acoustic and acousmatic are not opposed like objective and subjective', suggesting that he does not want to equate the acoustic and the non-acousmatic; but the issue is not clear ((1966), p. 92).

22 As discussed in Lippman, 'Spatial Perception and Physical Location as Factors in Music', in his *The Philosophy and Aesthetics of Music* (1999), pp. 26–39.

23 The important suggestion that non-acousmatic experience is essentially multi-modal – that it involves senses other than hearing – is discussed in Hamilton (forthcoming 2007a).

24 Scruton (forthcoming 2007a).

25 A fuller discussion of the timbral objection is found in Hamilton (forthcoming 2007a).

26 Stockhausen (1989), pp. 101–3.

27 A claim defended for instance by Lippman (1977), Chapter 7, and Nettl (2001).

28 It is notable that Walton (1988) omits the dimension of performance from the non-abstract features of music, when surely it is of the first importance.

29 Lippman argues that 'the solo voice has a pronounced externality [non-acousmatic nature] ... an individual singer remains an object that insists on an external status' ((1977), p. 70).

30 Rosen (1999), pp. 2–3.

31 As Jonathan Harvey put it, 'A smooth unchanging stream of neutral timbre invites attention mainly onto metaphysical events' (e-mail communication with author – and see below, Note 35).

32 For instance, in the passage quoted earlier: 'The person who listens to sounds, and hears them as music, is not seeking in them for

information about their cause, or for clues as to what is happening'
(Scruton (1997), p. 221).
33 Hamilton (forthcoming, 2007a).
34 Thomson (accessed 2004).
35 Harvey adds: 'A lot depends on changes in articulation. If Beethoven
was the first for our ears to emphasise violent changes of playing
articulation, he is also the most obvious start in history to "listening
to sound". A smooth unchanging stream of neutral timbre invites
attention mainly onto metaphysical events' (e-mail communication
with author).
36 Windsor (2000), p. 9.
37 Wollheim (1980), p. 213.
38 Scruton argued this in discussion.
39 Lachenmann, through his concept of *musique concrète instrumentale*,
explores new possibilities of sound production using traditional
instruments. The singing instrumental tone, which he regards as
'domesticated by tradition', is replaced by 'the detritus of sonic
phenomena', with a preponderance of toneless sounds, mostly
breathing, from wind instruments, and brutal grinding and scraping
of the strings. (See Heathcote (2004).)
40 Humanism in the philosophy of mind is defended in Hamilton
(forthcoming).
41 Harvey (1999), pp. 57, 62, and Harvey (forthcoming). Denis Smalley
writes that 'we detect the humanity behind [abstract musical
structures] by deducing gestural activity' – presumably, gestures
associated with the production of sounds: 'Music is always related in
some way to human experience' (Smalley (1986), p. 64).
42 Quoted in Swafford (1998), p. 570.
43 Jules Combarieu, quoted in Dahlhaus (1989), p. 3.
44 Hanslick (1986), p. 32.
45 The idea is developed in Julian Johnson (2002), especially pp. 61–2.
46 Davies (forthcoming 2007), and (2003), p. 114. See also Levinson
(2002).

CHAPTER 5

RHYTHM AND TIME

We are surrounded by rhythm. In the Western and Western-influenced world, public space is pervaded by music whose most obvious element is rhythmic – pop music that largely constitutes muzak, or the toneless hiss of rock or funk rhythms that emanates from personal stereos or iPods. But the ancient world was also pervaded by rhythm. The previous chapter referred to music's ancient connections with dance, physical labour and ritual, and with the movement involved in each, which are stressed by the humanistic account that I am defending. I have in mind, for instance, the way that musical activity arises out of, and indeed is part of, manual labour. Hammering, scything, pounding and other labouring activities essential to traditional societies are incipiently musical. Dance, poetry and music are conceptually inseparable in that rhythm is essential to each, and none can be understood independently of rhythm. In experiencing musical rhythm, one does not just experience music as behaving like a human body, but the human body as behaving musically – that is, the person as moving musically. Sound and bodily movement are intimately connected; life is interfused with music. Except perhaps in the case of Western art music, where these urges to move tend to be suppressed, music inspires movement in performers and listeners. The discussion of rhythm crystallizes the opposition between abstract and humane conceptions of music – in particular, between the ancient Pythagorean concept of music as number, discussed in Chapter 1, and the felt conception of music which the present book advocates. I focus on this topic because of its centrality to music and its humanistic implications but also because of its philosophical neglect since the time of the Greeks. We saw in Chapter 3 how Hanslick defined the content of music as 'tonally moving forms' or 'sound and motion', and there has been some discussion of melodic movement but very little of rhythmic movement. Rhythm, I believe, should be a core topic in aesthetics of music and is central to human life itself. It provides rich material for philosophical discussion.

MUSIC AS AN ART OF TIME

Music is often described as an art of time. For Stravinsky, 'music is a chronologic art as painting is a spatial art', while Stephen Davies regards it as an 'an art of temporal process'. Schopenhauer presents the extreme view that 'perceptions through hearing are exclusively in time' just as 'the way in which music is perceived, namely in and through time alone, [is] with absolute exclusion of space'.[1] Schopenhauer's metaphysical view is misguided; as we saw in Chapter 4, music has spatial features, and this chapter argues that rhythm itself also has spatial properties. Less dubious, perhaps, are claims that music gives a special insight into the nature of time. Zuckerkandl, for example, argues that the natural phenomenon of time is not just an empty, neutral vessel through which events pass but a real, active force, made available to experience through music.[2]

Clearly music – and, in light of the discussion in Chapter 2, non-musical sound-art also – is not an art of time in the sense in which it is an art of sound. Time, unlike sound, is not a medium. (It might be argued that sound is a phenomenon, and the air through which it is transmitted is the medium; but that claim is consistent with regarding sound as the musical medium in the sense that paint, canvas, wood and so on are the media of painting.) There are vital aesthetic questions arising from the timebound nature of our experience of music, in contrast, for instance, to that of painting – experience of painting takes place over time, but our attention is somehow less restricted than in the case of transient musical events in performance.[3]

My present concern, however, is not with the relation of music and time which has excited metaphysical pronouncements, but with musical time in the sense of rhythm. There has been much theorizing on rhythm and metre since the time of Aristoxenus –

the pupil of Aristotle whose empiricist views were discussed in Chapter 1 – especially concerning poetic rhythm and metre, applied to music through the pervasive rhetorical model. But discussion of rhythm features rarely in the philosophical literature, with Dewey and Scruton almost the only recent examples.[4] Even within musicology, Cooper and Meyer's ground-breaking *The Rhythmic Structure of Music* comments on the 'moribund state' of its topic – though their work can now be criticized for its narrow, almost exclusive concern with Western art music.[5]

There has been a philosophically important recent discussion of rhythm from a non-philosopher – Christopher Hasty's *Meter as Rhythm*.[6] The title does not fully convey the book's grand aspiration: to analyse the experience of music as an irreducibly temporal phenomenon, rather than the spatialized representation assumed by theorists, and which also figures in ordinary thinking. As Hasty puts it, music should be regarded as a process of becoming rather than a record of what has become. One of his central claims, discussed below, is that the metronomic image of metre is an artefact of a system of representation, and is opposed to the experience of the life in music. The philosophical influences behind Hasty's project are radical empiricists such as William James, and phenomenologists such as Husserl and especially Bergson, for whom awareness of duration involves experiencing something as present while also being aware of it as immediately past. Hasty's task is an almost impossible one – perhaps, as Wittgenstein would have put it, he is attempting to say what can only be shown. But his vision complements the account that I will give of music as motion.

Rhythm raises deep philosophical as well as purely aesthetic questions. Like the topic of picturing, traditionally discussed under the heading of aesthetics, it may not be an essentially aesthetic topic. But certainly, as with picturing, there are genuinely aesthetic issues which will be explored here. My central questions are: what is the difference between a mere sequence of sounds and movements and a rhythm? What is it for a sequence of sounds to be grouped into a rhythmic pattern? These questions are very close to 'What is it for a sequence of sounds to be music?', which shows how indispensable rhythm is to music – music could be defined as *the rhythmicization of sound*.[7] The aesthetic issues surrounding rhythm should be intelligible to non-musicians; in this discussion,

I try to explain musical terms and keep technicality to a minimum. Where such terms are not explained, they are not essential to the argument.

THE UNIVERSALITY OF RHYTHM

As noted earlier, rhythm is the one indispensable element of all music. In Western music, rhythm and pitch are regarded as the two primary parameters of musical structure, and music for unpitched percussion is comparatively unusual. But the music of traditional societies is often rhythmic without pitched tones. The so-called drone-musics of Eliane Radigue and Sachiko M are so non-rhythmic that they should be regarded as sound-art rather than music.[8] (To reiterate Chapter 2, this distinction is not in any way evaluative and is not intended to mark any great metaphysical divide.) John Cage's late 'number' pieces, based on duration, arguably do not exhibit rhythmic organization and so perhaps also belong in the sound-art category. Such cases should be distinguished from music where the rhythmic element, though attenuated, is undoubtedly present and not residual like the pitch element in percussion music. The mature work of Cage's younger New York contemporary Morton Feldman is rhythmically organized without generating propulsion, I would argue; in contrast, Webern's Quartet Op. 22 has both. (I will return to Feldman's work later.)

The flow of medieval plainchant, while almost without stress, still reveals a subtle rhythmic organization – although the metaphorical understanding of this music has as much to do with space, as it echoes through medieval or Renaissance churches to the glory of God, as time. Indeed, by the thirteenth century, the term 'plainchant' was used to denote the free, unmeasured rhythm of Gregorian chant, in contrast to the measured note values of polyphonic music. The Solesmes performance tradition attempted to remove rhythmic variation from chant, but several scholars argue that the plainchant or 'neume' notation indicated rhythm as precisely as modern-day notation.[9] In Renaissance polyphonic music such as the masses of Palestrina, stresses are even lighter than in the earlier work of Dufay and Josquin. The sound is very ethereal and rounded and – in contrast to plainchant – has a real if almost imperceptible internal propulsion.[10]

Figure 10 Tropaire de Saint-Martial de Limoges, eleventh century, neumes aquitains. Reproduced by kind permission of La Bibliothèque de France (BnF, Manuscrits, latin 1118, fol. 111). Neume notation represents only a few parameters of what was sung; in particular it does not represent precise pitches, or rhythm. But as Treitler (1982) stresses, although neumes are precursors of staff notation, they must not be viewed as imperfect ones; had it been desired to represent exact pitches, means to do so would have been found. Neumes remind the performer of the essential features of a melody that has already been learnt.

123

Separating rhythm from melody is not entirely unnatural; it is how many children are taught music. But there is a certain artificiality in treating rhythm in isolation from pitch, as this chapter inevitably does, since melody, harmony and rhythm are inseparably linked and work together. Harmonic resolution strongly suggests a downbeat, a 'ONE' on the tonic or home key. Indeed the very experience of a downbeat is infused with harmonic implications, as nineteenth-century music theorist Riemann realized when he argued that the contrast of upbeat and downbeat is the basic principle in the creation of musical form.[11] Rhythmic, harmonic and melodic aspects of musical language arise together. In Palestrina, for instance, voices rhythmically interlock, with dissonances and consonances alternating on strong beats; harmonic suspension and resolution is implicitly connected with rhythm. The tonal harmony which reached its apogee with Haydn, Mozart and Beethoven involves rhythmic gesture. In jazz, Thelonious Monk's spare, semitonal and tritonal harmonies and his percussive attack are fused in his artistic vision, while Bill Evans's fuller, more classical harmonies are inseparable from his more conventionally pianistic rhythmic approach. It is also true, however, that a composer or improviser can conceive a particular piece, or indeed their musical composition as a whole, in predominantly rhythmic (Monk), harmonic (Evans) or melodic terms. In works by contemporary composer James Tenney such as 'Koan' for string quartet, polymetre operates almost in synchronization with microtonal changes. Part of the difficulty in listening to atonal music, which rejects the tonal system of major and minor keys and thus harmonic resolution, is rhythmic as much as melodic or harmonic.[12]

Composers have attempted to separate rhythm and pitch as distinct parameters – notably Olivier Messiaen in his radical post-1945 compositions. Jonathan Harvey argues that these revolutionary experiments, which involved the exploitation of complex additive rhythms, seemed finally to free rhythm of its servitude to pitch: 'it was no longer the rhythm "of" something so much as a layer in its own right'. However, he adds, this was an intellectual illusion, which the holistic Stockhausen saw as such.[13] Electronic compositions by Stockhausen and Harvey himself later illustrated vividly the acoustic truth that pitches are really accelerated beats. But Meyer and Cooper's postulation of a hierarchical structure of rhythm provides a deeper explanation of the holism of rhythm and other musical features, placing rhythm within the larger structure of a musical work or performance.[14] The lowest level, note by note, is analysed as strong–weak–strong–weak, for instance; but every strong beat also belongs in a higher-level grouping. A wooden, unmusical performance of a waltz, in contrast to an authentically dance-like one, neglects this higher level. A genuinely musical performance, therefore, in addition to the note-by-note level, involves thinking in bars, in phrases (such as four or eight-bar units) and in larger structural units. The note-to-note level must not be neglected, however, as jazz pianist Alan Broadbent explained:

> [My teacher] Lennie Tristano used to have me sing Lester Young [solos], and in those days you could put the LP onto half speed, down to 16 ... What he was trying to get me to do ... was becoming involved in the creation of each note – the note-to-note process. To be aware of *every* note, full value, the tone you're making, with the metronome at 60 ... Lennie's ideal of that note-for-note process was Bud Powell – in his cleanest, his healthiest state. There are recordings where even if Bud plays a 64th note, you have the feeling that it's "that note, to that note" – it's not a run.

That is, there is a total awareness of each note following the other, in contrast to a scale or pattern produced from the muscular memory.[15]

Nonetheless, the alleged inseparability of rhythm, melody and harmony poses an aesthetic puzzle. Their fusion seems not to be a merely contingent feature of music but flows from the guiding ideal of the artwork's organic unity – the sense of inevitability and necessity of construction that one experiences with great art. (This ideal underlies Cooper and Meyer's hierarchical account, I believe.) A piece could be criticized for failing to develop one or other of the elements of melody, harmony and rhythm – hence, for instance, the (misguided) objection that there are no real melodies in Bruckner. But it may be that when all of these features are present, they are inevitably fused in some sense and are separated only when one of them is deliberately omitted. Thus, there is a feeling that the inseparability thesis is prescriptive rather than descriptive – it is a guiding principle more than a description of musical practice.

The *inseparability of rhythm, harmony and melody*, whether prescriptive or descriptive, suggests that rhythm is a specifically musical phenomenon. ('Harmony' is not meant in any ideological sense, as implying tonality; 'pitch' could be substituted for 'harmony and melody'.) However, that suggestion seems in conflict with *the universality of rhythm*: rhythm's presence in all the arts and in all kinds of human activity, and indeed, according to many writers, in nature itself.[16] Rhythm is essential to nearly all traditional forms of poetry, which perhaps are created more for the ear than the eye; it is exhibited in a less highly organized sense by prose, which is made more for the eye than the ear. Speech has metrical and rhythmical properties, and we talk of the rhythm of a line, reflecting the movement of the artist's hand. Rhythm is essential to many human activities such as physical labour, and we are conceived as the result of a rhythmic physical act.

I wish to argue that, contrary to appearances, the universality of rhythm does not really conflict with the inseparability of rhythm, harmony and melody. One assumption underlying the diagnosis of conflict is spelled out in Zuckerkandl's account. He rightly regards melody and harmony as essentially musical phenomena, applied only metaphorically outside the world of tone, but contrasts them with the truly universal and thus not specifically musical phenomenon of rhythm.[17] He cannot therefore account for the inseparability of these features, or with the essentially musical nature of rhythm. The resolution of this conflict, in my view, lies in the contrasting position that rhythm is like harmony and melody in being essentially musical, yet unlike them in being universal. Rhythm is both universal *and* musical. So there is only an apparent conflict between the inseparability of rhythm, harmony and melody and the universality of rhythm.

This reconciling claim is vindicated by contrasting the case of rhythm with that of harmony. As we saw in Chapter 1, ancient writers associated cosmic and musical harmony, and it is not clear that the musical use is primary and the non-musical one secondary; moreover, 'harmony' and 'discord' have non-metaphorical uses in discourse about colour. Although 'harmony' in all its uses describes a blending, sympathy, compatibility and unity, musical and non-musical uses seem to be distinct, and can be learned independently; 'rhythm', on the other hand, has a unitary meaning across music and human behaviour. If someone dresses stylishly and with excellent coordination of colours, fabrics and so on – that is, 'harmoniously' – no reference to their musical aptitude is implied; not so when they are described as walking very rhythmically, in a very loose, relaxed way for instance. Rhythm is essential to music, and – a stronger claim – rhythm and music cannot be defined independently of each other. They are internally related and form a conceptual circle or holism, on the model of music and tone as outlined in Chapter 2.

In contrast to harmonic properties, then, rhythmic properties are ascribed in the same sense to both music and bodily or human movement, and that sense is a musical one. Producing music is not more primitive or basic than moving rhythmically, or dancing. These activities arise together, both in the history of human society and in the lives of individuals. It is important to recognize that this is a conceptual and not an empirical claim – that is, any attempt to gather empirical evidence for it presupposes the application of the concepts in the way described, and would thus be pointless.[18] This is one central way in which music pervades ordinary life. Music arises from life, and, as a humanistic philosophy of music insists, it is infused with its features, both biological and cultural.

A PLATONIC, ORGANIC DEFINITION

I have been arguing that rhythm is essential to music, but this is not to say much until 'rhythm' has been characterized. This is far from easy. I referred to rhythmic organization with, and less commonly without, a feeling of propulsion. The paradigm case must be one which involves propulsion. Plato in *The Laws* describes rhythm as '*order in movement*' or '*order within movement*'.[19] Although he does not explain what kind of order, the Platonic definition is a promising start, certainly more promising than Dewey's 'ordered variation of changes'.[20] I will develop this Platonic definition first by proposing further conditions:

(1) Rhythm is order-within-movement that involves discontinuity, is perceivable through one or more of the senses, and generates immediate involvement by performer and listener.

There are two forms of movement which, in their limiting cases, are clearly non-rhythmical – kinetic chaos, such as an avalanche or explosion, and kinetic continuum, such as a smoothly gliding sailboat.[21] A piece of sound-art consisting of randomly generated noise would not have rhythm.[22] Neither would a smooth glissando – a steadily rising or falling pitch – or continuous tone, as in the work of Sachiko M mentioned earlier, unless perhaps it involves changes in dynamics or timbre. Obviously, chaos and kinetic continuum themselves form a continuum, and sometimes it will be undecidable whether rhythm is present or not.

I also wish to extend the Platonic definition by making sound as basic as movement. Thus rhythm is *order within movement or movement-in-sound.* I say 'movement-in-sound' rather than simply 'sound' since harmony and melody contribute to musical order – though given the inseparability of these factors, they may contribute to order within movement-in-sound too. What kind of order? Rhythm is more primitive than either convention or language, and a common and plausible view is that it is fundamentally a natural phenomenon, with a physiological basis in heartbeat and breathing and exhibiting the alternation of tension and relaxation characteristic of such bodily processes; musical tempos, it is claimed, are related to the normal human heart rate of 60 to 80 beats per minute.[23] One suggestion is that rhythmic movement arose from human awareness of pulse or breathing patterns. This organic image of rhythm suggests a humanistic treatment rather than one based on mechanical movement or abstract time. An organic treatment is found in Dewey's *Art and Experience*, though he argues that rhythm in the fine arts is not explained simply on the basis of rhythmic processes in the living body: 'the participation of man in nature's rhythms, a partnership much more intimate than in any observation of them for purposes of knowledge, induced him to impose rhythm on changes where they did not appear' – that is, through music and the other arts.[24]

However, the organic model covers only half the picture – order in movement, but not freedom in movement. Rhythm comprises both periodic phenomena that fall under the heading of metre, and freer, non-periodic and discrete phenomena such as compelling motion, the shape of a musical phrase, a fluid hand gesture, an expressive line in a drawing or painting, the course of a narrative. So the Platonic definition of rhythm as meaningful pattern of movement or movement-in-sound must be expanded to embrace the polarities of rhythm and *metre*, making explicit reference to *stress or accent*, and thus to *repetition*:

(2) Rhythm is order-within-movement or movement-in-sound that involves discontinuity, and is perceived through the senses; it involves the imposition of accent – whether by the performer or merely by the listener – on a sequence of sounds or movements, and creates non-periodic phenomena often within a periodic, repetitive (metrical) framework, giving rise to a 'feel' or pattern in which performers and listeners participate.

This final definition involves circularity – stress and rhythm are interdefined – though I think benignly so, as we will see. The definition does not state that rhythm always involves repetition – though this is a possible view – but it does hold that repetition is an essential part of the concept. Rhythm in music is commonly equated with pulse or beat. Beat is the kind of regular repetition or periodicity involving accent or stress which musicians call *metre*.[25] (It may seem that pulse does not have to exhibit stresses, but see below.) Like melody, rhythm involves a gestalt or unity – a 'feel' or pattern – which generates involvement in the movement by performers and listeners. Indeed, we talk of a rhythmic 'feel' for the very good reason that it is felt. The use of 'rhythm' to describe non-periodic phenomena – the particular rhythm patterns that metrical rhythm contains – is not in any sense metaphorical, and we must now explore the relation and interdependence between these two senses.

Rhythmic accent – which I regard as the core case of accent – comprises the metrical downbeat and also, as we will see, cross-accents or syncopation which set up tensions with it. Music without metrical regularity, such as plainchant, can still have a downbeat – plainchant has accent if not metre, generated by words rather than tones – while free or irregular rhythms also exhibit non-metrical stress without downbeats. Does rhythm have to involve accent? Most of the music which Western listeners hear today has rhythm in the sense of accent, but perhaps the very creation of sounds and silences creates accent and non-accent; certainly if a sound has a definite attack, rather than appearing imperceptibly out of silence, it thereby seems to acquire a stress. (Morton Feldman was very concerned with removing the characteristic attack from the production of tones, which is another reason why his music barely conforms to the Platonic definition.) I wish to resist the static conception of rhythm as essentially a pattern of possibly unstressed sounds and silence. In order to consider these issues, we need first to discuss the contrast between rhythm and metre.

RHYTHM AND METRE

Although metre is a more technical concept, it is as hard to characterize as rhythm. The most developed theories of metre have concerned poetic language. In music, the duration of tones is precisely established, whereas in language the duration of the syllables remains indefinite – long and short are indicated but not how long or how short. What all metric systems, however complex, depend on is *pulsation* – they are repetitive and thus offer a framework for rhythmic design, even if the frame is sometimes inferred only on the basis of the design which it frames.[26] Rhythm is essentially related to accent, metre and tempo. However, while all music involves rhythm in some sense and therefore, I will argue, accent, not all music involves metre.

The present Western concept of musical metre is conditioned by its role in written music – the staff notation which is familiar even to non-readers.[27] Musicologists dispute when the modern system of rhythm and metre appeared, but most likely it was during the twelfth and thirteenth centuries. They agree that it arose from the development of polyphonic music, that is, music involving more than one voice which is too complicated to be easily memorized, and which requires precision in synchronizing the performance.[28] As we have seen, whereas notation began as a means of communicating music that had already been made, it eventually became a driving force in the evolution of music.[29] From the mid-seventeenth century, barlines were employed to denote metrical periodicity, and time signatures in their present form appeared during the Baroque era of the eighteenth century. However, while strong and weak accents replaced long and short durations as the basis of rhythmic theory during the seventeenth century, medieval mensural notation, with its tendency to undermine metre, remained influential.[30]

In Western staff notation, a time signature of 3/4, 4/4 ... normally denotes the metre, which is often stable throughout the piece, and determines the order and subdivision of beats or pulses. Thus 4/4 stipulates four beats to the bar: ONE, two, three, four,

ONE, two, three, four ... where 'ONE' is the downbeat. The beat 'four' is in the same 'place' in every bar, and we constantly return to it throughout the piece, or pass through it if no note is played. Bars have a fixed number of pulses, but they may vary in the durations they contain – that is, in the number and lengths of notes. These are cumbersome descriptions of phenomena that every musician, professional or amateur, knows well, and it is interesting how hard it is to capture them in words. This difficulty is a mark of a philosophical problem, and the idea of 'returning to the same place' is very significant, as we will see.

Figure 11 Metre and rhythm: We keep returning to the beat 'four' in every bar, or pass through it if no note is played, as here in bar 2. Illustration by David Lloyd.

Metre, therefore, is usually defined as a context of regularly occurring structural accents and weak beats with which, or against which, freer rhythmic design may play.[31] In Western popular and art music, metre generally involves clearly articulated, easy-to-tap beats – we could call this the *4/4 model*. But outside Western music, the model is far from pervasive. In Japanese *gagaku* or court music, one beat is noticeably longer than the others, while much African and Indonesian music is polymetric – the listener can appreciate the total effect or attend to one metre out of the several presented. Examples are the traditional African music which inspired Ligeti's polyrhythmic – or polymetric – *Études* for piano, and Javanese gamelan.[32] This process of attending to one metre out of several involves a kind of aural aspect-perception, comparable to the 'seeing-as' explored by Wittgenstein, who cited Jastrow's duck–rabbit figure among many examples.[33] Just as in a contrapuntal piece – music with two or more independent but harmonically related melodic parts sounding together – one can focus on one part or line, so in Ligeti's 'rhythmic counterpoint' one can focus on one metre or rhythm.

Figure 12 'Jig Piano' (2004–5) by Philip Clark is highly polymetric – for instance, bars 113–14 set up a 'six against five' metre. Bars 113–17 show rapid changes of time signature – 5/8 to 2/4 to 2/4 to 5/16 to 2/4.

In fact, time-signature does not have to denote metre, though the assumption in the common practice or tonal era, from the eighteenth century onwards, is that it does. Even in nineteenth-century Western art music, barlines were not an infallible indication of true metric structure. For example, Beethoven's fast scherzo movements are in 3/4, but can be heard as groups of three or four measures, or alternating these; first beats are not stressed equally because this higher-order metre is involved. In metrically complex music of the past century by Stravinsky, Webern and their successors, barlines and time-signatures might only be a tentative analysis of stress pattern, or else serve merely to synchronize the ensemble.[34] Even in the case of metric music, one could notate everything in 4/4 and mark stresses where needed; in this notation, the first beat of the bar would not imply a stress. On the other hand, to change the time-signature every bar, as in some Stravinsky or Bartók, would be pointless if no stress is implied on the first beat. 'Non-metric' time-signatures are a deviation which has acquired currency only following the rhythmic revolution of Stravinsky's *The Rite of Spring*.

Non-metric music is not a modern invention, however. In the West before 1600, and in non-Western music from all eras, some music was metric, but much was not.[35] In Western pre-tonal music, as we have seen, the notational system does not clearly state a metre, but upbeats (anacrusis) are revealed, for instance, by an initial rest. In medieval motets there is no metre in the sense of a time-signature, but the 'proportion' by which one voice moves in relation to another can be specified. In three-voice motets by fifteenth-century composer Dufay, the two top voices have relatively fast-moving melodic material, with constantly changing rhythms. The bottom voice, however, is usually based on a plainchant motif, maybe of only three or four pitches, for instance, as we would say, three dotted crotchets followed by a dotted crotchet rest, repeating every fifth 'measure'. 'Measure' is in quotation marks because there are no barlines, and mensural notation only relates one voice's motion to that of another. Without barlines and a common metre to all three voices, there is no objective sense of pulse, just relationships between voices. Contemporary composer Harrison Birtwistle works with pulse but not metre, as in a very different way do free jazz-players Albert Ayler, John Coltrane and Charles Gayle, whose music has a

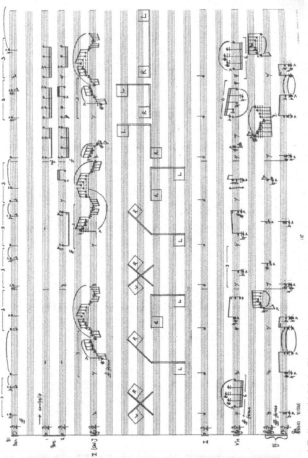

Figure 13 'Signal Failure' (1991–5) by Martyn Harry is an example of postmodern polyrhythm. He writes: 'The musicians in the ensemble are in different positions around the concert hall, with the conductor in the middle of the audience facing an actor on stage with semaphore flags. At this point the music is polyrhythmic – each part possesses a different relation to the conductor's beats, which seem at odds with what the audience hears. In a surreal effect, the actor mirrors the conductor's beats through semaphore flag movements. The audience thus experiences a dissonance between the silent "pulse" of the semaphore signals and the music, as if the actor were wading through a cacophony of conflicting sounds'.

strong residual swing without a foot-tapping pulse.[36] Like plainchant in this if nothing else, their music has accentuation without metre.

Free rhythm or free tempo – that is, non-metric rhythm without an obvious pulse – involves a more radical departure from the 4/4 model than metrically complex phenomena such as polymetre, divisive rhythms, the long beats of *gagaku* and the ambiguous status of medieval motets. (More on tempo later, but it is interesting to note that 'free rhythm' and 'free tempo' appear to be co-extensive.) Free rhythm is widespread in non-Western music – Gypsy violinists, traditional lullabies, vocal and instrumental forms across the Arab world, Indian *alap*, Chinese *qin* and Japanese *shakuhachi* music, where speech rhythms are an important influence.[37] Such music is usually performed solo or without a synchronized ensemble; it transmits a text or expresses a melody and is not used for dancing. While Western art music since 1600 has been predominantly metric, there have been examples of free rhythm – unaccompanied recitative in opera, for instance, or the unmetred keyboard preludes of the French baroque composer Louis Couperin, and in the twentieth century, some free improvisation and some avantgarde composition. Though free rhythm is undeniably rhythm, one can imagine the same debate as with melody – rhythms outside the 4/4 model could be described as arhythmic, just as the apparently unsingable 'melodies' of Webern or Boulez appear non-melodic. It might be argued that free rhythm involves a flexible beat or *rubato* – a proposal which extends considerably the province of loosely metric music. (*Rubato*, briefly defined, is the expressive alteration of rhythm or tempo.)

Until now I have been running together pulse and beat, but these should be distinguished. Beat has to be metric, but pulse does not, though as I will suggest, pulse may imply accent. As we have seen, the traditional conception underlying Western art music tends to divide rhythm and metre, treating the latter as a temporal grid for musical events or rhythmic structures. Scruton thus contrasts 'rhythm' with 'beat' in the sense of metre: '"Beat" denotes a pattern of time-values and accents, while "rhythm" denotes the movement that can be heard in that pattern'.[38] 'Rhythmic freedom' is often contrasted with 'the tyranny of the barline', and a performance can be criticized as unfeelingly metrical and metronomic, but only exceptionally as too rhythmic.[39] Learning to read music involves counting beats, but in any but the most complex contemporary composition, anyone who continues to rely on counting will not play rhythmically.[40] The traditional opposition does allow that rhythm plays expressively with and against metre. In Ravel's 'Bolero', for instance, sinuous rhythms are foregrounded against an unambiguous metrical backdrop, in emulation or caricature of the syncopated figures, asymmetrical phrase structures and groundbeat of jazz. In some genres, metre seems to overwhelm non-periodic rhythm; rap replaces speech-rhythms with chant-rhythms based on a single pulse, while drum 'n' bass consists largely of a single, often sampled, uninflected pulse.[41]

I wish to question the traditional division of rhythm and metre, at least in order to reject its abstract conception of metre. Opposing the traditional division, ethnomusicologist Curt Sachs argued that they are shades of the same phenomenon: 'Rhythm is flowing metre, and metre is bonded rhythm'. According to Zuckerkandl, musical metre is not simply the scaffolding for rhythm or the ruler which measures it, but an active force, a series of 'waves' or continuous cyclical motions, away from one downbeat and towards the next.[42] Most radically, the musicologist Christopher Hasty regards metre as an *aspect* of rhythm. Rejecting what he regards as the deterministic image of metre as the measure of time in which genuinely rhythmic events occur, he argues that it is essentially a felt or aesthetic category displaying creativity and spontaneity. Hasty argues plausibly that Western notational practice encouraged this image of an abstract grid of durations, while musical analysis deals in a timeless present – each blinds us to the fundamental nature of felt regularity.[43]

Hasty's concerns are justified. The traditional image neglects the felt regularity of the *underlying pulse or groundbeat* – abstract 3/4 time should be contrasted with felt waltz rhythm. Flexibility of pulse and rhythm exists even in non-*rubato* playing.[44] Tiny irregularities or elasticities characterize the time-feel of peerless jazz drummers such as Elvin Jones, Max Roach or Han Bennink, making their work human and musical. Almost all current drum machines play 'elastically', irrespective of whether they sample or synthesize their sound sources, showing their ability to mimic – even if crudely – human performance. Hasty's argument that metre as well as rhythm implies movement supports a humanistic account. While the distinction between rhythm and metre usefully applies to many kinds of music, it is essential is to avoid a merely abstract conception of the latter.

RHYTHM AND ACCENT

The final statement of the Platonic definition linked accent and metre. But is my subsequent claim correct – that even non-metric music involves accent? Music with an entirely uninflected pulse seems conceivable. 'X for Henry Flynt', written in 1960 by American minimalist composer La Monte Young, consists of a sound selected by the performer and repeated exactly uniformly, a chosen number ('X') times every second. The composition, if played with complete fidelity, eliminates metre in favour of perfect periodicity. Young, like Cage, was interested in making the listener perceive great diversity in such uniformity. However, exact uniformity is impossible for a human performer, a fact which Young also seems concerned to exploit. As avant-garde composer Cornelius Cardew commented, the interest of the piece lies in:

(1) Its duration, and proportional to that (2) the variation within the uniform repetition (3) the stress imposed on the single performer and through him on the audience ... These elements occur rather *in spite of* the instructions, although naturally they are the *result* of them. What the listener can hear and appreciate are the *errors* in the interpretation. If the piece were performed by a machine this interest would disappear and with it the composition.[45]

'X for Henry Flynt' seems to have a pulse, but does this amount to a rhythm? Can a monotonal pulse, a single repeated attack without the light and shade of stresses, be regarded as rhythmic? Even if it cannot, and so the result is strictly not music, 'X' is an implicit commentary on musical practice which presupposes the existence of music that does vary rhythmically and in other ways – just as Duchamp's readymades presuppose a traditional art world against which they are a reaction. 'X' calls for musicianship and so is parasitic on the aesthetic concerns shown by performers of conventional music. (I am concerned to locate salient features of rhythm and music, rather than necessary and sufficient conditions, and counterexamples may not refute claims of salient features.) The most pressing considerations, however, are that the piece as specified is impossible to perform – and probably impossible to hear as monotonal even if it were possible to perform. This is because the performer cannot avoid introducing unintentional stresses that shape the listener's perception; and that even if they could, listeners presented with an unaccented, fixed-pitch pulse will hear it as a stressed pattern, as psychological research, especially in the Gestalt tradition, has shown.[46] Indeed, the urge to perceive pulse in music, and to generate a pulse in it, may be so strong that there is little music which cannot fail to suggest pulsation.[47] There is no clear distinction between accent as a measurable acoustic phenomenon and as a phenomenological one – a deep issue that cannot be fully explored here.

It is also important to note that before the electronic era, it was simply not possible to create a fixed pulse without accent or differentiation. It is doubtful that an organic or even a mechanical pulse could be monotonal. A heartbeat, for instance, involves systole and diastole, or contraction and expansion, while even the clicks of a mechanical metronome at each end of its swing differ subtly in quality, giving the impression of a beat. My suggestion is that a subtle difference between two very similar sounds yields a beat, rather as the juxtaposition of two colours gives an impression of pictorial depth. (Perhaps the heart has a pulse but not a rhythm, while in contrast there is a rhythm to breathing; however, while we are not normally aware of the heart expanding and contracting, we do talk of cardiac arrhythmia.)

Not all accents are metric accents. Metric music often has accents off the beat. What makes a lot of metric music exciting and compelling is the play between metrical structure and offbeat, backbeat or syncopated stresses; there is a parallel here with the role of dissonance in tonality. It is not quite right to say that *syncopation* is the stress of a normally unstressed beat – often stress will be expected on such beats – but rather, it is stress that is not placed on the metrical downbeat. Syncopation occurs in many kinds of music and should not be confused with swing in jazz, though jazz can be syncopated also. For instance, funk has stress on '4' – the 'backbeat' – and tango on '2 *and* '. It is essential that the metrical downbeat is felt, even though the backbeat can appear the most stressed beat and so in tension with it; performers

Figure 14 'Thelonious Dreaming' (1990) by Philip Clark is highly syncopated – the opening bars for instance have heavily stressed offbeats (marked >). The piece is an attempt to find a notated response to the soundworld of jazz improviser and composer Thelonious Monk – a composition that is meant to give an impression of improvisation (on which, see Chapter 7)

can push that effect to the limit, leading to what in jazz is called 'turning the beat around'.[48]

But what exactly is accent? As with rhythm, the question is very hard to answer. Accent is not merely a physical feature of sounds which musical perception transforms into rhythm; rather, it is conceptually interlocked with rhythm. Accent makes essential reference to human activity in music-making, dancing and movement in general and can be created by changes in intensity, pitch, harmonic function or timbre.[49] It cannot be characterized simply in terms of decibel-level intensity but depends crucially on context. For instance, what is known as agogic accent extends a note slightly beyond its normal time value; while the highest note of a melody that leaps upwards and then falls back is experienced as accented, irrespective of its loudness. Where the metrical context is one of movement, even a rest can be accentuated:

Figure 15 Rests that make a rhythmic contribution: the downbeat in each bar is 'silent'. Illustration by David Lloyd.

Sudden quiet can constitute an accent. The climax of the *Liebestod* to Wagner's *Tristan and Isolde*, when the famous 'Tristan' chord resolves very quietly, or the 'Adagietto' of Mahler's Fifth Symphony, constitute a quiet structural downbeat – although these cases are metaphorical extensions of the concept of accent, as the qualification 'structural' suggests.

It may be objected that these considerations, instead of showing that rhythm is not a matter of physical intensity, show that rhythmic accent is not the only kind of accent. Thus the *New Grove Dictionary of Music and Musicians* defines accent as

The prominence given to a note or notes in performance by a perceptible alteration (usually increase) in volume ('dynamic accent'); a lengthening of duration or a brief preceding silence of articulation ('agogic accent'); an added ornament or pitch inflection of a melodic note ('pitch accent'); or by any combination of these.

Thus to accent a note, the player could pause, use vibrato or portamentos (sliding up or down to it), or add an ornament as well as stressing it. Instruments not capable of much or any dynamic nuance, such as the harpsichord and organ, simulate dynamic accentuation by agogic accents. On this view, accent itself is simply a 'drawing-attention-to'. As one authority wrote in 1779: 'The affections of *heavy* and *light* were always felt in music, though erroneously called by some moderns *accented* and *unaccented*; however, the *accented* or heavy note, was never understood to be *necessarily loud*, and the other *necessarily soft*'.[50] The idea of accent as drawing-attention-to does not imply movement, even if the production of a rhythmic accent generally does involve movement; it draws instead on the inseparability of rhythm and pitch discussed earlier.

However, I am still inclined to maintain that the core sense of accent is rhythmic, and that the preceding arguments complicate but do not undermine the necessary connection of rhythm and accent. Accent makes essential reference to movement. Rhythm, I have argued, is order in movement. But I wish to extend this common picture by arguing – against Cooper and Meyer, and Scruton – that accent also involves movement and is not merely a matter of pattern. My position is that rhythm, metre, stress and accent cannot be understood independently but are internally related and form a circle of concepts – just like rhythm and music, in the manner described earlier. It follows that Cooper and Meyer's definition of rhythm as 'the way in which one or more unaccented beats are grouped in relation to an accented one' cannot constitute an introductory explanation for someone who lacks an understanding of rhythm, since they could not understand what 'accent' means. This definition is informative only when interpreted as asserting an internal relation between rhythm and accent. Cooper and Meyer almost realize this when they allow that accent is an 'axiomatic concept' which remains 'undefined in terms of causes', and that since duration, intensity, melodic contour and regularity are all involved, 'one cannot at present state unequivocally what makes one tone seem accented and another not'. However, this is not, as they seem to think, a result of our present ignorance of psychological or physiological causes of human responses. Rather, it follows from the conceptual truth that any definition of accent will itself refer to rhythm; that the concepts of rhythm and accent are interdependent.[51]

RHYTHM AND MOVEMENT

Movement is, I believe, the most fundamental conceptualization of music – the basic category in terms of which it is experienced. To reiterate the Platonic definition:

> Rhythm is meaningful order within movement or movement-in-sound, involving the imposition of accent on a sequence of sounds or movements; it creates non-periodic phenomena often within a periodic, repetitive (metrical) framework, and gives rise to a 'feel' or pattern in which listeners participate.

Most kinds of music have 'swing', not in the precise jazz sense but in this broad sense of rhythmic feel. Tempo is an essential element here – the precise speed affects the feel greatly. Despite his tendency to treat metre as an abstract and mathematical rather than a phenomenal feature of a sequence of sounds, the core of truth in Scruton's account is that rhythm 'belongs not to number but to life ... [it is] the virtual energy that flows through the music, and which causes me to move with it in sympathy'. He argues convincingly that to hear rhythm is to hear a kind of animation: 'Rhythm involves the same virtual causality that we find in melody. Beats do not follow one another; they bring each other into being, respond to one another, and breathe with a common life'.[52]

Although these claims are absolutely correct, the way that Scruton develops them is questionable, however. He argues that the attribution of motion to music is just as metaphorical as ascriptions of emotion; nothing relevant in the music literally moves, just as nothing in it is literally sad. Musical experience involves the importation of a spatial framework – the organization of the auditory field in terms of position, movement and distance – though these spatial concepts do not literally apply to the sounds that we hear: 'Rather they describe what we hear *in* sequential sounds, when we hear them as music'.[53] Scruton's claim may be expressed as follows: the experience of hearing sounds as music has two intentional objects – sounds and silences (whose content features in an asserted thought) and life and movement (whose content features in an unasserted thought, involving the imagination). That is, we literally hear sounds and silences, and through a process of imaginative, metaphorical perception, we also hear life and movement in them.

Scruton thus interprets the basic claim that movement is a fundamental conceptualization of music – a claim that certainly needs interpreting – through two further claims: the movement is spatial and is perceived metaphorically. The first of these claims could be queried on the grounds that the movement in question is not along a continuum, as pitch appears to be; rather it is contraction and dilation as in a heartbeat, or movement about a point, or back and forth, like a pendulum.[54] This is the correlate in movement of the repetition inherent in rhythm. Marching across a parade-ground is rhythmic, but directional movement in space is not essential; marching on the spot could exhibit the same rhythm. This repetitive bodily movement is equivalent to, or expressive of, the returning to or passing through the beats of the bar such as 'and two', discussed earlier under the heading of metre. We always return to the beginning of the bar, as it were. Variation on an underlying repetitive structure occurs at different levels in music. It occurs also in pitch, though in this case we are not aware of it – wave forms are cyclical – and, as noted earlier, Stockhausen and others have accelerated regular pulses in the studio to produce wave forms.

Against the assertion that movement is fundamental to experiencing music, Malcolm Budd objects that rhythmic movement is not spatial and that it is not essential: 'to hear rhythm – acousmatically – is not to hear imaginatively any kind of spatial movement'. (By 'acousmatically' he means 'musically' – see Chapter 4.) These claims, I believe, commit him to an unacceptably static conception of rhythm: 'at the basic level, we hear rhythm in music, not as beats causing one another to come into being, but as an intentionally designed process in which sounds and silences are grouped into units in which an element is heard as accented relative to the others, patterns of stressed and unstressed moments'.[55] (In fact, silences are not essential; rhythm requires only change or discontinuity, as the Platonic definition asserted, and this might just involve relative shifts in volume or even timbre.) Budd does not say that we never hear rhythm as a form of animation, imagining the tones to be the expression of life's pulsations. Rather, he argues that such imagining is not necessary – by which I take him to mean that the metaphor of movement is not essential for any kind of music, not merely that it is essential only for some kinds. For him, talk of musical motion is an eliminable, non-explanatory metaphor.[56]

We have already encountered music where a more static conception seems appropriate. Morton Feldman's is the music of near-stasis, in which the model for rhythm seems to be blocks of almost sourceless sounds and silences – which is not, of course, to say that his music is 'going nowhere', rather that it achieves its purposes without resorting to conventional rhythmic practices. In John Cage's late 'number' pieces, which earlier I assimilated to sound-art, these practices are actively undermined. Cage's pieces 'stretch' time in that sound events are situated far apart and are causally disjunct; even when events coincide within this conceptual framework it appears to be an accidental occurrence rather than a contrivance. (There is something of this feeling with Feldman's music also.) Jonathan Kramer interestingly characterizes a category of musical stasis or non-linearity which he refers to as the 'verticality of time'.[57]

However, the existence of this category does not support the application of the static conception as a paradigm. (Again, as with sound-art, no relative evaluation is implied.) The static conception should be rejected, I believe. The question remains how music is conceptualized in terms of movement; is this, as Scruton argues, a matter of metaphorical perception? I think not. This is because one consequence of the universality of rhythm discussed earlier is that not only do we conceptualize music in terms of human movement; we also conceptualize human movement in terms of music. Scruton therefore understates the case when he writes that, 'The musical phenomena that we group together under the rubric of rhythm have their counterparts in other areas of human activity' – speech, dancing, physical labour.[58] For these are not counterparts, they are the same phenomenon. Dance, poetry and music are conceptually interdependent in that rhythm is essential to each, and none can be understood independently of rhythm. The experience of musical rhythm does not only involve experiencing music as behaving like a human body; it also involves experiencing the human body as behaving musically – that is, the person as moving musically. A piece of music can be in waltz time or feature dotted rhythms; likewise, someone can tap their foot or hammer a nail in waltz time, or in dotted rhythms. On the Indonesian island of Bali, for instance, rice is pounded, usually by several women with bamboo poles working on the same or adjacent containers of unhusked rice, creating complex rhythms while doing so.[59] In contrast to work songs such as sea shanties, which accompany the work as opposed to being generated by it, this is not music, though it is musical. We can see, therefore, that rhythmic descriptions apply to categories or behaviour that are not immediately regarded as music but are at least incipiently so.

In order to advance the debate over movement and metaphor, it is necessary to understand metaphor, and this is no easy matter. There is a large philosophical literature on the topic. However, it should be agreed that metaphor involves a primary and a secondary use – an origin and a target. To describe a tree as a human body swaying is to attribute properties of the human body (the metaphor's origin) to properties of the tree (its target). But the universality of rhythm means that human bodily movement is as much the target of metaphorical projection as music itself. A contrast with the ascription of emotions makes this point clear. In order to learn to ascribe emotions, one does not have to experience music as well as human reactions and behaviour; emotion-ascriptions to music are secondary compared with those to people. In contrast, we do not project from a primary sense of rhythmic bodily movement to a secondary sense of musical rhythmic movement because we have already reached the musical level of description in describing human bodily movement as rhythmic. To master rhythmic ascriptions, it is necessary to grasp both musical and bodily descriptions; the description of human behaviour is not the primary description of which the musical description is secondary. Rhythm is an essentially musical feature of apparently non-musical, but incipiently musical, events or processes. Music and life are interfused.

The same fusion is shown by those movement ascriptions to music which probably are metaphorical. The sound of John Lee Hooker's foot-tapping, which his producer captured vividly on disc, adds to the intensity of his classic 1940s and 1950s recordings.[60] Indeed, it is as integral to the appreciation of Hooker's music as his guitar-playing or singing. We might describe the blues master as tapping his foot with great momentum. This use is metaphorical, I think. A fairly slow piece can have great momentum in this sense – Muddy Waters' 'Hoochie Coochie Man' or funk classics by James Brown – and here the origin of the metaphor is an object of large mass and slowly incremental acceleration. Neither the music nor the foot-tapping literally have great momentum; they will not, for instance, power industrial machinery. Putting John Coltrane's free-jazz classic *Ascension* on the turntable was said to heat up a New York apartment on a cold winter's day, but no one actually reduced their heating bill that way. The ascription of momentum here is metaphorical both in the case of music *and* bodily movement. Music itself does not move literally as dancers' limbs do; but in order to describe those bodily movements in the dance, it is necessary to use musical terms. It is not as if there is a complete set of non-musical descriptions of bodily movement, which are then projected onto music – and this fact applies also to the metaphorical cases such as 'momentum', which derive from the movement of physical bodies as such. Projection between human bodily movement and music is entirely two-way, whether literal or metaphorical.

It may be the case that proponents of metaphorical projection are really objecting to the claim that rhythmic movement of music can be captured in purely physical terms. It is not, for instance, the movement of air molecules energized by a player blowing through their horn. But then neither can rhythmic *bodily* movement be captured in such terms. A purely physical description refers to a foot moving up and down and exerting a certain force or pressure on the ground. But this description applies to the situation where a machine grasps someone's foot while they are unconscious and raises and lowers it, perhaps every fourth time lowering it with more force. This would only be a simulation of a beat. A rhythmic action is one intended under a certain description, where that description is not a purely physical one. This may just be the traditional philosophical question of whether describing human action in physical terms can permit a distinction between action and mere movement – to which the answer, in my view, would be 'no'. The paradigm of rhythmic movement is human action with a feeling or sense of involvement – originally, a communal activity of making music. This may not be present in absolutely all cases of rhythm, but it is the paradigm from which the concept arises.

To claim that there is literally no movement in the music may be to claim no more than that there is literally no physical movement. But implicit in the claim is the assumption that the paradigm of movement is spatial, and this is questionable. Many familiar kinds of movement, for instance the movement of temporal processes such as the Stock Exchange index, do not involve a change in location, yet they are at most dead metaphors – that is, literal near enough.[61] Hence the earlier claim that music is an art of temporal process. Tempo does indeed seem to involve literal ascriptions of movement to music, because there can be literal movement in time as well as in space. 'Rapid' is ambiguous between 'many events in a short period of time' and 'fast movement between two points in space'. A rapid speech, for instance, is one which is spoken fast and is over quickly – many vocal 'events' occur in a short space of time. An event that is rapid is not one that moves at a faster rate through time, rather, it occurs within a shorter period of time. Though these descriptions are not spatial, to talk of a short or a long game is not to talk metaphorically. The application to music is obvious. A fast piece normally contains many notes in a short space of time – it would be a feeble joke to say, of a piece consisting entirely of long notes, 'This is a very fast piece, but it hasn't got many notes in it', and mark it *presto*. A slow piece can have rapid ornamentation, since if rapid notes are rightly heard as decorations and ornaments surrounding a basically slow melody, the piece is not literally fast. ('Presto lamentoso' is a different phenomenon – the final movement of Mozart's Symphony No. 40 is an uptempo tragic lament.) Thus there is a connection between tempo and frequency of notes, even if it is not direct. A piece that presents many notes in a short space of time is literally fast in the sense of moving rapidly in time.

It would be wrong, therefore, to say that the basic sense of 'rapid' refers to velocity in a certain direction. As well as the rapid oscillation associated with rhythmic movement discussed earlier, it also refers to movement in time. A spatial metaphor such as 'the flow of time' notoriously causes metaphysical problems, but there is a real phenomenon to which it refers. Here a general issue opens up. As we saw in Chapter 3, even for Hanslick, allegedly the paradigm formalist, music consists in 'tonally moving forms'. I believe that he is referring primarily to movement in time, not in space, which returns us to the questions at the start of this chapter concerning music as an art of time. It is not possible to pursue these questions, or that of metaphorical projection, any further here. But I hope to have cast doubt on the conventional or received view – it is not, as Paul Boghossian writes, the beginning of wisdom about aesthetics of music that the descriptions under which we hear sounds, when we hear them as music, are not literally true of anything.[62] To hear music as movement is a fundamental way of experiencing and conceiving it, but one that does not have to involve metaphorical projection in the way that is commonly assumed.

This chapter, more so than others in this volume, has raised more questions than it has answered. But what it suggests is that the treatment of rhythm is a central part of the case for a humanistic conception of music, one that richly repays further philosophical investigation. In the next chapter, we return to the historical issues presented in Chapter 3 on absolute music and take the story into the era of modernism through an analysis of the work of Theodor Adorno.

NOTES

1 Stravinsky (1970), p. 1; Schopenhauer (1969), Vol. I, section, pp. 52, 266; Davies (1994), p. 235. Davies has a particular reason for referring to 'temporal process', as we will see below. Edward Lippman ((1977) pp. 55–6) writes: 'Sound is intrinsically temporal; it does not merely depend for its existence on the temporal continuity of consciousness the way stationary visual objects or concepts do'.

2 Zuckerkandl (1969), Chapter 11, 'Metre and Rhythm'.

3 These issues are interestingly discussed by Alperson (1980) and Levinson and Alperson (1991).

4 Scruton (1997), Dewey (1980). Bergson, the philosopher of time, has almost nothing to say on rhythm.

5 Cooper and Meyer (1960).

6 Hasty (1997).

7 As Hasty (1997) argues. The closeness of these questions illustrates the inseparability of rhythm, melody and harmony, discussed below. Poetry is the rhythmicization of speech rather than sound.

8 Excellent examples are Radigue (2002) and Sachiko M et al. (2005). Sachiko M's sine tones are continuous, and such changes as occur in them are textural rather than dynamic. Drone-music is diffuse compared to the more precise and – I would say – rhythmic music of slow change produced by such composers as James Tenney; see Szlavnics (2006).

9 From the late nineteenth century, the monks of Solesmes attempted to 'reform' plainchant and return it to what they perceived to be its original purity. (See Sadie and Tyrrell (2004), entry under 'Solesmes'; Hoppin (1978), pp. 88–90.) We will return to the issue of notation shortly.

10 An excellent recording of Palestrina's *Missa Papae Marcelli*, which displays that propulsion, is found on Tallis Scholars (1990).

11 Quoted in Dürr and Gerstenberg (1980), p. 806, who defend the holism of rhythm, melody and harmony. Tonal or functional harmony contrasts with the non-functional harmony of much twentieth-century music, for instance, the minimalism of Reich, Riley and Glass.

12 As Scruton suggests in his *The Aesthetics of Music* (1997). Schoenberg's revolution is discussed in Chapter 6. Dahlhaus (1987), pp. 45–61, argues that discussion of this revolution has attended one-sidedly to atonality at the expense of equally important developments in rhythm. While Webern's music is atonal, Schoenberg's and Berg's – and the twelve-tone compositions of Stravinsky – tends to have tonal centres; Schoenberg's rhythmic language was conservative in comparison to Webern's.

13 Harvey (1980). Post-Renaissance Western music mostly uses *divisive rhythms* or metres, whose basic units are bars, which are broken down into smaller units (crotchets, quavers and so on). *Additive rhythms* do not require regularity at the level of the bar, only at the level of the individual pulse; they start with a small pulse-unit and build rhythmic blocks from them. Examples of the latter date back to fifteenth-century *ars nova*, and are found in Indian classical music, in Bartók's 'Bulgarian' rhythms and in Stravinsky, Messiaen and Tippett. The distinction is a difficult one, however, on which see Sadie and Tyrrell (2004), entry under 'Rhythm' by Justin London.

14 Cooper and Meyer (1960), for instance p. 2.

15 Quoted in Hamilton (forthcoming 2007b), Chapter 4. Lee Konitz comments: 'I'm talking about note-to-note responsibility ... I'm trying to tune in to every note – how it feels in itself, and how it connects with the next note, whether I'm tonguing it or legato-ing it, or vibrating it' (Hamilton (forthcoming 2007b), Chapter 6). The issue is pursued in Chapter 7.

16 Hanslick (1986), for instance, refers to rhythm as 'the sole musical element in nature' – in contrast to harmony and melody (p. 69). He neglects birdsong, however.

17 Zuckerkandl (1969), *The External World*, pp. 156–7. A very different claim of universality is found in London (2004), who argues that metre is a particular kind of more general entrainment behaviour, not fundamentally musical in origin (see, for instance, p. 4). *Harmonic rhythm* or *speed* is the rate of change of harmony – a rather different matter.

18 Scientific psychology has a tendency to attempt to establish what are in fact conceptual truths on an empirical basis; for instance, as we

will see below, it tries to justify empirically the conceptual connection between rhythm and accent. In the field of memory, it tries to justify empirically the conceptual distinction between autobiographical memory of what one has witnessed or experienced, and factual memory based on other sources (Hamilton (forthcoming)).

19   Depending on the translation – Plato (1970), Book 2, 665.

20   Dewey (1980).

21   As Dewey comments, 'A gas that evenly saturates a container, a torrential flood sweeping away all resistance, an unbroken waste of sand, and a monotonous roar are wholes without rhythm' ((1980), p. 155).

22   Blamey and Denley (2006) is an example of random noise-based sound-art – and a very tough listen.

23   Dürr and Gerstenberg (1980), p. 805. In fact, starting with bebop, much jazz, pop and rock is considerably faster than 80 beats per minute; a sympathetic quickening, rather than imitation, of bodily rhythmic processes is intended.

24   Dewey (1980), pp. 147–51.

25   The existence of additive metres shows that there is more to the distinction between metre and rhythm than regularity versus non-regularity – or that regularity should be understood as relative. See Sachs (1953), pp. 24 ff.

26   As Clayton (1996) comments.

27   Six-year-olds can read music with ease; many great jazz musicians could not. It is just a tool.

28   See Treitler (1979), p. 524, and also Hoppin (1978), especially Chapters 14 and 15. As we saw earlier, some theorists argue that certain earlier plainchant notation implied rhythm, but these theories are controversial and have not gained wide acceptance.

29   See Box ('Musical Notation'), Chapter 1, p. 35.

30   Sadie and Tyrrell (2004), entry under 'Rhythm'.

31   Yeston (1976), pp. 32–3, argues that this has been the dominant definition for the past 300 years.

32   Ligeti's music and its African models can be heard on pianist Pierre-Laurent Aimard's (2003). Javanese gamelan is gong-structured music in 4/4, but Westerners usually hear the gong as sounding the beginning of a bar, whereas Indonesians hear it as the closing note of a cycle as long as 128 beats. Tenzer (1998) is an excellent introduction to Balinese gamelan.

33   Wittgenstein (1953), Part II.

34   Hasty argues that Webern's Quartet Op. 22 shows no clear pulse and may not be genuinely metrical, while Whittall comments more cautiously that in such compositions, the concept of metre is under strain (Hasty (1997), p. 257, Whittall (1999)).

35 As Sachs observes: 'We might look over hundreds and hundreds of polyphonic pieces from the Middle Ages and the Renaissance and never find an upbeat ... An actual upbeat – like winding up for a throw – prepares a stress; it is necessarily four-ONE. It was out of place in the polyphonic forms which depended, on the whole, upon an even, little-stressed flow' ((1953), p. 261).

36 An excellent example is Ayler's 'Holy Ghost', from Ayler (1998).

37 These and other forms are discussed in Clayton (1996). Fine performances of music for *shakuhachi* are found on the Ongaku Masters (2004).

38 Scruton (forthcoming 2007b).

39 Schumann rejected the 'tyranny of the bar-line', stressing the supposed origins of music in 'free speech ... a higher poetic form of punctuation, as in the Greek choruses, the language of the Bible or the prose of Jean Paul' (quoted in Sadie and Tyrrell (2004), entry on 'Accent').

40 John Tilbury remarks that one cannot play Morton Feldman's late piano pieces without counting the repetitions and rhythmic displace-ments – which must be true also of early minimal music by Reich and Glass, where the interest is almost entirely rhythmic. However, he adds, this is human counting, and ideally there comes a point when the performer transcends the notation (e-mail conversation with the author, January 2007).

41 I would question London's contention that rhythm is the 'temporal stimulus' that is 'phenomenally present' in the music, while metre is our perception and anticipation of such patterns, not least because 'phenomenally present' implicitly refers to the listener's response (Sadie and Tyrrell (2004), entry under 'Rhythm').

42 Sachs (1953), pp. 20–1 – the quotation is from Roman grammarian Charisius, in Sachs (1953), p. 13; Zuckerkandl (1969), Chapter 11. A tone acquires its special rhythmic quality from its place in the cycle of the wave, from 'the direction of its kinetic impulse', Zuckerkandl argues.

43 Hasty (1997), for instance p. 12. His position is criticized by London (2004), who regards metre as a mode of attending, and rhythm as that to which we attend (for instance, p. 4).

44 Psychological research on this question has involved precise measurement of note lengths on recordings of a single piece, for instance Repp (1992).

45 Cardew (1971), p. xiv. Drum 'n' bass produced from samples might achieve the same metre-less pulse, though it would resemble the mechanistic performance which Cardew found uninteresting. Per-haps, through its strong attack, everything in drum 'n' bass is stressed.

46 Composers such as Brian Ferneyhough and Chris Dench also create a friction between ideal score and realized performance, not really expecting their incredibly complex scores to be actualized perfectly.

47 As Clayton (1996) argues, p. 330.

48 Charlie Parker's metrically free-floating flurries of notes could make fellow musicians think that he had missed a beat, and so they would drop a beat in response, thus 'turning the beat around'. See, for instance, Davis (1989), p. 101.

49 See, for instance, London (2004), p. 19.

50 Sadie and Tyrrell (2004), entry under 'Accent'. See also entry under 'Rhythm'.

51 Cooper and Meyer (1960), p. 6; as argued in Chapter 2, there is nothing particularly unusual in such a holism of concepts – it is a common if neglected feature of language.

52 Scruton (forthcoming 2007b), and (1997), p. 35. Here he does distinguish felt beat from abstract metre.

53 Scruton (forthcoming 2007b).

54 Budd (2003), pp. 221–2, makes the point about contraction and dilation.

55 Budd (2003), pp. 221–2.

56 He also seems to hold the assumption, found in writers as diverse as Meyer and Scruton, and which I disputed earlier, that 'accent' or 'stress' can be understood independently of rhythm.

57 Kramer (1988), pp. 382–8.

58 Scruton (forthcoming 2007b).

59 Discussed in Eiseman (2004), p. 296.

60 An excellent example is the instrumental 'Stomp Boogie' from 1948, on John Lee Hooker (2002).

61 As Davies argues (1994), p. 236. However, my concern is with rhythmic rather than melodic motion – which is a separate problematic issue – and in the case of rhythm, the metaphor seems more compelling.

62 Boghossian (2002), pp. 50–1. In place of Scruton's synthesis of metaphorical and aspect perception he proposes what he calls 'normatively constrained projection' – a property is projected onto the sounds, and the projection may or may not be appropriate (hence, 'normative').

CHAPTER 6

ADORNO AND MODERNISM

Music as autonomous and 'social fact'

Any contemporary aesthetics must take modernism seriously. Philosopher, sociologist and music theorist Theodor Adorno (1903–69) was a totally committed modernist and avant-gardist and the most important writer on aesthetics of music in the twentieth century. For him, the most authentic art is modernist art which reflects in its own fragmentation the fragmentation of society, and he held that modernism's admission of the ugly and dissonant shows art's increasing capacity for self-interrogation. The task of this chapter is to assess his view that as artists became free of church and aristocratic patronage towards the end of the eighteenth century, their work simultaneously became autonomous – that is, free of direct social function – and entered the marketplace. Thus, autonomous music, for Adorno, stands in a dialectical relation to commodification. Adorno wants us to be struck by how such an extraordinary and exotic phenomenon as autonomous music, and autonomous art in general, could arise, and he sees its implications as no other writer has done. This central concern with music's autonomy is accompanied by other key issues in Adorno's very rich treatment, including the historical nature of artistic material and the language-like character of music.

THE ADVENT OF MODERNISM

Some of the implications of modernity – its associated system of the arts and the growing aesthetic and social autonomy of music –

were traced in Chapter 3. 'Modernity' is a general term for social and cultural developments arising with the Enlightenment at the end of the eighteenth century – a sociological and historical phenomenon. *Modernism*, in contrast, is primarily an artistic phenomenon, a sharpening and intensifying of modernity, or a response to it – some writers describe it as a reaction.[1] Modernity and modernism should not simply be equated, therefore.[2] The fact that German and other languages have no separate term 'modernism' may create some confusion, though in context it is clear that 'modern' or '*Die Moderne*', when used for instance by Adorno, refers to modernism.[3]

Modernism is a problematic and highly contested concept. The consensus is that artistic modernism arose in the later nineteenth century, flourished in the first three decades of the twentieth and still persists in the face of postmodernism. Many authorities date it from the 1880s, but Adorno claimed a slightly earlier date, arguing that 'the category of "the modern" ... emerges for the first time with Baudelaire'.[4] It may be that modernism did not appear in all the arts simultaneously – arguably, literary modernism began in the 1860s with Baudelaire, followed by painting with impressionism and, finally, in the 1890s, music – Debussy's 'Prélude à l'après-midi d'un faune' (1894), inspired by a poem of Mallarmé, is often cited as the first fully modernist work. Any listing is contestable, but principal modernist artists from the early decades include painters Cézanne, Kandinsky, Picasso and Matisse; architects Le Corbusier, Gropius, Mies van der Rohe and Frank Lloyd Wright; composers Debussy, Schoenberg, Stravinksy and Varèse; and writers and poets Baudelaire, Rimbaud, Valéry, Yeats, Eliot, Pound, Joyce, Conrad, Kafka and Proust. Maverick avant-gardists such as Satie, Ives and Duchamp enjoy a problematic relationship with modernism and may be better regarded as proto-postmodernists.

Modernism saw itself as progressive, and in both the visual arts and music, modernists rebelled against classical standards imposed by the academy. In contrast to classicism's sceptical attitude towards the new, 'modern' became a positive description of revolutionary avant-gardism – the French poet Baudelaire, who defended Wagner against his critics, used it in this sense in 1863.[5] Wagner regarded the history of music as progressive – art should disrupt conservative tastes to reveal hidden truths and make prophetic criticism – and his successors Mahler, Strauss, Schoenberg and Debussy engaged in a self-conscious search for a new musical language.[6] But it is impossible to give any account of modernism without taking sides on the question of how radical the break with past tradition really was – that is part of its essential contestability. Even if one accepts the idea of a radical break, there are opposed accounts of what the modernist movement represented. This second issue will be addressed at the end of the chapter.

Concerning the first issue, I must own up to being a card-carrying supporter of modernism, someone who regards the movement's products as revolutionary and immensely rewarding. Modernist Herbert Read was right when in 1933 he referred to 'a difference in kind in the contemporary revolution' compared to earlier ones – an abrupt break with all tradition and the abandonment of five centuries of European effort.[7] A defining feature of modernism is its self-conscious attention to the artistic medium itself. If 'medium' is taken to be genre – 'string quartet' in music, 'still life' in painting – then music was as self-conscious as the other arts; for instance, Stravinsky's 'Three Pieces for String Quartet' radically questions the traditional medium in this sense. But taking medium in a larger sense as sound itself, a concern is apparent in music in the work of Edgard Varèse from the 1920s, and before then more crudely in the work of the Italian futurists, while it could be argued that painters became self-conscious about the activity of placing marks on surfaces even earlier. In the words of modernist art critic Clement Greenberg, 'Modernism used art to call attention to art' – the movement's persistent experimentalism put into question the very concept of what art is. Critics of modernism would regard such claims as exaggerated, but, for its proponents, modernist art is self-conscious, self-reflective and self-critical, rejecting aesthetic norms.

Modernists were eager to break down barriers between the arts. As we saw in Chapter 3, they especially took the growing abstraction of music during the nineteenth century as a model for painting – Kandinsky's *Concerning the Spiritual in Art* is a manifesto for this ideal.[8] There are interesting congruences between the different arts in the heroic early decades of modernism, in their overturning of traditional aesthetic values. In architecture, modernism is expressed in the dictum 'form follows function' and the rejection of decoration. In literature, traditional linear narrative was supplanted by traditional forms such as stream of consciousness writing, and realism and naturalism were attacked; in poetry, conventional metrical and rhyming patterns were abandoned, and all that remained was the line. But the most interesting congruence is between visual art and music, which abandoned post-Renaissance perspective and tonality respectively. On an influential modernist view, painting and picturing became separated – abstract paintings were those which no longer depicted, and at most represented, conceptual or emotional content.[9] (However, realism is also a strand and so not all modernist painting is abstract.) In music, the eighteenth- and nineteenth-century 'era of common practice', based on the tonal system of major and minor keys, came to an end.

For Schoenberg and later theorists, the music of Wagner, Strauss, Debussy and Mahler showed the breakdown of tonality. From the first decade of the twentieth century, Schoenberg and fellow modernists fragmented common-era syntax, replacing the tonal system with various strategies, most radically through what became known as atonality, discussed below. In his 1941 essay 'Composition with Twelve Tones', Schoenberg explained how his 'new style', after 1908, emancipated dissonance: 'The term *emancipation of the dissonance* refers to its comprehensibility, which is considered equivalent to the consonance's comprehensibility. A style based on this premise treats dissonances like consonances and renounces a tonal centre'.[10] Stultification of the tonal system made this 'emancipation' necessary and inevitable, Schoenberg believed.[11] However, to talk of the collapse of tonality and emancipation of the dissonance is itself to subscribe to a Schoenbergian vision of modernist history. An alternative view refers instead to the *evolution* of tonality, citing many modernist composers, notably Stravinsky and Bartók, who continued using key signatures.

Many of its proponents regarded modern art as a necessary response to the contemporary world of industrialization and mass culture, and the artistic movement was spurred by technological revolution. Russian abstract pioneer Kazimir Malevich commented extravagantly in 1916 that,

The new life of iron and the machine, the roar of automobiles, the glitter of electric lights, the whirring of propellers, have awoken the soul, which was stifling in the catacombs of ancient

156

reason and has emerged on the roads woven between earth and sky. If all artists could see the crossroads of these celestial paths ... then they would not paint chrysanthemums.[12]

The shock and devastation of the First World War and economic instability of the post-war years, deepened the modernist impulse among composers, particularly in France and Germany; in conservative England, Frank Bridge, teacher of Benjamin Britten, was drawn to European modernism as a result. But this was also the era of neoclassicism, which reacted against romantic expressionism by offering a pastiche of classical ideals – both Stravinsky and Schoenberg went through neoclassical phases, and lesser figures such as Hindemith and Poulenc were largely identified with it.[13] After the Second World War, modernism persisted through composers such as Boulez, Stockhausen, Nono and Carter and painters such as Jackson Pollock and Barnett Newman. The 1960s are often described as the crisis of modernism – with its subversion by Cage and later the American minimalists, and in visual art, Pop art, Op art and sculptural minimalism. Through the era of *postmodernism* from the 1970s onwards, *high modernists* such as Lachenmann, Harvey and Ferneyhough, or in visual art, Noland and Caro, continue to define themselves in opposition to postmodern fragmentation and eclecticism.[14]

Modernism was never embraced by more than a minority of artists, critics or the public, and an aura of difficulty still surrounds the work of leading exponents such as Schoenberg, Eliot and Joyce. The immediate success of his opera *Wozzeck* paradoxically undermined the confidence of Schoenberg's pupil Alban Berg. Adorno, who was involved with the première, reported Berg's feeling that 'if a piece of music nowadays won over the public so immediately, there must be something wrong with it'.[15] Modernism deepened the rupture between art music and popular music, well under way at the time of Wagner; understanding modernist art seemed to require a specialized language. The poet Philip Larkin – ironically himself a representative of modernism – condemned the 'life-denying' modernist trilogy of Charlie Parker, Ezra Pound and Picasso:

How glibly I had talked of modern jazz, without realising the force of the adjective ... I went back to my books: "After

157

Parker, you had to be something of a musician to follow the best jazz of the day". Of course! After Picasso! After Pound! There could hardly have been a conciser summary of what I don't believe about art'.[16]

Many commentators argue that not only does modernist art deepen the rupture between high and popular culture, it actively sets itself against popular culture. Thus, in his classic article *Avant-Garde and Kitsch*, Clement Greenberg argued that 'In turning his attention away from subject matter of common experience, the poet or artist turns it in upon the medium of his own craft'. And Ortega y Gasset commented in 1925 that 'Modern art will always have the masses against it. It is essentially unpopular; moreover, it is anti-popular'.[17]

The truth of this assertion depends on the artform in question, however. The impact of modernist painting and architecture on commercial design and the media still endures – Bauhaus products would not be out of in place in a store like Habitat or Ikea. Kandinsky and Rothko reproductions appear on café walls, but never Webern or Morton Feldman as piped music. Modernism in music did not fundamentally affect the tastes and practices of twentieth-century mass culture, though its effect on film music and, less directly, popular music has been significant.[18] The rift between modernist art music and popular music is therefore a salient feature of Western musical life. It is a key issue in the work of Theodor Adorno, whose philosophy and aesthetics of music is a product of the modernist movement. A high-art standpoint often led to aestheticism, and critics of the central modernist narrative argue that it neglects the social context of art.[19] As we will now see, this charge cannot be levelled at Adorno's version of the narrative – though it appears in various forms as a criticism of his work and will have to be addressed more than once.

ADORNO'S AESTHETICS OF MODERNISM

'The fundamental problem addressed by Adorno's aesthetics is how to philosophize about art in the absence of aesthetic norms', writes Max Paddison.[20] In the era of modernism, on this view, prescriptive maxims either for the production of, or critical response to, artworks, are no longer available. As we saw in Chapter 3, Kant denied that such norms, either for artists or audiences, could ever exist – there are no a-priori principles of taste, and though rules can be derived from the creations of geniuses, genius itself follows no rules. However, countless critical authorities in the immediate pre-modernist era seemed to remain in ignorance of Kant's dictum, codifying the era of common practice through rules for harmony and counterpoint which expressed the solidification of bourgeois culture. While pre-modernist autonomous artworks accepted criteria for genre and form, and for harmony, unity and integration, modernist works subverted such specifications and thus became incommensurable with what went before.

Adorno was a precocious adherent of the ideals of the modernist avant-garde. Brought up in a rarefied artistic milieu, from the age of fifteen, Kant's *Critique of Pure Reason*, together with the work of Hegel and Marx, was his primary philosophical influence. He studied at Frankfurt University, and from 1925 to 1928 was a composition student of Alban Berg. He eulogized Berg's teacher Schoenberg as the paradigm modernist, though the puzzled composer did not return the compliment. Teaching philosophy at Frankfurt University, he also became associated with the Institute for Social Research, but after the Nazi rise to power in 1933 he became exiled to England, then the USA, where he continued sociological research on popular music. In 1949 Adorno returned as co-director of the re-established Institute for Social Research, becoming a leading member of the so-called Frankfurt School of contemporary Marxist philosophy. *Philosophy of Modern Music* (1949), the book that made him famous, presented Schoenberg and Stravinsky as opposed poles of modernism, with Stravinsky the reactionary. During the 1950s and 1960s he was a regular contributor at Darmstadt summer schools, focus of modernist musical activity, debating the music of Stockhausen, Boulez, Ligeti and Cage. Adorno died in 1969; his classic work *Aesthetic Theory* was published posthumously in 1970.

Paddison describes Adorno's work as a critical sociological aesthetics of music. He was almost exclusively concerned with Western art music of the eighteenth to twentieth centuries, and within that the Austro-German tradition – Classical and Romantic – and its avant-garde wing, the Second Viennese School of Schoenberg, Berg and Webern. His elitist rejection of popular culture discomforts his natural philosophical allies on the left.[21]

For someone whose musical world-view was so narrowly focused, Adorno's influence has been surprisingly broad. Even so there tends to be an insider quality to discussion of Adorno which I hope to avoid, and his work poses intractable problems for those from other traditions, such as those like the present writer who come from the Analytic Tradition. As Paddison puts it, 'Adorno's work is interdisciplinary, densely formulated, deeply paradoxical, anti-systematic and fragmented'.[22] His articles and correspondence exhibit less of the involuted dialectical extravagance that characterizes his major works. For all the complexity of his writing, he is an impressive stylist nonetheless, though perhaps, in contrast to his sometime literary model Nietzsche, when he strains for effect, the substance does not always justify the rhetoric.[23] The rich and subtle *Aesthetic Theory* demonstrates Adorno's uncompromising commitment to the union of philosophical aesthetics and the criticism and history of art – a union which, I argued in the Introduction, is essential to aesthetics. As Jarvis writes, 'The unique significance of Adorno's work on art lies in the unparalleled determination with which it dashes itself against [the] apparently natural and irresistible opposition [of art history and philosophical aesthetics]'.[24] Hence the quote from Schlegel which Adorno intended as the epigraph for *Aesthetic Theory*, and which I have appropriated for the present book: 'One of two things is usually lacking in what we call philosophy of art: either the philosophy or the art.'[25]

ADORNO AND KANT: ART AS AUTONOMOUS AND PURPOSELESS

As with other philosophical works of great complexity and difficulty, Adorno's *Aesthetic Theory* is best considered in relation to the writers that its author draws on and opposes. This strategy is particularly appropriate in the case of Adorno, since his 'Negative Dialectics' – an interpretation of Hegelian dialectics in which opposites remain unreconciled – operates through a critique of existing systems, in the case of aesthetics those of Kant and Hegel. But although Adorno criticizes Kant's aesthetics for being 'transcendentally abstract', in ways to be outlined shortly, he regards its core achievements as irreversible. One cannot return to rationalist ideas of timeless rules of taste, while pure subjectivism in aesthetic judgement is equally unacceptable, he maintains.[26]

Adorno takes from Kant the fundamental idea that aesthetics is concerned with appearance or semblance (*Schein*) – it is the domain of the unreal, of images.[27] Kant's concept of *purposiveness without a purpose*, discussed in Chapter 3, is a key concept for Adorno also, but radicalized. Adorno holds the view, often wrongly imputed to Kant, that artworks – the great artworks of the bourgeois era, at least – are functionless: 'Insofar as a social function may be predicated of works of art, it is the function of having no function'.[28] This feature, he holds, defines *autonomous art*, which has as its 'purpose' the creation of something without direct function – in contrast, pre-bourgeois art, in the form, for instance, of religious or theatre music, does have a direct social function. According to Adorno, autonomous artworks have a social *situation* but no direct social *function*. This is a key theme of his aesthetics to which we will repeatedly return.

Although his aesthetics shares profound affinities with Kant's, therefore, Adorno criticizes Kantian aesthetics, first on the broadly Hegelian grounds that it neglects the specificity of artworks and rarely discusses particular cases in detail. Adorno, in contrast, aims to unify aesthetics and artistic criticism. For him, aesthetic appearance or semblance does not arise from a Kantian aesthetic attitude, nor from an item's membership of the art world; it is a concrete particular that presents itself with each individual work. Relatedly, and also a criticism from Hegel, he holds that Kantian aesthetics fails to address the *historicity* of art and wrongly assumes that there are absolute aesthetic norms independent of history. Third, Adorno develops from Marx – as well as from Hegel – the criticism that Kantian aesthetics ignores the socially conditioned character of autonomous art. Finally, in place of Kant's allegedly *aesthetic conception of art*, with the judgement of taste based on disinterested pleasure, Adorno emphasizes the Hegelian notion of *truth-content*. His view is that the value of modernist artworks lies in their truth and not in any pleasure that they may occasion. As a response to 'the real fear triggered by [Kafka's] *Metamorphosis* or *The Penal Colony*, that shock of revulsion and disgust', he writes, 'disinterestedness would be crudely inadequate ... Ultimately disinterestedness debases art to what Hegel mocked, a pleasant or useful plaything'.[29]

This final criticism of Kantian aesthetics is unfair, and Adorno's elitist and puritan tendencies come together in further dubious characterizations of Kant's so-called 'taste' aesthetic: 'Only once it is done with tasteful savouring does artistic experience become autonomous. The route to aesthetic autonomy proceeds by way of disinterestedness; the emancipation of art from cuisine or pornography is irrevocable. Yet art does not come to rest in disinterestedness'. And also: 'Whoever concretely enjoys artworks is a philistine; he is convicted by expressions like "a feast for the ears" ... What opened up to, and overpowered, the beholder was their truth, which as in works of Kafka's type outweighs every other element. They were not a higher order of amusement'.[30] These criticisms are dubious, because, like a surprising number of commentators, Adorno treats the theory of aesthetic judgement in the early part of the *Critique of Judgment* (the Four Moments) as if that were the sum total of Kant's treatment of art, ignoring the later discussion of artworks' cognitive as well as purely aesthetic appeal – or rather, the arguments that the aesthetic embraces the cognitive as well as the sensuously pleasurable. For instance, Kant argues that the invention of aesthetic ideas belongs to genius, while their expression in beautiful forms depends on the faculty of taste. The demands of Negative Dialectics – the need to present Kant in a certain argumentative light – lead Adorno to ignore or suppress these aspects of his discussion.

Adorno is, in any case, mistaken – in this context at least – in assuming that modernist artworks afford no pleasure, or that to gain pleasure from art is to regard it as amusement. Indeed, the vague phrase 'Whoever concretely enjoys' shows that he is aware of these objections. In continuing to read Kafka or to go to performances of Alban Berg's harrowing operas, one does gain pleasure – even though it would be crass to say, after reading 'In the Penal Colony' or seeing *Wozzeck*, 'I enjoyed that'. A great performance of *Wozzeck* will be a shattering experience which one might well want to repeat eventually but not often.[31] Some experiences which one desires to repeat, such as visiting a parent's grave, are not pleasurable; however, most artistic examples are not in this category. They stimulate and give pleasure, despite the disturbing nature of the experience – hence the paradox of tragedy, which shows that although the desire to shock is important in modernist art, it is not unique to it. A similar response applies to Adorno's rejection of beauty in modern art, 'all of [whose] beauty consists in denying itself the illusion of beauty' – there is beauty in the sounds and structure of *Wozzeck*, and the words and structure of Kafka. Here Adorno exaggerates – though he does not fabricate – the distinctive aesthetic problems arising from modernism. Those problems remain challenging enough.

ADORNO AND HEGEL: DIALECTIC, HISTORICISM AND TRUTH-CONTENT

We have seen that Adorno's critique of Kantian aesthetics – in which he is nonetheless immersed – is conditioned by the philosophies of Hegel and Marx. Indeed, Adorno's theoretical works are profoundly indebted both to Hegel's dialectical method and to his historicism. However, in contrast to Hegel's 'Positive Dialectics', he denies the reconciliation of contradictions, stressing instead their irreconcilable antagonism. In titling his major work *Negative Dialectics*, Adorno is saying that in the historical process opposites negate each other yet refuse reconcilement or synthesis in a concept of the whole. Hence Adorno's pessimism is as pervasive as his elitism and puritanism, and of a piece with them, while his historicism is also ubiquitous in his work. It is shown in the concept of immanent critique, which says that an artwork must be interpreted in its own terms and not by applying external philosophical categories; and in his aesthetics of music, in the discussion of artistic material. It is a truism at least of post-Romantic thought that the artist must remain 'true' to the requirements of the material, but Adorno interprets this truism to mean that material is not a previously inert substance transformed by the artist but is ineliminably historical: 'material is what artists manipulate: everything from words, colours and sounds through to connections of any kind ... Forms, then, can also become material'.[32] That is, the material that the composer addresses is historically 'pre-formed'. (This claim arose in connection with the discussion of 'tone' in Chapter 2.) Genres are passed down, forms and gestures show their historical derivation, but within the structure of the autonomous artwork, this material is 're-formed'.[33]

These claims are developed by Adorno in an important correspondence from 1929 to 1932 with modernist Austrian composer Ernst Krenek (1900–91). Krenek saw the composer as an autonomous creator with absolute freedom to select material, but

Adorno responded that their choice was restricted by historical possibilities:

When I maintain that atonality is the only possible manner of composing today, it is not because I consider it ahistorically to be 'better', a handier referential system than tonality. It is rather because I think that tonality has *collapsed*, that every tonal chord has a meaning that we can no longer grasp.[34]

In the early twenty-first century it is impossible to write without irony in the style of Mahler, let alone Mozart; tonality, for instance, no longer has the meaning it had for them. For Adorno, music of the past is understood from the avant-garde's position, and progressive composers respond to the objective demands of the material. A 'tonal conservative' composer, in contrast – one who rejects modernism and in particular Schoenbergian serialism – maintains that they can reject these demands and continue using tonal or classical forms and language without irony. Examples would be Britten, Shostakovich, Vaughan Williams, Robert Simpson and, less convincingly, Penderecki (in his Brucknerian incarnation). But Adorno dismissed such conservatism as inauthentic, and allows re-use of tonal material only in the form of what he calls 'surrealist music', or neoclassical pastiche, as it is by Weill, Stravinsky and Krenek. Such music understands that 'original meaning cannot be restored' and creates a new unity from historical fragments: 'surrealist composing makes use of devalued means ... *as* devalued means, and wins its form from the "scandal" produced when the dead suddenly spring up among the living ... a montage of the debris of that which once was'.[35]

This technique of pastiche has become an essential strategy of postmodernism, found in present-day composers from Ligeti to Thomas Adès and, most strikingly, in avant-garde visual artist Joseph Beuys. The originality of modernism here should not be overstated – there is pastiche in Mozart. But such imitations as 'Turkish Rondo' are not ironic. And quotation from a language regarded as dead, in the sense of Adorno's 'surrealist music', is hard to find before modernism – Bruckner refers to Beethoven, but as a living inspiration. More important, Adorno, in stressing the extremes of avant-garde and reaction, neglects the possibility of 'tonal radicalism'. Although he discusses Weill and 'surrealist music', he does not recognize the enduring possibilities of this approach, demonstrated in the later twentieth and twenty-first centuries by such composers as Tippett, George Rochberg, Kagel, Finnissy, Rihm and Saariaho.

We have been talking of 'valid' artistic procedures and authentic art. For Adorno, validity and authenticity crucially depend on what he terms 'truth-content'. This concept, originating in Hegel's cognitivist conception of art discussed in Chapter 3, is captured in the quotation from the latter which heads the introduction to Adorno's *Philosophy of Modern Music* (1949): 'In art we have to do not with any agreeable or useful child's play, but with an unfolding of the truth'.[36] Adorno believes that there is a suppressed cognitive element in mimesis – the ancient conception of art as imitation of nature. While he takes the concept of truth-content from Hegel, he takes from Marx as well as Hegel the idea that it is a social truth – and from modernism that it is a fragmented and not a unitary one. But what exactly is truth-content? It may seem that while artistic truth in imaginative literature is comprehensible, in music it is obscure. The 'untruthful' crime fiction of Agatha Christie, with its wooden characterization and clichéd social settings, contrasts with the psychologically compelling characterization and social realism – the well-observed social, class and political distinctions – found in the novels of Joseph Conrad. However, Adorno holds that all artworks, and not just those whose medium is language, possess a 'language-character', which he links with truth-content.

By this he means that elements which are not meaningful in themselves are organized into a meaningful structure:

> Music resembles language in that it is a temporal sequence of articulated sounds which are more than just sounds. They say something, often something human. The better the music, the more forcefully they say it. The succession of sounds is like logic: it can be right or wrong. But what has been said cannot be detached from the music. Music creates no semiotic system.

The truth-content of a Mahler symphony is not captured by the metaphysical pronouncements favoured by programmatic interpretations; nor are Wagner's music-dramas decoded by a process of literal motif-identification. In contrast, Adorno gives the example of musical affirmation, 'the judicious, even judging affirmation of something that is, however, not expressly stated', in the first movement recapitulation of Beethoven's Ninth Symphony. On the strength of its similarity to language, Adorno believes, music constantly poses a riddle, which it never answers – but he insists that this is true of all art. Even when its medium is linguistic, what the artwork says is not what its words say, and so the cases of music and literature are not so distinct: 'No art can be pinned down as to what it says, and yet it speaks'.[37]

In talking of truth-content, Adorno often compares composers to philosophers and describes their work in philosophical terms – for instance, he links Beethoven's dialectical treatment of sonata form with Hegel's dialectical method. He compares Hegel's emphasis on the 'labour of the concept' with the way that, in the history of music, motivic or thematic material must increasingly be worked on, not just recapitulated. Thus Beethoven carries out development even in his recapitulation sections – it is no longer sufficient simply to repeat material, it must be altered or transformed. The hard-to-grasp notion of truth-content will now be pursued further in the context of Adorno's individual brand of Marxism.

ADORNO AND MARX: ART AS COMMODITY OR SOCIAL FACT

Adorno's work arises from the Idealist tradition of Kant and Hegel, but also from Marx's materialist critique of that tradition. Classical Marxism, commonly taken to derive from the later Marx, is a materialist theory of society and history according to which the economic circumstances under which people produce and consume conditions their politics and culture. Like the core ideas of Darwin and Freud, this theory has entered the lifeblood of twentieth-century Western thought. Economic determinism is a rigid form of this view, but Marx himself usually allowed an interaction between economic base and political, social and cultural superstructure, such that cultural conditions exercise some reciprocal influence on economic ones. Adorno's Frankfurt School – under the influence of Hungarian Marxist philosopher György Lukács – cited the younger Marx in favouring historical rather than scientific, deterministic materialism and stressed the importance of culture. Thus Adorno is a heterodox Marxist who questions what he regards as the 'vulgar Marxist' privileging of production and rejects the linear evolutionary scheme of classical Marxism. This position has become known as Western Marxism, as a contrast to the traditional Soviet version; it questions whether proletarian revolution is any longer possible, since the working-class has ceased to be a vehicle for social change.[38] It is against this sceptical background that Adorno's notorious ambivalence towards student revolt in 1968 should be judged: 'I had set up a theoretical model, but I could not suspect people would want to put it into action with Molotov cocktails'.

Adorno's sociological critique treats art in the context of its use in industrialized societies and holds that while it lacks the direct social purpose of pre-autonomous art, it functions as a commodity; at the same time, its apparent autonomy is not mere bourgeois ideology but has an essential critical function. Progressive art embodies and exists within bourgeois culture whilst denying by its truth-content that very culture; it demythologizes late capitalism as a false totality. As Adorno puts it, 'truth-content [is] the task of critique'.[39] So he develops or qualifies Kant's pure autonomy aesthetic through the Hegel-inspired concept of truth-content and the historical conditioning of artworks and through the Marxist concept of art's social determination. His Marxism is filtered also through Freud, and Marxist thinkers Lukács and Walter Benjamin.

This discussion leads us to the central dichotomy in Adorno's aesthetic theory, between *art as autonomous* (from Kant) and *art as commodity* (from Marx): 'Art's double character as both autono-mous and *fait social* [social fact]' is a contradiction in the Hegelian or Marxist sense.[40] This dichotomy bears on the central concern of this chapter, the possibility of autonomous music. Adorno's key claim is that although autonomy and commodity status are in tension, yet each requires the other – the paradigm of dialectical opposition. In order to explain how art has this 'double character' as autonomous and commodified, we need first to understand exactly what Adorno means by 'autonomous art'. As we saw in Chapter 3, art in the pre-Enlightenment era had been in the service of a social function arising from court, aristocracy or church. On the modernist picture, music loses its direct function in society with the ascendancy of bourgeois culture from the late eighteenth century; aristocratic and church patronage declined, and a non-functional 'art music' developed. It was no longer the primary role of composers to write for religious services, military bands or the theatre or to produce *Tafelmusik* – literally 'table-music' – played during banquets. If artists stop working for a specific patron such as a church or a court and offer their work for sale to patrons whose identities are not fully specified in advance – that is, they begin to function within the market – it becomes easier for them to produce works that embody their own values rather than those of their patrons, thus increasing their autonomy.[41] Growing autonomy goes hand in hand with the commodification of artworks. As Jacques Attali pithily put it, 'The artist was born at the same time as his work went on sale'.[42]

This growing autonomization of art is a central theme of Adorno's *Aesthetic Theory*. For him, its key representative was Beethoven. Adorno understands that it is only because art became socially autonomous that it could become self-conscious and socially critical. He links the critical role of music with the focus on form which also arises with autonomy. As an heir to the tradition of absolute music discussed in Chapter 3, Adorno argues that the autonomous artwork creates its own inner logic, without referring to anything external to its form. In its consistency and total integration, form and content are identical; the work *is* its idea. In contrast, heteronomous art imitates, represents or expresses something outside itself. Adorno does not say that works of art 'ought' to become autonomous; the autonomization of the work of art is an inevitable historical process.

At the same time, though they may embrace the fact, reject it or appear unaware of it, socially autonomous works have no choice but also to be commodities. According to Adorno, high art's claims of autonomy – the implicit claim of artworks to be more than a mere thing, to have a non-exchangeable dignity – are strictly illusory.[43] The concept of autonomous art has probably always been 'ideological' in Marx's sense – necessary in order for art to take on a critical function towards society – but it is not thereby false: 'Artworks are plenipotentiaries of things that are no longer distorted by exchange, profit, and the false needs of a degraded humanity'.[44] There is a dialectical relation between the aspiration to autonomy and the reality – whether an artwork recognizes it or not – of commodification.

I have defined autonomy as lack of *direct* social function, since in his formulation of art as social fact, Adorno absolutely recognizes that all art has a social function in some sense. The point that he is making about autonomous art is that its social function arises precisely *because* of its apparent functionlessness – hence the importance to him of Kant's concept of 'purposiveness without a purpose'. The most obvious function of functionless art is as a badge of conspicuous consumption and a statement of prestige – as in corporate hospitality events hosted at the Tate Modern or the Royal Festival Hall. Indeed, Adorno argues, a 'false reconciliation' with society has 'paved the way in the sphere of radically abstract art: Nonrepresentational art is suitable for decorating the homes of the newly prosperous'. But the principal social function of autonomous art in the era of modernism and after, Adorno believes, remains social critique – in virtue of the artwork's form not its content. For

> Art ... is social not only because of its mode of production ... nor simply because of the social derivation of its thematic material. Much more importantly, art becomes social by its opposition to society, and it occupies this position only as autonomous art. By crystallising in itself as something unique to itself, rather than complying with existing social norms and qualifying as 'socially useful', it criticises society by merely existing ... through its refusal of society, which is equivalent to sublimation through the law of form, autonomous art makes itself a vehicle of ideology.[45]

We return to the question of the critical role of autonomous art, and its reciprocal or dialectical relation to commodification, in the final section of this chapter.

We have just seen Adorno comment on the 'social derivation' of musical material. For him, art is 'concentrated social substance' and so contains within itself the contradictions of social reality. Its material is a sediment of social relations and is 'historical through and through'. Again Adorno's profound historicism is evident: 'If art opposes the empirical through the element of form ... the mediation [of form and content] is to be sought in the recognition of aesthetic form as sedimented content. What are taken to be the purest forms (e.g. traditional musical forms) can be traced back even in the smallest idiomatic detail to content such as dance'.[46] Adorno has in mind the way, for example, that trumpet flourishes in a classical symphony are derived from music for military bands, and that movements such as minuet and scherzo originated in dance forms – recent research suggests direct allusions to French revolutionary songs in the finale of Beethoven's Fifth Symphony.[47] The historical progress of mediated musical material is, for Adorno, an aspect of what he calls the Dialectic of the Enlightenment – the progressive domination of nature and the rationalization of all aspects of social life.

Adorno regards sociology of art as embracing all elements of the relationship between art and society, and treats it dialectically in a sense that I will explain shortly: 'It is impossible to restrict it to any simple aspect, such as the social effects of works of art. This effect is in itself only a moment in the totality of that relationship'. Hence his claim that 'Art perceived strictly aesthetically is art aesthetically misperceived' – the result would be 'aestheticism' in the bad sense of 'art for art's sake', a socially irresponsible misunderstanding.[48] Even a retreat from the market is a symptom of its dominance. The amateur composer or Sunday-afternoon painter, apparently working in isolation, has to confront social forces from within the material itself – musical themes and forms, visual subjects such as bourgeois leisure activities. Artistic material is social sediment, and, for Adorno, individual artistic intentions are not enough to overcome this fact. His sociology of art permeates all levels of his aesthetics.

Adorno's picture is that as composers and artists gained independent social status and precarious economic power in a developing capitalist market during the late eighteenth and early nineteenth centuries, the liberal, 'bourgeois' art of Beethoven celebrated the class it represented and epitomised the socially and artistically progressive. In his time, the utopian notions of the French Revolution did not seem hopelessly idealistic: 'If [Beethoven] is the musical prototype of the revolutionary bourgeoisie, he is at the same time the prototype of a music that has escaped from its social tutelage and is aesthetically fully autonomous . . . His work explodes the schema of a complaisant adequacy of music and society'. Adorno stresses that through its organic form – the relentless development of thematic material, notably in the opening movement of the Fifth Symphony – Beethoven's music epitomizes socially progressive forces. He explains how it contains truth-content and how, through its dynamic form rather than its content, it is critical of society: 'The kinship with that bourgeois libertarianism which rings all through Beethoven's music is a kinship of the dynamically unfolding totality. It is in fitting together under their own law ... that his themes come to resemble the world whose forces move them; they do not do it by imitating that world'.[49] In the decades after the failed revolutions of 1848, Adorno argues, the bourgeoisie ceased to be the revolutionary class, and commodification became a prison rather than a liberation for the artist. With 'art for art's sake' in the later nineteenth century, art withdrew from political action; in the modernist era which followed, progressive art lost the self-confidence it possessed with Beethoven and turned against the bourgeois culture which produced it. During the twentieth century, Adorno concludes, there is a growing split between the music of the culture industry which embraces its commodity status and a high or avant-garde art which rejects it.

THE CULTURE INDUSTRY

The most influential concept from Adorno's sociology of art was taken up by the Frankfurt School as a whole – the *culture industry*, which diverts the revolutionary potential of the proletariat. Adorno first used the term in a chapter title from the *Dialectic of Enlightenment* of 1944, co-authored with Horkheimer, to denote a filtering mechanism, which preselects music and artworks and standardizes public taste according to the demands of the capitalist market. It constantly promises the new and 'perpetually cheats its consumers of what it perpetually promises'.[50] Adorno prefers the term 'culture industry' to 'mass culture' because it is not a culture that arises spontaneously from the masses but is administered from above:

The culture industry piously claims to be guided by its customers and to supply them with what they ask for. But while assiduously dismissing any thought of its own autonomy and proclaiming its victims its judges, it outdoes in its veiled autocracy, all the excesses of autonomous art ... It drills them in their attitudes as if it were itself a customer.[51]

Adorno seems to hold the elitist belief that nothing can be both popular and artistically valuable; his critique of mass culture is unusual in being left-wing elitist rather than right-wing elitist.

During their debate in the 1930s, Marxist essayist Walter Benjamin took the opposed view that film and radio politicize the masses and that mechanical reproduction (for instance, recordings) is progressive in undermining the traditional aesthetic 'aura'.[52] Adorno questioned both moves. Concerning the second, he confesses his disquiet 'that you now casually transfer the concept of magical aura to the "autonomous work of art" and flatly assign to the latter a counter-revolutionary function ... it seems to me that ... within itself [the autonomous artwork] juxtaposes the magical and the mark of freedom'.[53] Concerning the first, Adorno's 'On the Fetish Character in Music and the Regression of Listening' (1938) argued that the mass arts resist innovation. 'The composition hears for the listener' is his verdict on popular music – no listening effort is required – and he draws implausibly dark, totalitarian conclusions from the mass crazes and infatuations of contemporary popular culture. His essay 'On Popular Music' (1941) diagnoses the standardization of popular material – he was struck by Abner Silver and Robert Bruce's *How To Write and Sell a Song Hit* (1939), with its ten cardinal rules for successful songwriters.[54]

The culture industry is often assumed to embrace only popular music and arts, but this is a misinterpretation of Adorno's concept. It also includes art music of the past that has been transformed into 'museum-art', as well as 'moderate', non-modernist music of the present time that makes compromises in order to be accessible. For instance, Mozart's Symphony No. 40 and Vivaldi's 'The Four Seasons' have become popular classics and, hence, commodified – Adorno would have marvelled at, and been appalled by, their appropriation by the mobile ring-tone industry. But unlike commodified pop music, the work of Vivaldi and Mozart was not originally a product of the culture industry. Thus, the same work might in one era be autonomous and in a later era entirely commodified; its aesthetic value can change over time, or maybe one should say that the identity of the work changes: 'Works are usually critical in the era in which they appear; later they are neutralised, not least because of changed social relations. Neutralisation is the social price of aesthetic autonomy'. Paddison comments that for Adorno the split is not so much between serious and popular music as such – a division which has become, in his view, increasingly meaningless due to the almost inescapable commodity character of all cultural products

in the twentieth century: 'The split is much more between ...
music which accepts its character as commodity, thus becoming
identical with the machinations of the culture industry itself, and
... *self-reflective* music which critically opposes its fate as
commodity, and thus ends up by alienating itself from present
society by becoming unacceptable to it'.[55]

Adorno's elitist assault on popular culture has long been an
embarrassment to his adherents on the left. In his notorious polemic
'On Jazz' (1936), written under the pseudonym Hektor Rottweiler –
Adorno's sense of humour was no laughing matter – he confused
commercial danceband music and improvised jazz.[56] This is rather
like writing an essay 'On Rock Music' focusing on the Spice Girls
and *Pop Idol* winners, or 'On Cinema' on the basis of having seen a
few 'Carry On' films – or, indeed, writing 'On Classical Music' and
looking at Manuel and His Music of the Mountains, or Mantovani.
'Farewell to Jazz' (1933) implausibly claims that classical music
anticipated jazz syncopation, but its criticism of jazz's often
predictable use of standard, thirty-two-bar song forms has some
validity. Moreover, Adorno deserves credit for taking dance music
seriously as a social fact, rather than dismissing it as harmless
entertainment.[57] He was not the first philosopher to draw insightful
conclusions about an area of artistic endeavour that he only
imperfectly understood, and his grudging conclusion is not
completely without foundation: 'What it was possible to learn from
jazz is the emancipation of the rhythmic emphasis from metrical
time; a decent, if very limited and specialized thing, with which
composers had long been familiar, but which, through jazz, may
have achieved a certain breadth in reproductive practice'.[58] (This
question is taken up in Chapter 7 on improvisation.) The lofty high-
art standpoint from which Adorno delivers this verdict is echoed in
his rejection of art-house cinema: 'all intentions to ennoble films
artistically do indeed look awry, falsely elevated, out of keeping with
the form – imports for the connoisseur. The more pretensions a film
has to art, the more bogus it becomes'.[59]

The later Frankfurt School philosopher Jürgen Habermas must
be almost alone in maintaining that 'by all notable standards,
Adorno remained anti-elitist', though he did concede that 'it was
denied him, in a clearly painful way, ever to be trivial'.[60] Lukács
added the charge of 'champagne socialism' to that of elitism,
arguing that the Frankfurt School took a pessimistic view of

capitalism while enjoying its benefits – taking up residence in *Grand Hotel Abgrund* ('Grand Hotel Abyss'), a luxury hotel on the edge of the Abyss, they contemplate the void 'between excellent meals or artistic entertainments'.[61] It should, however, be noted that according to Adorno's philosophical stance, only the extremes embody historical truth – Negative Dialectics focuses on extreme autonomy and extreme commodity.[62] The fracturing of the social totality – the disintegration of late capitalist society – is reflected in the split between the avant-garde and popular culture, the autonomous work and work as commodity: 'Both bear the stigmata of capitalism, both contain elements of change (but never, of course, the middle-term between Schoenberg and the American film). Both are torn halves of an integral freedom, to which however they do not add up'.[63] Hindemith's attempt to create *Gebrauchsmusik* ('useful music') for amateur performers is futile – there is no middle way between the avant-garde's rejection of an audience (Schoenberg) and the purely commercial product (Hollywood).

The poignancy of Adorno's pessimistic vision should not blind us to the existence of such middle terms.[64] Popular culture is not as cohesive as he claims and embraces both 'opiate' and autonomous expression in forms such as jazz, electronica, art-house cinema and experimental rock. The reification of extremes – austere, audience-alienating modernism and commodified pop music – is a misconception at the heart of Negative Dialectics. Current extremes of commodification are, however, as shocking as any conceived by Adorno. It is unlikely that in his worst nightmares he could have envisaged such paeans to inanity and imbecility as Reality TV's *Big Brother* and the manufactured democracy of *Pop Idol*. He may even have underestimated the disastrous cultural consequences of late capitalist affluence, as the fabulous wealth of consumer society cascades in evermore fatuous directions, while so-called high art thrives only at the service of the culture industry. In the face of such developments, an Adorno-like pessimism and despair is the only sane reaction.

MUSIC OF THE AVANT-GARDE: ADORNO'S LIMITED GROUNDS FOR OPTIMISM

We have seen that through his theory of the culture industry, Adorno diagnoses a divide in twentieth-century music between, on the one hand, a progressive, self-reflective and critical music that resists commodification in the marketplace, while alienating itself from its public and, on the other hand, a regressive, assimilated music that uncritically accepts its commodity character as entertainment. In the earlier nineteenth century, when art music and popular music were less divided, Stendhal could begin his *Life of Rossini* as follows:

> Napoleon is dead; but a new conqueror has already shown himself to the world; and from Moscow to Naples, from London to Vienna, from Paris to Calcutta, his name is constantly on every tongue. The fame of this hero knows no bounds save those of civilisation itself.

No biography of a contemporary classical composer could make such grandiose claims – we have no Rossini, only all-conquering Andrew Lloyd Webber.[65] (Though, on reflection, maybe the difference is not so great.)

In the modern divide, Adorno believes, only authentic avant-garde art, which resists its social commodification, could be both socially conditioned and aesthetically autonomous. Avant-garde music ultimately alienates itself from its audience, which is bourgeois; Schoenberg and his followers most radically, but also Stravinsky, Bartók and Hindemith. The extent of their alienation is shown in the way that, after the First World War, modernist composers sought refuge in organizations such as the Society for Private Musical Performances, and fought against the domination of the arts by business interests.

For Adorno, Schoenberg remained the exemplar of authentic art, especially through his freely atonal works of 1907–14, with their remarkable structural freedom which raised expression to a new level. The expressionist monodrama '*Erwartung*', written in a stream-of-consciousness style, seemingly avoids thematic recurrence in its fragmented form. This genuinely 'new music', Adorno wrote, 'breaks from the continuity of musical development. It is shockingly alienated from [normal] musical speech, and it declares war upon the dispassionate, hedonistic popular taste'.[66] During the 1920s, unable to sustain the intensity of creative effort, Schoenberg codified atonality in the serial or twelve-tone system – almost a replacement for the tonal system which he had rejected.

Adorno was, at best, ambivalent towards this development, regarding it as a neoclassical prison and 'spurious harmony' – it was no coincidence, he felt, that Schoenberg turned to baroque forms and simple binary structures at this time.

As Paddison notes, Analytic aestheticians have not been attracted by the concept of authenticity implicit in Adorno's notion of autonomous art, and instead emphasize authentic performance in the sense of original instruments, composers' intentions and expression, as well as the issue of originals, fakes and copies.[67] However, Adorno's is arguably the most important sense of 'authenticity'. Authentic art of the avant-garde is distinctive in both social and aesthetic terms. We have seen how, according to Adorno, the conflict between autonomy and commodity results in music's 'alienation': 'Through the total absorption of both musical production and consumption by the capitalist process, the alienation of music from man has become complete'.[68] The result is music into which no social function falls – indeed, which even severs the last communication with the listener. *The Philosophy of Modern Music* describes authentic modern music which rejects its audience as like the messages of bottles thrown into the sea by shipwrecked sailors, in the hope, but not the expectation, of finding a reader.[69] Milton Babbitt, a serialist successor of Schoenberg, made this aim explicit in a notorious article published in 1958 under the title 'Who Cares if You Listen?'.[70] The difficulties of grasping contemporary music – and indeed of composing it – in the absence of the comprehension-inducing language of tonality, haunted Adorno throughout his career.[71]

Authentic avant-garde art is distinctive also in more narrowly aesthetic terms. An influential post-Romantic view of artistic creation holds that artworks set up conflicts which are resolved within the frame of the work. But, for Adorno, the modernist work sets up conflicts which cannot be resolved, thus rupturing the form of the work – and reflecting the impossibility of reconciliation within society. This fracturing process can be traced back as far as Beethoven's late string quartets and piano sonatas, whose disintegration of form created bafflement in their own time: 'The utmost integration is utmost semblance [illusion] and this causes the former's reversal: Ever since Beethoven's last works those artists who pushed integration to an extreme have mobilised disintegration. The truth content of art, whose organon was

integration, turns against art'.[72] According to Adorno's Negative
Dialectics, 'A successful work is not one which resolves objective
contradictions in a spurious harmony, but one which expresses the
idea of harmony negatively by embodying the contradiction, pure
and uncompromised, in its innermost structure'.[73] 'Success' is
relative; even the authentic works will fail, but the effort must be
made. For Adorno, indeed, 'the authentic works are the failures' –
late Beethoven, Schoenberg, Samuel Beckett – and he would have
appreciated the line from Beckett's *Worstward Ho*: 'Ever tried.
Ever failed. No matter. Try again. Fail again. Fail better.'[74]
Adorno asserts so often that Art may no longer be possible –
most famously in his remark about the impossibility of poetry
after Auschwitz – that his aesthetics of music provides very limited
grounds for optimism.[75]

His defence of art as socially critical separates Adorno's
position from 'art for art's sake', but it is essential to understand
that this socially critical role does not imply a defence of 'political
art'. Here is another dialectical opposition: 'It was plausible that
socially progressive critics should have accused the programme of
l'art pour l'art, which has often been in league with political
reaction, of promoting a fetish with the concept of a pure,
exclusively self-sufficient artwork', he writes. However, this sympathy with progressive critics of art for art's sake does not mean
accepting political art: 'What is social in art is its immanent
movement against society, not its manifest opinions'.[76] Though he
praises the socialist playwright Bertolt Brecht, Adorno has little
time for the politically committed art which Brecht represents, and
he was highly critical of Hanns Eisler, a student of Schoenberg who
wrote 'songs for the masses' in the 1930s and became an 'official'
composer of post-war East Germany. Adorno argues that Eisler's
enterprise risks degenerating into mere propaganda, which, like the
banal products of Socialist Realism or Nazi art, betrays its own
'law of form', the demands of its material. Art should oppose
capitalist coercion indirectly through form, not directly through
content: 'It is not the office of art to spotlight alternatives, but to
resist by its form alone the course of the world, which permanently
puts a pistol to men's heads'.[77] The way things are constricts the
imagination; it is the role of art to resist this.

This critique of politically committed art is a political one –
Adorno's point is that it may end up as bad art without becoming

good politics either.[78] The autonomous modernist artwork is, he maintains, at least as valid politically as committed art. Kafka's work represents for Adorno an ideal of this politically engaged art which resists capitalism by its form alone and not by stirring proclamations: 'In [it] monopoly capitalism appears only in the background; yet it codifies in the flotsam of the administered world what human beings have experienced under the total social spell, more faithfully and more powerfully than novels about corrupt industrial trusts'.[79] Although it would be absurd to regard Adorno, as some writers have, as an 'apolitical aesthete', Martin Jay's description of a 'political deficit' in Adorno's theorizing is justified; his interest was in culture, society and the human psyche rather than the political realm.[80] Understandably, for one who lived through the Weimar Republic and the Nazi and Stalinist eras, he was pessimistic about the emancipatory potential of modern liberal societies.[81]

Adorno's critique of political art is, I believe, a persuasive one. Political art can be regarded as a development of the pre-Romantic category of didactic art. Autonomous art has a meaning, even a message that the artist wishes the audience to grasp, but according to the *post-Romantic conception of art* this is not a didactic one – the audience must be free to recognize and perhaps accept it in their own way. Thus, the greatest art is not prescriptive but allows for freedom of response – a freedom that does not rule out the possibility of misinterpretation. In contrast, political or propaganda art – Michael Moore's film documentaries such as *Fahrenheit 9/11* are a striking recent example – tells the audience what to think. It is authoritarian art that leaves little room for freedom of response. (Religious art may not be explicitly didactic – more like a shared assumption of a religious world-view.)

It might be thought that so-called absolute music could hardly be political. But debates within the school of John Cage with his student Christian Wolff and disciple Cornelius Cardew – who we encountered in Chapter 5 discussing 'X for Henry Flynt' – show that this assumption is mistaken. Wolff has said that he does not think that music should be manipulative, in contrast to Cardew's proselytizing streak: 'For me, the aim is not to say "This is what you must think", but to get people to look at things and think about them. Basically people have to do that for themselves'. He continues:

Anything to do with culture or art, which by necessity has some public character to it, is political ... The performance of music always has a social setting where it's part of some kind of establishment or power centre – a concert for some kind of community, elite or variously interested parties.

Wolff explains the variety of responses to that situation. One is 'political music' of the kind Eisler wrote. 'Another way is to think of the music as a kind of model, say of cooperation', he continues, 'the interaction, both free and contingent, of performers ... there's the possibility of having the music such that in its performance it doesn't simply convey some simple message: get rid of all nuclear technology, for instance. The point's really more to help people focus certain energies'. This is the kind of freedom of response encouraged by the post-Romantic conception of art.[82]

DIALECTICS AND THE AUTONOMY OF ART

It is necessary to evaluate Adorno's claims as well as interpret them, and this final section addresses his core claim that the art of modernity is both autonomous and commodified. We saw how, from the social perspective, the autonomy of music is, for Adorno, a kind of illusion, and vice versa – each position is false from the terms of the other. They are not two sides of one coin but are irreconcilable. To understand these central claims we must backtrack to the pre-dialectical opposition between classical Marxism and the aestheticist position of art for art's sake and contrast it with the dialectical opposition which Adorno postulates. Art for art's sake regards autonomy – the detachment of art from everyday life – as an absolutely real phenomenon. The orthodox Marxist responds that art for art's sake is a false ideology; in our capitalist age, art cannot be autonomous, given the economic reality of commodification. I call the opposition between art for art's sake and orthodox Marxism pre-dialectical, because there is no sense in which these positions fit together even in a dynamic tension. Adorno's dialectical position is both more subtle, and more elusive, in seeming to recognize the truth in each position: he regards art aesthetically (as autonomous) and sociologically (as product) at the same time.

Adorno's logical and conceptual system assumes Hegel's dynamic concept of contradiction, pervasive in nineteenth-century

German philosophy, which holds that in positing any position, opposite is also present in its exclusion. For Hegel, contradiction is resolved only by appeal to an absolute, but Adorno's Negative Dialectics denies any such notion and, thus, the possibility of resolution. As he comments in *Minima Moralia*, 'the whole is the untrue'.[83] Negative Dialectics constitutes a rejection of what Adorno terms 'Identity Thinking', the dominant mode of cognition in modernity, which holds that concepts fully contain the object conceptualized; in contrast, dialectics 'says no more, to begin with, than that objects do not go into their concepts without leaving a remainder'.[84] To take the kind of everyday example that does not much occupy Adorno, dialectics would hold that a particular chair is not wholly contained under the concept 'chair', but has an indefinite number of other properties – being wooden, painted, solid, graceful, comfortable and so on. The remainder is the Non-Identical; there is always something Other than the posited concept. Objects thus have to be understood through a constellation of concepts. A parallel Adorno used is a Charlie Chaplin film where, at the end, the tramp tries to pack too many clothes in a suitcase. He forces the lid closed, but still there are trousers and shirts hanging out – so he cuts them off! That, for Adorno, is Identity Thinking.[85]

Adorno's denial of Identity Thinking is reminiscent of Nietzsche's, who, like him, also rejects the conception of truth as timeless, unchanging and ahistorical.[86] From an Analytic perspective, it may appear that these writers simply misunderstand the nature of concepts. Why should one hold that if an object is subsumed under the concept 'chair', its properties are exhausted by that concept? Anyone capable of philosophical thought can recognize the perils of disregarding particularity and concreteness, of making the material world fit the abstract idea and of ignoring the status of concepts as artefacts of human intellectual organization. However, the characterization of Identity Thinking in these conceptualist terms may not be helpful. Adorno's target is really much broader; he objects to thinking which is static, simplifying and ahistorical – in contrast, dialectical thinking is dynamic, historicist and recognizes complexity. The contrast is abundantly exemplified in *Aesthetic Theory*, for instance by the interplay of nature and culture in the aesthetics of nature, by the venerable idea that time is the test of artistic value and by the way that music is like a language, yet not a language, discussed earlier.[87] And we will see in Chapter 7 how improvisation and composition stand in a dialectical relation.

The nature of dialectical thinking bears on our central concern, the interplay between the autonomy and commodity status of artworks, which Adorno believes can be captured only through such thinking. There is no fixed relation between autonomy and commodity, he maintains; it changes over time. Adorno's core insight is that art can become fully autonomous only by becoming fully commodified. Thus, two apparently contradictory features stand in a reciprocal or symbiotic relationship – something which, he believes, identity thinking cannot capture. As Fubini puts it,

> For Adorno, aesthetic value is not an optional extra which can be added to the social import of the musical idiom ... social criticism and aesthetic criticism involve one another reciprocally in a subtle dialectic relation ... a relation which is complex, dynamic and two-way [and not] an ordinary relation of cause and effect: music exists within society, and is thus an essential component of society.[88]

For Adorno, music is not simply a reflection of society, and so he does not subordinate aesthetic values to social and economic ones as classical Marxism does.

A fundamental question concerning Adorno's treatment is whether so-called autonomous art really is autonomous. We saw earlier that to regard the art of modernity as autonomous itself involves a modernist assumption – the quasi-political narrative of the 'emancipation' of music is not a neutral history. Adorno, with contributions from other Frankfurt School figures such as Ernst Bloch, had a central role in establishing this narrative.[89] The ideal of absolute music had only established half the picture – the non-political, non-social half. Hanslick's formalism was politically neutral, though, as we saw, it had proto-historicist aspects, while in complete contrast, classical Marxists dismissed the emancipation of music as bourgeois ideology and illusion.

The modernist narrative began to be challenged in the late 1960s, as modernism entered a crisis represented by Pop Art and minimalism – the latter in the visual arts and music – and by the powerful maverick influence of John Cage. Social historians of art started to consider the representation of class, gender and ethnicity which mainstream modernist writing had neglected, readdressing art movements with a strong socio-political dimension such as Dadaism and Surrealism which it had occluded or dismissed. Musicology later followed suit. From a different direction, post-Adorno Marxists reiterated the charge that he neglected the social dimension. Peter Bürger, for instance, argues that that the 'autonomy of art' thesis is ideological: 'The relative dissociation of the work of art from the praxis of life in bourgeois society [which has an element of truth] thus becomes transformed into the (erroneous) idea that the work of art is totally independent of society'.[90] An opposed line of objection, which takes a very different message from Hegel than Adorno did, is that art has indeed become autonomous, but disastrously so. Thus, Jay Bernstein, although sympathetic to Adorno, argues that the art of modernity has lost its truth-function, resulting in 'aesthetic alienation'.[91]

I believe that these criticisms of the modernist narrative are largely misguided. As we have seen, Adorno's account is certainly Eurocentric and it ignores gender issues, but it is equally clear that his treatment of the autonomy of art has the social dimension at its core; and he would certainly insist that autonomous art has a truth-content. To reiterate, for Adorno, autonomy is lack of *direct* social function. He would not deny that concerts have various social functions – just that they do not have an instrinsic or direct function of the kind found in heteronomous music. The social functions of autonomous art, including concert music, arises precisely as a result of its apparent functionlessness – whether as symbol of conspicuous consumption or as social critique. Adorno has penetrating insights into how the lack of direct social function gives rise to unique secondary functions: 'In a society that has been functionalised virtually through and through, totally ruled by the exchange principle, lack of function comes to be a secondary function'. Later he comments on the way that music can be 'the decoration of empty time'.[92]

But what is direct or primary social function, as opposed to secondary function? A direct social function, I would argue, is one which has to be grasped, in order to have any understanding at all of the event or process in question. Until I know that a certain event is a religious service rather than a university graduation ceremony, I will not be in any position to know what secondary functions it may have. A primary function makes essential reference to participant understanding. Perhaps what has to be grasped about the direct function of a concert is that the music performed has no direct social function. A cultural outsider could ask, during a church service, 'what is the function of this music?'. The answer is: religious – to uplift the spirits of the congregation and turn their thoughts to God and so on. A corresponding answer could be given in all cases of music with direct social function. These would all be cases of art that is *not* for art's sake, but which is for the sake of any of the things that art can be contrasted with – religion, entertainment, instruction, politics, commerce, advertising. (On the modernist story, prior to the separation of the value spheres in the eighteenth century, all art was for the sake of one of these other things.)[93] In contrast, if the outsider went to a concert and asked, 'what is the function of this music?', no comparable answer could be given. One could only say, in the case of a Bach cantata given in a concert performance, for instance, 'This music was composed for church services'. To add, 'but now it has a purely aesthetic function' is not to point to a *social* function in the same sense. Today, in concert performance, Bach's music exhibits purposiveness without a purpose. Music for dancing or a military pageant is part of, or contributes to, the social occasion; but to say that the music contributes to the social occasion of a concert is absurd. The music *is* the social occasion. It is, however, important to note that the functions of serving the dancing, or military or religious ritual, reflect the ancient origins of music, in the way that the function of serving advertising – Dvorak's 'New World' Symphony used in the soundtrack of a Hovis advert – clearly does not.

Functionless art, which acquires functions in virtue of its functionlessness, is a deeply paradoxical or dialectical notion. It is precisely through their refusal of social function that, according to Adorno, autonomous music and art acquire a critical function. It is by standing apart from society that autonomous art becomes most powerfully critical – more genuinely critical than so-called political or propaganda art. It is a model of emancipation, of life lived under non-oppressive conditions – the most one can hope for from art in the present age, Adorno believes (so he was not a *total* pessimist).

But functionless art also acquires non-critical and other secondary functions – as Adorno would also recognize. He would not deny that concerts have various social functions – just that they have an intrinsic or direct function of the kind found in heteronomous music. Corporate hospitality events in the Tate Modern or the Royal Festival Hall trade on the perceived social value of functionless art – which is vulnerable to exploitation or co-option by the capitalist marketplace. Autonomous art will also acquire functions of the kind that Bourdieu describes, as cultural capital and expression of social status.[94] Knowledge is power, and knowledge of the arts can be used to impress and oppress; so, in a different way, can 'street credible' knowledge of popular musics. (Intimate knowledge of hip-hop is also cultural capital.) But this is a sociological truth; it is a mistake to infer from this that the classics are inherently a bourgeois category and that an alternative art for the people is required. The sociological truth is secondary to a genuine, aesthetic interest in art, in the broad sense of 'aesthetic' defended earlier.

According to the standpoint of absolute music or formalism, understanding and evaluating functional music as music has nothing to do with its social function. On this view, the best minuets or waltzes are not necessarily those that are the best for dancing to; what makes Bach's religious music valuable aesthetically has nothing to do with how well it performs its religious function. This position is too purist, I believe. It makes sense to look for some link between the form and content of the music and the function it was written or performed to serve. One can always ask what there is in functional music that enables it to fulfil its function – music for marching bands is in 4/4 with strong emphasis on the first beat; religious music in the Christian tradition is often ethereal, disembodied, without sharp attack, stressing otherworldly concerns, perhaps. In contrast, for music performed today in the concert hall, it makes no sense to look for such a link – because concerts have no direct social function of the kind required. By the same token, music originally written with a religious or military function can be performed today in the concert hall and still fulfil the secondary functions we have discussed – if not as social critique, then certainly as backdrop to corporate hospitality. Direct social function in the act of performance – music for church services or military pageants – should be contrasted with indirect social function found in political and religious art intended for concert performance or exhibition. Thus Socialist Realist art can achieve its social function directly by integration in activities not primarily artistic – Moscow military rallies for instance – and indirectly through exhibition in art galleries. In the latter case, it trades on the credentials of purposeless art, that is, art without direct social function.

Adorno's picture requires some qualification, as indicated by Berger's discussion, which sensibly puts the modernist claim in terms of a practice. Berger asks: 'At which point did European music acquire the unmistakable characteristics of an autonomous practice ... [one which has] aims of its own and does not derive them from another practice?'. His answer is that autonomous and functional (heteronomous) music are 'ideal types', and that most European music since ancient times falls between them: 'Rather than expecting to find the point at which the era of autonomous music began, we should look for partial autonomy in all music'.[95] Certainly there is evidence that some arts achieved significant autonomy before the eighteenth century. Painters with their artisanal tradition began to exploit market mechanisms from the sixteenth century – as the careers of Michelangelo and Raphael and, more markedly, the studios of Titian and Rembrandt, show.[96] Indeed, it has been argued that in China a commodified art market existed as early as the Song Dynasty (960–1368) and that faking and copying with dishonest intent, corollaries of an art market, became prevalent during the fifteenth to sixteenth century Ming Dynasty.[97] In the West, music was slower than other arts in gaining social autonomy, hence its lower artistic status up to the later eighteenth century. Only from that time, and not always successfully, did composers begin to market their products; hence the not entirely romanticized story of Mozart dying in poverty. However, it is striking how few composers of art music since Mozart's time – compared to painters or novelists – have managed to make a living as composers.

It is the great achievement of Adorno's treatment that he sees the deeply paradoxical status of autonomous music and art. His approach to the understanding of music transcends the unfortunate division found in the visual arts in particular, between 'connoisseurship' or attention to aesthetic features and the social history of art which has largely replaced it. This is shown by his comments in *Introduction to the Sociology of Music* on Beethoven's bourgeois revolutionary critique. If we do not hear such a critique in Beethoven's music, Adorno argues, then we understand him no better than someone who cannot follow the purely musical content of the work: 'the musical experience has been insulated from the experience of the reality in which it finds itself ... and to which it responds'.[98] It would be a simplification to say that Adorno was committed to the concept of absolute music; proponents of that ideal neglected music as social fact, he would argue. But he would regard absolute music as the core of the ideology of autonomous music, and he was recognizably an heir to its tradition.

In the final chapter we look at the concept of the musical work through the contrasting concept of improvisation, which Adorno and proponents of Western art music's Great Tradition have shown little interest in. However, the opposition between improvisation and composition, and the rival aesthetics of perfection and imperfection, turns out to exhibit some very Adornian dialectics.

NOTES

1   Gildea (2003) writes that modernism 'was essentially a revolt against modernity. It was a critique of the mechanization of life, of materialism ... of the tyranny of the masses' (p. 395).

2   'By "modernism" we refer to those new social practices in both "high art" and "mass culture" which engage with the experiences of modern life, with *modernity*, by means of a self-conscious use of experiment and innovation' (Blake and Frascina (1993), p. 127).

3   See Eysteinsson (1990), pp. 1–2.

4   Adorno (1973), quoted in Paddison (2002), p. 327.

5   Baudelaire (1964).

6   See, for instance, Bottstein's entry under 'Modernism' in Sadie and Tyrrell (2004).

7   Read (1960), first published 1933, p. 44. Also quoted in West, S., ed. (1996).

8   Kandinsky (1982).

9   See, for instance, Harrison (1993). Realism and naturalism appear in the 1840s, replacing idealism.

10   Schoenberg (1984), pp. 216–17.

11   Rosen (1975) provides an excellent discussion of Schoenberg and modernism.

12   Kazimir Malevich, 'From Cubism and Futurism to Suprematism', in Andersen (1968), p. 29.

13 Pierre Boulez commented tartly: 'Both [Schoenberg and Stravinsky] adopt dead forms, and because they are so obsessed with them they allow them to transform their musical ideas until these too are dead' (quoted in Sadie (1980), entry under 'Neo-classical').

14 Confusingly, 'high modernism' is also used, like 'high Renaissance', to describe the first flourish of modernism in its earlier decades – for instance, the English translation of Rudolf Frisius' sleevenote essay in Rihm (2006), though the German text has *klassichen Moderne*.

15 Adorno (1970), Vol. XVIII, p. 492, trans. R. Geuss, in his work (2005), p. 237 n.

16 Larkin (1985), pp. 22–3. A case for Larkin as modernist, influenced by Baudelaire, Yeats and Eliot, is presented in Motion (1982).

17 Greenberg (1992), p. 6; Ortega y Gasset (1968), p. 5. Against Greenberg, as noted earlier, there is also a realist strand in modernism.

18 Entry under 'Modernism' in Sadie and Tyrrell (2004).

19 '[O]ne particular, much contested account [of modernism] stresses "art for art's sake", artistic autonomy, aesthetic disinterestedness and the formal and technical characteristics of works of modern art. It systematically relegates the social [dimension]' (Blake and Frascina (1993), p. 128). See Box 'Aestheticism', pp. 85–6.

20 Paddison (1993), p. 2. Paddison notes the claim that modernism has its own norms, made, for instance, by art critic Clement Greenberg, but wishes to reject it.

21 His narrow interests led contemporary modernist composer Helmut Lachenmann to comment bluntly that 'I have a great deal of respect for Adorno, but he was a fossil from the nineteenth century' (quoted Heathcote (forthcoming 2007)). In his late essay 'Vers une musique informelle' from 1961, Adorno wrestled with his response to contemporary music after Webern but, except for Cage, restricted himself to high modernism (Adorno (1998), pp. 269–322).

22 Sadie and Tyrrell (2004), entry under 'Adorno'.

23 The compendious anthology Adorno (2002) is an excellent place to start.

24 Jarvis (1998), p. 91.

25 Adorno (1997), p. 366 – regrettably, in reprinting this translation, Continuum, also the publishers of the present book, have changed the pagination. The story of the motto comes from Rolf Tiedemann, and is reported in Adorno (2000), p. 239.

26 'Subjective and objective aesthetics, as counterpoles, are equally to be criticised by a dialectical aesthetics: the former [Kant] because it is either transcendentally abstract or contingently dependent on the taste of individuals; the latter [Hegel] because it misrecognises the objective mediatedness of art through the subject' (Adorno (1997),

p. 166).

27 Discussion of Kant is found in Adorno (1997), pp. 9–13, 61–78 (natural beauty), 163–6 (subjectivity and objectivity), 196–9 (the sublime).
28 Adorno (1997), p. 227.
29 Adorno (1997), p. 12. Kafka's story is in fact 'In the Penal Colony'.
30 Adorno (1997), pp. 9–13.
31 I am thinking in particular of Keith Warner's taut, compelling production of *Wozzeck* which opened at the Royal Opera House Covent Garden in 2002.
32 Adorno (1997), p.148.
33 The issued is addressed in Adorno (1973), for instance, pp. 36–7.
34 Letter to Krenek in 1929, quoted in Paddison (1993), p. 83; the issue is also discussed in Paddison (2004). Krenek had popular success with his 'jazz opera' *Jonny Spielt Auf* (1925).
35 'Reaktion und Fortschritt' (1930), quoted in Paddison (1993), pp. 90–1. A striking case is American composer Easley Blackwood, for instance, his Cello Sonata – see Blackwood (1992).
36 Adorno (2006), p. 7; Hegel (1975), Vol. II, p. 1236.
37 Adorno, 'Music and Language: a Fragment', (1992), p. 1.
38 On Adorno's heterodox Marxism and his questioning of the concept of reification, see, for instance, Jay (1984), Chapters 2 and 3.
39 Adorno (1997), p. 194.
40 Adorno (1997), p. 5. The term 'social fact' comes from French sociologist Émile Durkheim.
41 As Berger (1997) notes, p. 6.
42 Attali (1985), p. 47.
43 Adorno (1997), p. 132.
44 Adorno (1997), p. 227.
45 Adorno (1997), pp. 229, 226–7.
46 Adorno (1997), p. 5.
47 The political context of Beethoven's middle and late period output – unusually he concentrates on the latter – is charted in Rumph (2004), who declares that 'Beethoven was a political composer' (p. 1). It is an interesting question how far this description differs from that of politically committed composers discussed below – is Beethoven just a greater but equally political composer?
48 Adorno (1997), p. 6.
49 Adorno (1976), p. 209.
50 Adorno and Horkheimer (1972), p. 139.
51 Adorno (1974), pp. 200–1. See also 'Culture Industry Reconsidered' in Adorno (2001), pp. 98–106.
52 See, for instance, Taylor (1977), 'Presentation III'.
53 Letter to Benjamin, 18/3/36, in Taylor ed. (1977), p. 121. Later in the

same letter he comments rather patronizingly that 'it is my task to hold your arm steady until the sun of Brecht has once more sunk into exotic waters' – that is, until Benjamin ceases to be attracted by the lure of politically committed art.

54 Adorno (2002), pp. 437–69.
55 Adorno (1997), p. 228; Paddison (1982) p. 204. We will return to this 'self-reflective' music – music of the modernist avant-garde – shortly. In fact, Adorno traces the roots of the culture industry as far back as the kitsch of antiquity: 'The stagnation of the culture industry is probably not the result of [capitalist] monopolisation, but was a property of so-called entertainment from the first' (Adorno (1974), p. 147).
56 This essay and other jazz writings are collected in Adorno (2002), edited by Leppart, who defends Adorno against the charge of confusion. Perhaps in Germany in 1936, when the article appeared, commercial danceband music was still often confused with genuine jazz – small group improvised music originating in the USA (Adorno (2002), pp. 357–60). As Müller-Doohm (2005) comments, it is no surprise that Adorno refers by name to scarcely any genuine jazz musicians (p. 201). However, it is worth noting that at the time, there was virtually no serious critical writing on jazz. Gracyk (1992) argues that Adorno's writings support the appraisal of jazz in its own terms.
57 As Müller-Doohm (2005) notes (p. 199).
58 Adorno (2002), p. 499 – from the essay 'Farewell to Jazz', first published 1933.
59 Adorno (1974), p. 203 – the aphoristic collection *Minima Moralia* was first published in 1951.
60 Habermas (1992), p. 119.
61 Quoted in Paddison (1993), p. 37. *Abgrund* is a pun on 'grund' – Adorno was born Theodor Adorno Wiesengrund.
62 '[T]he dialectic advances by way of extremes, driving thoughts with the utmost consequentiality to the point where they turn back on themselves' (Adorno (1974), p. 86).
63 Letter to Benjamin, in Adorno and Benjamin (2003), p. 130.
64 The issue is debated in Paddison (1996), focusing on the figure of Frank Zappa, and also taken up by Watson (1995).
65 Stendhal (1970), p. 3. The example is used by Subotnik (1991), p. 253, though without the reference to Andrew Lloyd Webber.
66 'Neue Musik', written 1942, in Adorno (1984), p. 80.
67 Paddison (2004), p. 206.
68 'On the Social Situation of Music' (1932), Adorno's first extended essay on the sociology of music.
69 Adorno (2003), p. 88; Adorno (2006), p. 102.

70   Reprinted in Babbitt (2004).

71   See, for instance, Weber Nicholsen (1997), pp. 44–9.

72   Adorno (1997), p. 45.

73   'Cultural Criticism and Society' in Adorno (1967), p. 32.

74   Beckett (1983), p. 7.

75   Adorno (1967).

76   Adorno (1997), p. 227.

77   Taylor (1977), p. 180 – from the 1962 essay 'Commitment', on the work of Bertolt Brecht.

78   As Jarvis (1998), p. 121 puts it.

79   Adorno (1997), p. 230; see also p. 31.

80   Jay (1984), p. 86.

81   The issue needs careful handling. Adorno and Western Marxists offer a critique of what they regard as bourgeois liberalism; they do not believe that Western liberal democracy delivers freedom. But clearly Adorno is not an authoritarian in the Soviet Marxist mould; if anything, he is an extreme libertarian.

82   Interview with Christian Wolff in Hamilton (2000).

83   Negative Dialectics is not a system opposed to Hegel's 'Positive Dialectics', but may simply constitute a way of keeping Hegel's system fluid, of making German Idealism 'dance to its own tune' as Marx put it. See, for instance, Jarvis (1998), pp. 165–8. (As well as a term for Adorno's approach, Negative Dialectics is also the title of one of his books.)

84   Adorno (1973b), p. 5.

85   Adorno often refers to Chaplin; Max Paddison related this example to me, though we have not been able to find a reference in Adorno for it.

86   For instance, Nietzsche (1990), p. 83.

87   Adorno's aesthetics of nature is discussed in Hamilton (2006); as Jarvis comments, he is 'rewriting the oldest maxim of aesthetics. Art imitates nature: but nothing like "nature" exists as yet: art imitates what does not yet exist' (Jarvis (1998), p. 100). On the test of time, Adorno as usual comes close to outright self-contradiction in claiming both that 'the course of history as such in no way makes common cause with what is good', yet 'the idea of the judgment of history is not simply nugatory', at p. 195. A good discussion of dialectical thinking is Jay (1996), Chapter 2.

88   Fubini (1991), pp. 445–6.

89   The musicologist, not to be confused with composer Ernest Bloch.

90   Bürger (1984), p. 46.

91   Bernstein (1992).

92   Adorno (1976), pp. 41–3, 47. He continues: 'If something simply exists, without a raison d'être, and that is enough to console us for

the fact that everything else exists for something else ... [then this] anonymous solace to the congregation of the lonely, ranks surely not lowest among the functions of music today'.

93 I would argue that the autonomous–heteronomous distinction in art is underwritten by Kant's contrast between free and dependent beauty, discussed in Chapter 3. The artforms which he describes as dependent beauties are the heteronomous forms; the only autonomous forms – notably instrumental music – are free beauties. If there is a genuine contrast between free and dependent beauty, there can be a genuine contrast between autonomous and heteronomous art. But that is a large issue that cannot be discussed further here.

94 Bourdieu (1987).

95 He continues: 'It is precisely the continuity of music's internal aims ... that made possible the inclusion of the works of Bach, Monteverdi, and Josquin in the canon of great art music even though the external functions of their music changed' (Berger (1997), pp. 115–16, 153). On this view, in aiming to demonstrate the musical practicability of the system of twenty-four well-tempered keys, Bach's *The Well-Tempered Clavier* at its creation conformed to the ideal of absolute, autonomous music. Ledbetter comments: 'The purpose of the collections was ... for young people wishing to study composition and performance, and for the more advanced to refresh their spirits, a concept deeply rooted in the Lutheran tradition as the purifying function of music' (Ledbetter (2002), p. 34). See also Wolff (2000), pp. 225–30.

96 See for instance Goffen (2004), pp. 19, 44.

97 Clunas (1997), Chapter 5, especially pp. 173, 176, 190, 194.

98 Adorno (1976), p. 62.

CHAPTER 7

IMPROVISATION AND COMPOSITION

There is an extensive literature on the concept of the musical work – the ontology of music, as philosophers call it. Readers interested in pursuing its ramifications are referred to Stephen Davies' magisterial *Musical Works and Performances.*[1] Here, instead, I focus on the rather neglected converse question, the aesthetics of improvisation. Davies sensibly comments that if ontology is to be more than a philosopher's game, it should respond to the ways we actually engage with and discuss music and its works. This is the approach I adopt towards improvisation.

Improvisation is a near-universal tendency in music and needs no defence. However, from the viewpoint of Western art music, it appears to have the deficiencies highlighted by Ted Gioia:

> Improvisation is doomed, it seems, to offer a pale imitation of the perfection attained by composed music. Errors will creep in, not only in form but also in execution; the improviser, if he sincerely attempts to be creative, will push himself into areas of expression which his technique may be unable to handle. Too often the finished product will show moments of rare beauty intermixed with technical mistakes and aimless passages.[2]

Gioia is concerned to show why we are, nonetheless, interested in the 'imperfect art' of improvisation. His defence he labels 'the aesthetics of imperfection', in contrast to 'the aesthetics of perfection' which takes composition as the paradigm.

As we saw in Chapter 4, the *aesthetics of perfection* emphasizes the timelessness of the work and the authority of the composer, and

192

in its pure form is Platonist and anti-humanistic. In contrast, the *aesthetics of imperfection* is humanistic. It values the event or process of performance, especially when this involves improvisation – though again, these opposites turn out to be dialectically interpenetrating. Thus, the contrast between composition and improvisation proves more subtle and complex than Gioia and other writers allow. The focus in this chapter is mainly on jazz and related popular music, but much of the discussion applies to other kinds of improvised music.

THE AESTHETICS OF PERFECTION AND IMPERFECTION

We saw in Chapters 1 and 5 how the development of Western musical notation, at least until some avant-garde developments in the past century, has been one of increasing specification and prescription in the requirements it placed on performers. This process reached its highest point during the nineteenth and twentieth centuries and was associated with the increasing hegemony of the work-concept. Performers who had once had an improvisational freedom now interpreted an essentially fixed work. The dichotomy between improvisation and composition lacked its present meaning, or perhaps any meaning at all, before this process was well advanced. As Lydia Goehr writes, 'By 1800 ... the notion of extemporization acquired its modern under-standing [and] was seen to stand in strict opposition to "composition" proper'.[3] Philosophers, apparently mesmerized by the vision of the scored musical work espoused by the aesthetics of perfection, have mostly not thought enough about the dialectical opposition to composition which improvisation constitutes. In Roger Scruton's *The Aesthetics of Music*, for instance, the work-concept dominates, and an improvisation is treated as a work that is identical with a performance. George Lewis rightly argues that since 1800 there has been an 'ongoing narrative of dismissal' of improvisation by Western composers, though, like Scruton, he rather neglects the historicity of the concept and its dialectical opposition with composition.[4] I will argue that this narrative of dismissal expresses an aesthetics of perfection which arose with the work-concept and which is opposed by an aesthetics of imperfection associated with improvisation.

Classical music

'Classical' is a term used at least from the seventeenth century onwards to describe an artistic or literary work involving formal discipline, that is, a model of excellence. Often such works derived from ancient Greek or Latin models – hence the use of 'Classics' to describe the study of ancient civilization. Since music had no Greek or Latin masterworks, the application of the term 'Classical' lacked such associations. However, Mozart's biographer Niemetschek, describing the 'classical worth' of Mozart's music, wrote that 'The masterpieces of the Romans and Greeks please more and more through repeated reading, and as one's taste is refined – the same is true for both expert and amateur with respect to the hearing of Mozart's music' (1797, rev. 1808). Forkel in 1802 described J. S. Bach's main keyboard works as *klassisch*, while in eighteenth-century England 'classical' first came to stand for a particular canon of works in performance, distinct in quality and also age. By the 1830s, 'classical' music had become increasingly identified with the 'Viennese classics' of Haydn, Mozart and Beethoven. This use, followed for instance by Charles Rosen in *The Classical Style*, conforms with that of the other arts in referring to a period of particular excellence or influence. However, as European art and popular music became separated during the nineteenth century, 'classical music' came to refer to the entire output of what in this book I term *Western art music* – signaling the construction of the 'museum of musical works' that makes up the modern concert repertoire. In fact, the classical style was a popular one in the context of the audience of its time, limited to the bourgeoisie and aristocracy. The 'classical' artist attempted to fulfil this public's expectations. Haydn's instrumental works were widely printed, and he told Mozart that his language had become understood by all the world; Mozart said that he wrote for 'all kinds of ears – tin ears excepted'. Beethoven also aimed at first to please a wide public, but in later years turned inward to become an original and isolated 'romantic'.

This opposition offers a fruitful framework for looking at certain aesthetic questions in the performing arts. It is illustrated by the debate between Busoni, the defender of improvisation, and Schoenberg, the compositional determinist.[5] We have already looked at Schoenberg's ideas in the context of modernism – both he and Busoni were committed modernists. Schoenberg emphasized the autonomy of the composer-genius in the creation of masterworks, which, he insisted, required the complete subservience of the performer; Busoni, however, found virtues in improvisation and in the individual contribution of the performer-interpreter. Busoni writes:

> Notation, the writing out of compositions, is primarily an ingenious expedient for catching an inspiration, with the purpose of exploiting it later. But notation is to improvisation as the portrait is to the living model ... What the composer's inspiration necessarily loses through notation, his interpreter should restore by his own ...

He defends his practice of transcription – the arrangement of a composition for instrumental forces different from those for which it was originally composed – and argues that 'Every notation is, in itself, the transcription of an abstract idea. The instant the pen seizes it, the idea loses its original form'. The purity of the improvisation is one step less removed from the locus of artistic inspiration.

For Schoenberg, in contrast, there is only gain in the working-up of an improvisation into a crafted composition. He rejects Busoni's claim that improvisation has artistic priority: 'the portrait has higher artistic life, while the model has only a lower life'. The interpreter is the servant of the work – 'He must read every wish from its lips' – and any attempt to express his own individuality is regrettable: 'And so the interpreter mostly becomes a parasite on the exterior, when he could be the artery in the circulation of the blood'. Elsewhere, however, notably in his valedictory tribute to George Gershwin, Schoenberg is less hostile to improvisation:

> the impression [of his songs] is that of an improvisation with all the merits and shortcomings appertaining to this kind of production. Their effect in this regard might be compared to that of an oration which might disappoint you when you read and examine it as with a magnifying glass – you miss what touched you so much, when you were overwhelmed by the charm of the orator's personality. One has probably to add

something of one's own to re-establish the first effect. But it is always that way with art – you get from a work about as much as you are able to give to it yourself.[6]

Despite these mollifying sentiments, there is no doubt that Schoenberg stands squarely on the side of increasing individuality for the composer at the expense of that of the performer. This is a dilemma which Western art music has found it very hard to resolve. As Rose Rosengard Subotnik puts it: 'when efforts to preserve the autonomy of the composer's vision are unbounded, the performer is turned into a kind of automaton'.[7]

The aesthetics of imperfection questions these developments in Western art music, focusing on the event or process of performance, while the aesthetics of perfection endorses them and emphasizes the timelessness of the work. The dichotomy, as will become clear, implies others: process and product; impermanence and permanence; spontaneity and deliberation. A contemporary expression of an aesthetics of perfection is found, for instance, in comments by British composer Thomas Adès, who is evidently more interested in product than process: 'I'm trying to fix something ... I don't know how a jazz artist or improviser goes about their work, it's a mystery to me. And I would think that what I do is rather a mystery to them'. Adès is not tempted, like other contemporary composers such as Mark-Anthony Turnage, to incorporate passages of improvisation in his compositions. Revealingly, he says that if he did, 'in 70 or 80 years' time there'll be this very weird situation where you'll have these scores with holes in them, and the people won't be there to fill the holes in'.[8]

The idea of an 'aesthetics of imperfection' may appear overly paradoxical, its connotations too negative – how could imperfection be an aesthetic value? However, 'perfection' and 'imperfection' have a descriptive sense close to their Latin derivation – *perficere* means 'to do thoroughly, to complete, to finish, to work up'; '*imperfectus*' means 'unfinished, incomplete'. The aesthetics of imperfection finds virtues in improvisation which transcend the errors in form and execution we saw acknowledged in the quotation by Gioia. Indeed, it claims, these virtues arise precisely because of the 'unfinished state' of such performances.

However, I do not fully endorse the aesthetics of imperfection.

While acknowledging the unique value of improvisation, the argument of this chapter progressively qualifies the rival aesthetics, and in particular rejects their common assumption that improvisation is a kind of instant composition. My argument is that 'improvisation' and 'composition' denote ideal types or interpenetrating opposites. A feature that seems definitive of one type also turns out to be present, in some way, in the other – or so I will argue with regard to preparation, spontaneity and structure. For readers who followed the chapter on Adorno, this is, I hope, an example of dialectical thinking.

The continuum runs like this. Pre-realized electronic music stands at the far limit of pre-structuring since, although possibly possessing spontaneity at the level of composition, at the level of performance or 'sounding' it is fixed. Trial-and-error compositional efforts of students in a recording studio contrast with the organically structured through-composed works of Brahms and Schoenberg in their development of motivic material. Within the improvised sector, pre-performance structuring ranges from the work of jazz composers such as Ellington and Gil Evans to the very loose frameworks brought along by Miles Davis to the *Kind of Blue* recording session. At the furthest 'improvised' limit of the continuum stands free improvisation, a development from 1960s free jazz, which abandons the recurring harmonic structures and groundbeat of earlier jazz. Thus the aesthetics of perfection and imperfection apply not just at the level of performance but within the process of composition itself. Or rather, these levels overlap; there may, for instance, be little difference between a loosely constructed studio composition and the recording of an improvisation. For some purposes it may be useful to divide the continuum into works and improvisations, but this simple division glosses over continuities and similarities.

The rival aesthetics extend into other aspects of artistic production, such as recording, where again there is a contrasting focus on the moment of performance (imperfection) or the timelessness of the work (perfection). Recording offers new possibilities of vindicating an aesthetics of perfection, since allegedly contingent conditions of live performance can be screened out – an approach expressed most thoughtfully in the creative recording techniques of pianist Glenn Gould. The imperfectionist view, in contrast, is that recording should be

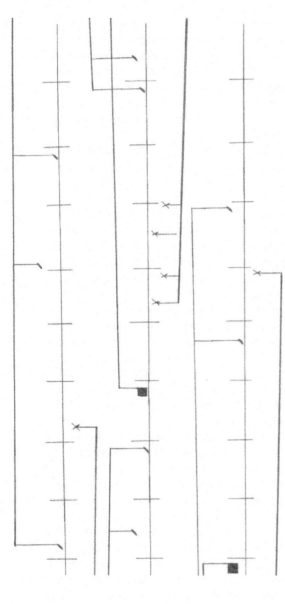

Figure 16 'Composition's Finished?' (2006) by Philip Clark, is a grand open-form graphic score for improviser, performed in 2006 by multi-instrumentalist Orphy Robinson. It is an open-ended piece of 60 free-floating pages – of which this is one – which can be played in any order, placed any way on the music stand, and with pages taken away and added to for each performance. The piece can never, therefore, properly be finished – the title also suggests that the era of the fixed composition is finished. The symbols are defined by performers to mean what they want; the recurrence of a symbol can indicate repetition of whatever gesture the performer has decided that it denotes – or not. The score is therefore a means of guiding the improviser into territory that they would not normally find. It is both improvisation and composition. Clark says: 'The whole point of the piece is that it cuts across the boundaries between them – that it makes the distinction seem meaningless'.

treated as a transparent medium giving a faithful representation of a particular performance, with only the grossest imperfections eliminated.[9]

Although an aesthetics of perfection seems to demand absolute fidelity to the composer's intentions – or rather, has a very narrow and stringent conception of what such fidelity involves – it should be separated from a commitment to authentic performance in its usual present-day sense.[10] The aesthetics of perfection perhaps implies a Platonist conception of the musical work as an eternally existing sound-structure detachable from its original conditions of performance, instruments as well as locations. The converse implication, from Platonism to perfectionism, is stronger, as Glenn Gould's remarks illustrate: 'Music need not be performed any more than books need to be read aloud, for its logic is perfectly represented on the printed page; and the performer ... is totally unnecessary except as his interpretations make the music understandable to an audience unfortunate enough not to be able to read it in print'.[11] The current concept of authenticity, in contrast, is more ambivalent between perfection and imperfection. It has been argued that it rejects the 'portability of music' in favour of an ideal of acoustic interdependence of composer, ensemble and environment, but it may also be regarded as the confused expression of a timeless Platonist conception.[12]

THE CONCEPT OF IMPROVISATION AND 'IMPROVISED FEEL'

The core idea of improvisation is that of a spontaneously improvised musical statement. But how should this idea of spontaneity be interpreted? The idea that improvisation involves 'pure transmission of the musical idea' is emphasized by many proponents of an aesthetics of imperfection, including Busoni and Bill Evans. W. F. Bach wrote of his father, J. S.:

> his organ compositions were indeed full of the expression of devotion, solemnity and dignity; but his unpremeditated organ playing, in which nothing was lost in the process of writing down but everything came directly to life out of his imagination, is said to have been still more devout, solemn, dignified and sublime.

This view is echoed by Leo Smith, avant-garde trumpet-player and ideologist of free jazz:

> improvisation ... is not like composition ... [where an] idea [is conceived] at one instant, only to be funnelled at a later time through a standard system of notation onto paper as merely a related idea, and finally interpreted and performed ... as an idea removed at least three times from the original.[13]

These writers regard improvisation as a kind of instant composition, a natural picture which I hope to undermine, first by examining the spontaneity which performers actually exhibit.

'You will hear something close to pure spontaneity in these performances', Evans wrote in the liner-notes to Miles Davis's *Kind of Blue*. This claim is an essential element of an aesthetics of imperfection, though it has not always been the improviser's ideal. According to a report of the 1760s, Austrian composer and violinist Carl Ditters von Dittersdorf performed a violin concerto followed by an encore of brilliant 'improvised' virtuosity which, he later admitted, had been prepared in advance.[14] With some key exceptions, such as Louis Armstrong, early jazz did little to undermine this attitude to improvisation. Most jazz musicians up to the swing era of the 1930s felt no compunction in rehearsing and working up their solos. Billie Holiday was one among many whose performances of the same song varied only in minor details, though her interpretations evolved over time.[15] Harry Carney from the Ellington orchestra rarely varied his solos on given numbers at all, it seems. Coleman Hawkins' 'Wherever There's a Will, Baby' from 1929 is an interesting case; the two issued versions show that patterns are memorized and repeated exactly at crucial points, such as the beginning and the middle, but that the rest is freely improvised.[16] The overwhelming influence of Charlie Parker in creating an artistically self-conscious modern jazz in the 1940s overturned these attitudes – if not perhaps jazz practice – and was decisive in generating an ideal of spontaneous creation. But performers with his genius, where alternative takes of the same song at the same recording session will be radically different, remain very rare.[17]

What does spontaneity amount to in improvised performances? And how does it matter aesthetically? These questions bring us to the heart of the concept of improvisation. A useful case study is the contemporary von Dittersdorf apparently observed by a journalist from *Downbeat* magazine:

> How much is improvised? Tonight, [Ray] Bryant played 'After Hours' in a note-for-note copy of the way he played it on the Dizzy, Rollins and Stitt album on Verve some fifteen years ago. Was it written then? Or worse. Has he transcribed and memorised his own solo, as if it were an archaeological classic? It was fine blues piano indeed, but it was odd to hear it petrified in this way.[18]

If it was 'fine blues piano', would it matter that it was 'petrified'?

Writers who adopt a purely genetic or causal account of the concept of improvisation imply that its presence is of little aesthetic consequence. Stanley Cavell claims that the standard concept of improvisation 'seems merely to name events which one knows, as matters of historical fact ... independent of anything a critic would have to discover by an analysis or interpretation ... not to have been composed'. And Eric Hobsbawm writes: 'There is no special merit in improvisation ... For the listener it is musically irrelevant that what he hears is improvised or written down. If he did not know he could generally not tell the difference'. However, he continues, 'improvisation, or at least a margin of it around even the most "written" jazz compositions, is rightly cherished, because it stands for the constant living re-creation of the music, the excitement and inspiration of the players which is communicated to us'.[19]

Now, of course, the concept of improvisation does have an essential genetic component. Although it glosses over crucial complexities, a succinct definition of 'improvised' would be 'not written down or otherwise fixed in advance' – Ray Bryant's performance was apparently fixed though not written down. A purely genetic account claims that whether a performance is improvised may not be apparent merely by listening to it and suggests, furthermore, that the mere fact that a performance is improvised is not an aesthetically or critically relevant feature. (There are several possible variations on the latter claim.) This account in fact diagnoses what amounts to an 'intentional fallacy' concerning improvisation – reminiscent of the familiar suggestion that extraneous knowledge of authorial intention is irrelevant to critical evaluation.

I believe that the genetic account exaggerates the extent to which improvisation is undetectable. There is a genuine phenomenon of an *improvised feel*, which is gestured at by Hobsbawm's comments on what improvisation symbolizes. Curiously, the best description of it is found in a book aimed at the few remaining improvisers in the church organ-loft. In *The Art of Improvisation* from 1934, T. C. Whitmer offered a set of 'General Basic Principles' which included the following description, one which justifies the term 'aesthetics of imperfection':

> Don't look forward to a finished and complete entity. The idea must always be kept in a state of flux. An error may only be an unintentional rightness. Polishing is not at all the important thing; instead strive for a rough go-ahead energy. Do not be afraid of being wrong; just be afraid of being uninteresting.[20]

From this 'feel', I think, arises the distinctive form of melodic lines and voicings in an improvised performance. The qualities that Whitmer cites are salient features, present to varying degrees. Although Bill Evans' beauty of tone seems in conflict with a 'rough go-ahead energy', there is an understated tensile quality in his work. In contrast, recordings of Evans transcriptions by classical pianist Jean-Yves Thibaudet, though tonally even more perfect than the original perhaps, do not sound improvised.[21] It is interesting that Lee Konitz describes a 'very obvious energy' in improvisation which he believes does not exist in a prepared delivery: 'There's something maybe more tentative about it, maybe less strong or whatever, that makes it sound like someone is really reacting to the moment'.[22]

One might say of a purported improvisation, 'That couldn't have been improvised' – meaning, for instance, that the figuration is too complex or the voicings too clear to be created under the constraints of an improvised performance. (Though J. S. Bach was apparently able to improvise music of such complexity.) Conversely, an improvised feel might be present in prepared playing which takes improvisation as its model – Ray Bryant's example might be a case in point – and possibly where a composer is looking to create an improvised effect. Would the fact that the performance was not improvised 'matter aesthetically'? It might justifiably alter one's view of the skill of the performer; but there is a more elusive sense in which it matters.

The sense of disappointment on discovering that the performer was a von Dittersdorf belongs to an interesting family of responses to what appears to be extraneous knowledge that some artistic ideal has been transgressed. The listener is surprised and disappointed to discover that an enjoyable piece by John Cage was created randomly using chance operations based on the *I Ching*; that a classical recording was constructed from tape-extracts of many separate takes; that an art photographer's work involves superimposition of figures or objects not in the original scene; that a putative abstract painting is in fact a piece of discarded interior decoration; or – a more extreme case – that a favourite painting is a fake. (Improvisation used to be called 'faking', hence 'fake books', collections of melodies and chord sequences of standard songs for improvisation; the idea, presumably, was that the player would be 'faking' that they were playing something composed, though the term may have arisen because this was pirated music on which copyright has not been paid.)

In the case of improvisation, the artistic ideal is part of what separates art from entertainment. If the reporter was correct, Ray Bryant's performance, for all its skill, seems indebted to the routine that wows the audience – Oscar Peterson might be a better example of this approach. A routine is something perfected by the performer, who knows that it works and sticks with it. Insofar as improvisation is present, it involves a 'bag of tricks' model. Routines are avoided by the 'modernists' who reject the culture industry – Bill Evans, Paul Bley, Lee Konitz, and all those who despise flashy virtuosity. There are obvious parallels here with the development of Western art music discussed in Chapter 6.

There are various senses in which improvisation matters aesthetically, therefore. Even assuming a viable notion of 'extraneous' knowledge, claims of an intentional fallacy are not vindicated. They are further undermined when the role of preparation is considered. Cavell and Hobsbawm seem to subscribe to the 'instant composition' view of improvisation. In my criticism of this view I will develop a positive definition of improvisation in terms of improvised feel. The idea of a continuum of composition and improvisation appears here in the idea of different kinds of preparation for performance, some of which aim at spontaneity while others do not.

SPONTANEITY AND THE AESTHETICS OF PERFECTION

The characterization of improvisation as instant composition is shared both by an aesthetics of imperfection with its ideal of complete spontaneity and by an aesthetics of perfection which denigrates improvisation. These positions have a common assumption; one praises instant composition while the other condemns it, but each assumes that improvisation *is* 'instant composition'. Later I will criticize the first position. Here I argue against the second, which claims that all improvisers, in their fruitless aspiration to spontaneity, are like von Dittersdorfs in recycling rehearsed material; on this view, improvisation is a barrier to individual self-expression, not a way of realizing it.

Adorno does not explicitly address this question, but, as we saw in Chapter 6, he treats jazz's aspirations to spontaneous improvisation as hollow, subjugated by the demands of the culture industry of which it is a part. Modernist composers are almost unanimous in their negative view of improvisation. Elliott Carter, for instance, argues that it allows undigested fragments of the unconscious to float to the surface, and since he is not an Expressionist, he does not approve: 'carefully written scores produce the most unroutinized performances because, in preventing performers from playing in their usual way, they suggest another kind of spontaneous reaction – to the musical concepts underlying the music – which has greater potential for liveliness than is usually the case with improvisation'. His conclusion is that 'improvisation is undertaken mainly to appeal to the theatrical side of musical performance and rarely reaches the highest artistic level of ... Western [art] music'.[23]

Pierre Boulez questions the more radical chance or aleatoric techniques deployed during the 1960s by Stockhausen and others, which leave much to the performer's decision:

If the player were an inventor of primary forms or material, he would be a composer ... if you do not provide him with sufficient information to perform a work, what can he do? He can only turn to information he has been given on some earlier occasion, in fact to what he has already played.

The criticism is that familiar patterns of notes are embedded in the performer's muscular memory as a result of countless hours spent with the instrument and regurgitated when there is no restraining score. Improvisers express themselves less than they think because so much of what they play is what they are remembering, including things that they do not even know they are remembering. In a later interview, Boulez was better disposed towards jazz than towards aleatoric improvisation, though he still stresses what he regards as its limitations: 'As long you have a solid ground on which to improvise, then the improvisation has a meaning of some kind. In jazz, you have chorus and then solo and then chorus and then solo, it's responsorial. It does not go very much out of this scheme, particularly'. However, he still affirmed that 'The [work-concept is the] top level not only of enjoyment, but also depth. I cannot consider improvisation as really the highest level ... I say that because the form is very important, and should be surprising ... really intriguing, challenging'.[24] This, then, is the Carter–Boulez line.

I believe that Carter, like Adorno, neglects those modernist improvisers who reject the 'theatrical side of musical performance'. Boulez's criticism begs the question against improvisation and amounts to an assertion of the classical hegemony expressed by the honorific title 'composer'. The aesthetics of improvisation precisely rejects the view that if the player were an 'inventor of primary forms or material', he or she would be a composer. (What the force of 'primary' is remains unclear.) It is true that the improviser has less chance than the composer of eradicating cliché in their work – as the aesthetics of imperfection recognizes. But Carter and Boulez fail to recognize the fact that the improviser's preparation and practice is precisely intended to 'keep [them] from playing what [they] already know'.

Saxophonist Steve Lacy, one of the most finest exponents of the art in modern jazz, puts the case strongly:

[There] is a freshness, a certain quality that can only be obtained by improvisation, something you cannot possibly get by writing. It is something to do with the 'edge'. Always being on the brink of the unknown and being prepared for the leap. And when you go on out there you have all your years of preparation and all your sensibilities and your prepared means but it is a leap into the unknown.[25]

And Lee Konitz, one of the most eminent living improvisers, who could never be accused of theatricality, describes the process of spontaneous creation and its limitations:

We talk about learning every change that existed, every inversion, every lick. And then when you play you forget about what you practised and try to really invent something for the moment, according to what the rhythm [section]'s playing, according to the acoustics, the audience, how you feel at the moment, and so on. And certainly I don't do it all the time. When I get in trouble, for acoustic reasons, or because it's the wrong band for me, or whatever, I have to rely on what I know more. And that's less satisfying, but necessary, certainly.

Konitz has 'complete faith' in the spontaneous process: 'I think most people think that can be very naive, and that you do your improvising at home, and when you go out, you play prepared material, so the paying customers don't get short-changed. It's the picture I've seen all of my life. And very talented people can do it effectively – the rest sound like hacks, to me'.[26]

Thus, there is a relation between performance and pre-performance activity not envisaged by Carter and Boulez – nor by the polar opposite of their view, the pure spontaneity assumed by a full-blown aesthetics of imperfection. The correct view, in contrast to the extremes of perfection and imperfection, is this, I believe. Interpreters think about and practise a work with the aim of giving a faithful representation of it in performance. True improvisers also practise, but with the aim of being better prepared for Lacy's 'leap'. Many improvisers will formulate structures and ideas, and, at an unconscious level, these phrases will provide openings for a new creation. Thus, there are different ways for a performer to get beyond what they already do, to avoid repeating themselves. For the improviser, the performance must feel like a 'leap into the unknown', and it will be an inspired one when the hours of preparation connect with the requirements of the moment and help to shape a fresh and compelling creation. At the time of performance they must clear their conscious minds of prepared patterns and simply play. Thus it makes sense to talk of preparation for the spontaneous effort. Lee Konitz puts it succinctly: 'That's my way of preparation – to not be prepared. And that takes a lot of preparation!'.[27] This is the qualified truth in the imperfectionist claim that improvisation is valuable because it is closer to the original idea.

These are elusive claims, vindicated only by critical examination of classic improvised performances. The contrast between relatively mechanical and spontaneous deployment of prepared ideas, for instance, is illuminated by Carl Woideck's discussion of Charlie Parker. One of Woideck's central claims is that Parker's creativity declined after 1950, for health and drug-related reasons. His huge repertoire of motifs was deployed increasingly mechanically – though still with a brilliance that his peers could not match – and no longer developed, Woideck argues. This does not mean that Parker was reproducing practised solos – part of the problem seems to have been that he ceased practising from the late 1940s onwards. This is a case of pre-existing structures being employed in progressively less spontaneous ways, compared to the brilliant performances of Parker's earlier years.[28]

FREE IMPROVISERS, INTERPRETERS AND 'IMPROVISATION AS A COMPOSITIONAL METHOD'

As noted earlier, the connection between preparation and performance is misconceived by proponents of a radical aesthetics of imperfection who eulogize improvisation, as well as by improvisation's perfectionist critics. Thus, some free improvisers claim to go beyond even Charlie Parker-like standards of freshness and improvise, in Ornette Coleman's words, 'without memory'. Leo Smith writes that 'at its highest level, improvisation [is] created entirely within the improviser at the moment of improvisation without any prior structuring'. Derek Bailey advocated 'non-idiomatic improvisation', apparently without a personal vocabulary – a paradoxical notion, given that he himself was such a highly idiomatic and individual improviser.[29] Against these authorities, I would argue that an improviser's individuality resides in, among other things, their creative development of

Figure 17 Steve Lacy's improvisation on Thelonious Monk's 'Misterioso', from the album 'Only Monk' (Omnitone).

Figure 17 Steve Lacy's improvisation on Thelonious Monk's 'Misterioso', transcribed (in C Concert) by Mike Baggetta, who writes: 'Steve Lacy's interpretation of "Misterioso" is an honest representation of his improvising. Lacy's playing often exemplified how phrasing and interpretation could be key elements in an improvisation, as well as striving to be consistently inventive rather than relying on idiomatic devices. In this piece, we see that he plays the melody, not strictly in time, but letting the natural feeling of the phrases lead to the initial interpretation. The improvisation that follows is based loosely on some elements of the melody, which constitutes a springboard for Lacy's own ideas on the subject of this twelve-bar blues form. Note the way he carefully builds his improvisation through from the very beginning. One gets from his connected ideas the sense of a complete statement, thoughtfully expounded throughout, to the end where Monk's melody is re-interpreted.

This piece was not performed in very strict time – however, some parts are definitely in rhythm. To this end I have left out all barlines, and notated pauses of phrasing with caesuras. Some of these pauses are shorter rests within a timed phrase and are notated as such. I have included dashed barlines in the playing of the melody so that the reader can relate it to its standard form. Be aware though that the rhythm in this piece does fluctuate and should be thought of as freely interpreted at points'. Reproduced by kind permission of Mike Baggetta.

favourite stylistic or structural devices, without which they risk incoherence and non-communication.

It is important to realize that the misconceptions shared by imperfectionists and perfectionists relate to the interpretation of composed works also. Many proponents of an aesthetics of imperfection believe that interpreters simply 'reproduce the score'. The dialectic here is the counterpart of that concerning instant composition: imperfectionists condemn interpretation as mere reproduction, while perfectionists praise it for the same reason, since – on their view – a reproduction allows no corrupting role for the performer's individuality. (These are extreme statements of the rival positions; the views of Busoni and Schoenberg are more subtle.) In fact, it is the achievement of the greatest interpreters to produce the illusion of spontaneous creation.[30] When artists of the stature of Lipatti, Brendel, Furtwängler or Kocsis perform or conduct, and the circumstances are propitious, the work is heard new and fresh, in a way that it never has been before. There is a genuine phenomenon here, not just an artistic illusion. Great performances can illuminate a truth about the work; the performer does not simply strive to 'do something different'. But as interpreters get to know a work intimately, they internalize it and make it their own – just as actors do not merely recite the lines of a play but become the part. A certain freedom then develops. In contrast to the macro-freedom of improvisers, there is a micro-freedom for interpreters to reconceive the work at the moment of performance, involving many subtle parameters such as tone and dynamics. A performance will then feel like a 'leap into the unknown' and will have an improvised feel. George Lewis is therefore wrong to contrast composition with 'real time music' – interpretation occurs in real-time too.

The process of interpretation is misunderstood by an aesthetics of perfection also. A well-rehearsed performance of a familiar work will, after all, involve something which the performer has already played, and this could become stultifying. So the interpreter must strive for that improvisational freshness which gives the illusion that they are not playing 'what they already know' – that is, a pre-existing work. (The quotation from Carter does acknowledge that scores 'suggest another kind of spontaneous reaction'.)

There seems to be a particular way in which improvisation makes the performer alive in the moment; it brings them to a state of alertness, even what Ian Carr in his biography of Keith Jarrett has called the 'state of grace'.[31] This state is enhanced in a group situation of interactive empathy.[32] But all players, except those in a large orchestra, have choices inviting spontaneity at the point of performance. These begin with the room in which they are playing, its humidity and temperature, who they are playing with and so on. Thus, interactive empathy is present in classical music too, at a high level for instance in the traditional string quartet, if not the orchestra (or jazz big band). Again, the rival aesthetics of perfection and imperfection fail to recognize that improvisation and composition are interpenetrating opposites – that is, features which appear definitive of one are found in the other also.

It remains finally to consider the view put forward by writers from various standpoints that improvisation should be regarded as a variety of composition – where this does not mean 'instant composition'. Now there is a sense in which recordings convert improvisation into composition. They can be subject to critical analysis, enter a canon and help to establish art music status – all of this is found in jazz.[33] Thus, improvisations can perhaps become works from the viewpoint of their reception. But it has also been argued that from the viewpoint of their production, improvisations can count as compositions. There may be an immediate practical impetus behind such claims. The Arts Council of England and Wales, for instance, operated a de facto policy that was product based, funding composers but not improvisers, encouraging jazz musicians to compose uninspired 'suites' when their true *métier* is improvisation.[34]

One advocate of improvisation as composition is Sidney Finkelstein, a classical-music critic who also wrote insightfully on jazz. He commented in 1948:

Improvisation is a form of composition. Improvisation is music that is not written down, composition is music that is written down ... The ability to write music makes possible a bigness of form and richness of expression that is beyond the limits of improvisation ... [But the] slow creation of a great jazz solo [from performance to performance] is a form of musical composition.[35]

I think that Charlie Parker, Lester Young or Lee Konitz are not unique in transcending Finkelstein's analysis; but his central claim has been echoed in different ways by later writers. Roger Scruton maintains that an improvisation is a work that is identical with a performance, but also seems to suggest that there is a stricter sense in which the work-concept supersedes improvised music:

> the distinction between work and performance grows sponta-neously in the practice of acousmatic hearing ... [involving] a peculiar experience of 'same again' ... There could not be meaningful improvisation without this experience, and the emergence of 'works' from a tradition of spontaneous perfor-mance is exactly what we must expect when people listen, and therefore recognize what they hear as 'the same again'.[36]

Scruton fails to recognize that the concept of improvisation, in its present-day sense, especially in jazz, arose precisely as a reaction to the emergence of works; while there is plenty of scope for 'playing it again' in the way that jazz utilizes the standard songs of Tin Pan Alley.

Some improvising musicians put a very different slant on the claim that improvisations are compositions. Evan Parker, one of the leading free improvisers, advocates 'improvisation as a compositional method', and describes his piece 'De Motu' as 'an improvisation composed uniquely and expressly during its perfor-mance in Zaal de Unie in Rotterdam on Friday May 15th 1992'. He continues: 'In the period of preparation I made notes of ideas and patterns ... in a method that can be seen as analogous to a painter's sketchbook where fragments of what might become the final work are treated in isolation from one another'. Possibly with Parker's view in mind, George Lewis objects to the claim that 'any kind of generating music is a kind of composing':

> the problem is not just taxonomical ... what you're doing is placing yourself under the hegemony of composers, or people who call themselves composers ... Once you decide you don't *need* to be accepted as a composer, then you should be accepted as doing what *you* do. You should be accepted as an improviser.[37]

Lewis is right – the issue is not taxonomic. Both his attitude and Evan Parker's can be seen as contesting the Western art music hegemony, possibly with equal effectiveness. They are right to give weight to the ideological import of the traditional vocabulary, and either view is defensible; what is essential is to avoid the picture of instant composition.

Although improvisers and composers are no longer in two mutually uncomprehending camps, many pervasive misunderstandings of improvisation remain, which this chapter has tried to correct. Despite the qualifications of it presented here, I believe that the aesthetics of imperfection is right to focus on music as event – a position which subverts the standard perfectionist account whereby works are merely exemplified in performance. This conclusion provides further support for the humanistic philosophy of music which I have been concerned to outline over the course of this short book.

I have ended with the problem that originally engaged me in aesthetics: does it matter aesthetically or artistically if an improvised performance is not truly spontaneous? Though that issue has seemed less urgent over the intervening years, another question, the status of jazz as an art music, has not. Why is this music so potent, despite evidently being less contrived than the great works of the canon of Western art music? Jazz has been called a miniaturist's art.[38] Perhaps in its most evocative moments – the three-minute classics on 78 rpm disc by Louis Armstrong, Billie Holiday or Lester Young – that description is correct. Ephemeral pop music has its own charm – what Noël Coward patronizingly called the 'potency of cheap music' – which arises precisely from its powers of association for the individual listener. When those materials are used as they have been in jazz, an art of great power can be created. This is a central issue to be debated in considering the contrast between popular and art music – a genuinely aesthetic question, but a topic for another occasion.[39]

NOTES

1 Davies (2001).
2 Gioia (1988), p. 66.
3 Goehr (1992), p. 234 – a brief account of the changing concept of

improvisation is found at pp. 188–9 and 232–4. Goehr may be influenced by Adorno's insistence on the historicity of the concepts of improvisation and composition, discussed in Max Paddison (1993), pp. 192–8.

4   Scruton (1997); George Lewis (1996), pp. 91–122.

5   The 'debate' consisted of Schoenberg writing marginal comments in his copy of Busoni's book; subsequent quotations are from Busoni (1962), p. 84, and Stuckenschmidt (1977), pp. 226–7.

6   Schoenberg (1984), pp. 476–7.

7   Subotnik (1991), p. 256.

8   Hamilton (1998), p. 13.

9   As discussed in Hamilton (2003).

10 On authentic performance in this sense, see Davies (2001), Chapter 5.

11 Quoted in Bazzana (1997), pp. 20–1. This comment echoes the quotation from Brahms on p. 113.

12 The former is the view of Robin Maconie (1990), pp. 150–1.

13 Bach quoted in 'Improvisation' by Eva Badura-Skoda, in Sadie (1980); Smith (1973) – the pamphlet has no page numbers.

14 Eva Badura-Skoda, 'Improvisation', in Sadie (1980) p. 43.

15 We know this from alternative takes of the same song. On improvisation in early jazz, see Schuller (1989), pp. 162 n. and 307 n.; and Cork (1996), pp. 81–6.

16 Entry under 'Coleman Hawkins' by Lewis Porter, in Sadie and Tyrrell (2004).

17 The issue is complicated by Parker's use of familiar motifs or building blocks for improvisation, which he assembled in ingenious and spontaneous ways. For this reason, Lee Konitz describes Parker as a 'composer' and contrasts this method with his own 'intuitive' approach to improvisation – discussed in Hamilton (forthcoming 2007b), Chapter 6.

18 *Downbeat* report from May 1978, quoted in Gioia (1988), pp. 52–3. In fact I doubt that the solos were, note for note, the same – for an accomplished jazz player like Ray Bryant, it would be more trouble to learn a solo than create a new one. But for the sake of argument I will go along with the journalist's report.

19 Cavell (1976), p. 200; Hobsbawm quote from *The Jazz Scene*, first published 1959 under the pseudonym of Francis Newton, quoted in Gottlieb (1997), p. 813. Cavell offers a more elusive sense of 'improvised' on pp. 200–1.

20 Quoted in Bailey (1993), p. 48.

21 Thibaudet (1997).

22 Quoted in Hamilton (forthcoming 2007b), Chapter 6.

23 Carter (1997), pp. 324–5. Carter's music has been much influenced

by jazz rhythms – maybe like Jelly Roll Morton he prefers his jazz well rehearsed.

24 Boulez (1986), p. 461; and interview with the author, Edinburgh International Festival, August 2000. Lukas Foss says that in improvisation 'one plays what one already knows', and John Cage agrees – see Lewis (1996), p. 106. Aleatoric music – music in which the effect of chance is a significant factor – is, in fact, only marginally influenced by improvisation, as argued in Hamilton (2002).

25 Weiss (2006), p. 51. A transcription of a Lacy improvisation, which shows these qualities of the 'leap into the unknown', is provided by Figure 17.

26 In Hamilton (forthcoming 2007b), Chapter 6.

27 Quoted in Hamilton (forthcoming 2007b); Konitz's ideas on improvisation are discussed especially in Chapter 6.

28 Woideck (1996), pp. 175–6, 199–200 and elsewhere. The distinction between creative and non-creative use of motifs is also well discussed by Porter (1986) and Cork (1996). Lewis (1996), pp. 106–7, discusses the 'motif theory' proposed by cognitive psychologists.

29 Smith (1973), Bailey (1993) *passim.*

30 Stressed by Gunther Schuller (1986), pp. 24–5. Despite the illusion of spontaneous creation, the present chapter has been reworked to death with almost all traces of the original idea completely obliterated – so in case you ask, 'No it wasn't improvised'.

31 Carr (1992). Jarrett's 'state of grace' makes perhaps too frequent appearances, on pp. 67, 72, 92, 104, 131, 151, 159, 163.

32 As described by Lee Konitz in Hamilton (forthcoming 2007b), Chapter 6.

33 The point is made by W. Brooks in 'Music in America: an overview (part 2)', in Nicholls ed. (1998), p. 269.

34 I owe this point to Conrad Cork, who was a panel member in the 1980s.

35 Finkelstein (1964), pp. 109, 111.

36 Scruton (1997), p. 111; (1999), pp. 157–8.

37 Evan Parker quotations from a manuscript written to accompany the performance at the Zaal De Unie and donated to the Rotterdamse Kunststichting; Lewis interview in sleevenote to George Lewis and Miya Masaoka (1998).

38 Harrison (1991), p. 128.

39 The ideas in this chapter arose through discussion over many years with Conrad Cork, David Udolf, Max Paddison, Ben Watson, Evan Parker, Berys Gaut and Gary Kemp. Thanks also to Peter Jones and Derek Bailey for the initial inspiration.

BIBLIOGRAPHY

Adorno, T. (1967), *Prisms*, trans. S. and S. Weber, Cambridge, MA: MIT Press.
—— (1970), *Gesammelte Schriften*, Frankfurt-am-Main: Suhrkamp.
—— (1973a), *Vorlesungen zur Aesthetik 1967–8*, Zurich: Mayer.
—— (1973b), *Negative Dialectics*, trans. E. Ashton, London: Routledge.
—— (1974), *Minima Moralia: Reflections from Damaged Life*, trans. E. Jephcott, London: Verso.
—— (1976), *Introduction to the Sociology of Music*, trans. E. Ashton, New York: Continuum.
—— (1984), *Gesammelte Schiften Bd. 18: Musikalische Schriften*, Frankfurt-am-Main: Suhrkamp.
—— (1992), *Quasi una Fantasia*, trans. R. Livingstone, London: Verso.
—— (1997), *Aesthetic Theory*, trans. R. Hullot-Kentor, London: Athlone.
—— (1998), 'Music and Language: A Fragment', in his *Quasi una Fantasia*, trans. R. Livingstone, London: Verso, pp. 1–6.
—— (2000), *The Adorno Reader*, ed. B. O'Connor, Oxford: Blackwell.
—— (2001), *The Culture Industry: Selected Essays on Mass Culture*, ed. J. Bernstein, London: Routledge.
—— (2002), *Essays on Music*, ed. R. Leppert, Berkeley, CA: University of California Press.
—— (2003), *Philosophie der neun Musik*, Frankfurt-am-Main: Suhrkamp.
—— (2006), *Philosophy of New Music*, trans. R. Hullot-Kentor, Minneapolis, MN: University of Minnesota Press.
Adorno, T. and Benjamin, W. (2003), *The Complete Correspondence 1928–1940*, Oxford: Blackwell.
Adorno, T. and Horkheimer, M. (1972), *Dialectic of Enlightenment*, trans. John Cumming, New York.
Agawu, V. Kofi (1991), *Playing with Signs: A Semiotic Interpretation of Classic Music*, Princeton, NJ: Princeton University Press.
Alcopley, L. (1968), 'Edgard Varèse on Music and Art: A Conversation between Varèse and Alcopley', *Leonardo* Vol. 1, No. 2, pp. 187–95.
Alexander, J. and Seidman, S., eds (1990), *Culture and Society: Contemporary Debates*, Cambridge: Cambridge University Press.

Alperson, P. (1980), ' "Musical Time" and Music as an "Art of Time" ', *Journal of Aesthetics and Art Criticism*, Vol. 38, pp. 407–17.
—— (1984) 'On Musical Improvisation', *Journal of Aesthetics and Art Criticism*, Vol. 43, No. 1.
Andersen, T., ed. (1968), *Malevich: Essays on Art, 1915–1933*, New York: George Wittenborn.
Aristides Quintilianus (1983), *On Music*, trans. T. Mathieson, New Haven, CT: Yale University Press.
Aristotle (1939), *On The Heavens*, trans. W. Guthrie, Cambridge, MA: Loeb Classical Library.
—— (1952), *Problems*, trans. W. Hett, London: Heinemann.
—— (1998), *Metaphysics*, trans. H. Lawson-Tancred, Harmondsworth: Penguin.
Armstrong, J. (2005), *The Power of Beauty*, Harmondsworth.
Attali, J. (1985), *Noise: Political Economy of Music*, Minneapolis, MN: University of Minnesota Press.
Babbitt, M. (2004), *The Collected Essays of Milton Babbitt*, ed. S. Perles, Princeton, NJ: Princeton University Press.
Bailey, D. (1993), *Improvisation: Its Nature and Practice in Music*, Cambridge, MA: Da Capo.
Barker, A. (1978), 'Music and Perception: A Study in Aristoxenus', *The Journal of Hellenistic Studies*, Vol. 98, pp. 9–16.
—— (1984), *Greek Musical Writings Vol. 1: The Musician and His Art*, Cambridge: Cambridge University Press.
—— (2004), *Greek Musical Writings Vol. 2: Harmonic and Acoustic Theory*, Cambridge: Cambridge University Press.
Barthes, R. (1977), 'The Grain of the Voice' in his *Music, Image, Text*, essays selected and translated by Stephen Heath, London: Fontana.
Baudelaire, C. (1964), *The Painter of Modern Life and Other Essays*, trans. J. Mayne, London: Phaidon.
Bazzana, K. (1997), *Glenn Gould: The Performer in the Work – a Study in Performance Practice*, New York: Oxford University Press.
Beckett, S. (1983), *Worstward Ho*, London: John Calder.
Beiser, F., ed. (1993), *The Cambridge Companion to Hegel*, Cambridge: Cambridge University Press.
Benson, D. (2007), *Music: A Mathematical Offering*, Cambridge: Cambridge University Press.
Berger, K. (1997), *A Theory of Art*, New York: Oxford University Press
Bernstein, J. (1992), *The Fate of Art*, Cambridge: Polity.
Blake, N. and Frascina, F. (1993), 'Modern Practices of Art and Modernity', in Frascina et al. (1993), pp. 50–140.
Boghossian, P. (2002), 'On Hearing the Music in the Sound: Scruton on Musical Expression', *Journal of Aesthetics and Art Criticism*, Vol. 60, No. 1, pp. 49–55.
Boretz, B. (1970), 'Nelson Goodman's Languages of Art from a Musical Point of View', *Journal of Philosophy*, Vol. 67, No. 16, pp. 540–52.
Boulez, P. (1971), *Boulez on Music Today*, London: Faber.

—— (1986), *Orientations*, London: Faber & Faber.

Bourdieu, P. (1987), *Distinction: A Social Critique of the Judgement of Taste*, trans. R. Nice, Cambridge, MA: Harvard University Press.

Bowman, W. (1998), *Philosophical Perspectives on Music*, New York: Oxford University Press.

Brooks, W. (1998), 'Music in America: An Overview (Part 2) in D. Nicholls ed. (1998).

Browne, R., ed. (1981), *Music Theory: Special Topics*, New York: Academic Press.

Buchanan, I., and Swiboda, M., eds (2004), *Deleuze and Music*, Edinburgh: Edinburgh University Press.

Budd, M. (1985), *Music and the Emotions: The Philosophical Theories*, London: Routledge.

—— (2003), 'Musical Movement and Aesthetic Metaphors', *British Journal of Aesthetics*, Vol. 43, No. 3, pp. 209–23.

Bujic, B. (1997), 'Delicate Metaphors', *Musical Times*, June 1997.

Bürger, P. (1984), *Theory of the Avant-Garde*, Manchester: Manchester University Press.

Burkert, W. (1972), *Lore and Science in Ancient Pythagoreanism*, trans. E. Minar, Cambridge, MA: Harvard University Press.

Busoni, F. (1962), 'Sketch of a New Aesthetic of Music', in *Three Classics in the Aesthetic of Music*, New York: Dover.

Cage, J. (1973), *Silence: Lectures and Writings*, London: Marion Boyars.

Cardew, C., (1971), 'On the Role of the Instructions in the Interpretation of Indeterminate Music', in his *Treatise Handbook*, London: Peters.

Carew, D. (2004), 'The Consumption of Music', in Huhn (2004).

Carr, I. (1992), *Keith Jarrett: The Man and His Music*, New York: Da Capo.

Carter, E. (1997), *Collected Essays and Lectures, 1937–95*, ed. J. Bernard, Rochester, NY: University of Rochester Press.

Case, B. (1982), 'Steve Lacy' (interview) in *The Wire*, No. 1, summer, pp. 6–7.

Cavell, S. (1976), 'Music Discomposed' in his *Must We Mean What We Say?*, Cambridge: Cambridge University Press, pp. 180–212.

Chion, M. (1983), *Guide des objets sonores: Pierre Schaeffer et la recherche musicale* [Guide to Sound Objects: Pierre Schaeffer and Music Research]. Paris: INA-GRM/Buchet-Chastel.

—— (1994), *Audio-Vision: Sound on Screen*, trans. C. Gorbman, New York: Columbia University Press.

Cicero, (1998), *The Republic*, trans. N. Rudd, Oxford: Oxford University Press.

Clark, P. (2005), 'James Tenney – All Shook Up', *The Wire*, No. 253, March, pp. 38–43.

Clarke, E. (2005), *Ways of Listening: An Ecological Approach to the Perception of Musical Meaning*, New York: Oxford University Press.

Clayton, M. (1996), 'Free Rhythm: Ethnomusicology and the Study of

Music without Metre', *Bulletin of the School of Oriental and African Studies, University of London*, Vol. 59, No. 2, pp. 323–32.

Clifton, T. (1983), *Music As Heard*, New Haven, CT: Yale University Press.

Clunas, C. (1997), *Art in China*, Oxford: Oxford University Press.

Collier, J. (1978), *The Making of Jazz*, London: Granada.

Comotti, G. (1991), *Music in Greek and Roman Culture*, Baltimore, MD: Johns Hopkins University Press.

Cooke, D. (1960), *The Language of Music*, Oxford: Oxford University Press.

Cooper, G., and Meyer, L. (1960), *The Rhythmic Structure of Music*, Chicago, IL: Chicago University Press.

Cork, C. (1996), *Harmony with Lego Bricks*, revised edition, Leicester: Tadley Ewing Publications.

Cox, C., moderator (accessed 2004), *Artforum* discussion, < http:// artforum.com/index.php?pn = symposium&id = 6682 >.

Cox, C. and Warner, D., eds (2004), *Audio Culture: Readings in Modern Music*, London: Continuum.

Craig, E. ed. (2000), *Routledge Encyclopedia of Philosophy*, London: Routledge.

Crofton, I., et al. eds (1988), *A Dictionary of Musical Quotations*, London: Routledge.

Curtin, D. (1982), 'Varieties of Aesthetic Formalism', *Journal of Aesthetics and Art Criticism*, Vol. 40, No. 3, pp. 315–26.

Dack, J. (1994), 'Pierre Schaeffer and the Significance of Radiophonic Art', in *Contemporary Music Review*, Vol. 10, No. 2, pp. 3–11.

Dahlhaus, C. (1982), *Esthetics of Music*, trans. W. Austin, Cambridge: Cambridge University Press.

—— (1987), *Schoenberg and the New Music*, trans. D. Puffett and A. Clayton, Cambridge: Cambridge University Press.

—— (1989), *The Idea of Absolute Music*, trans. R. Lustig, Chicago, IL: Chicago University Press.

Danto, A. (1964), 'The Artworld', *Journal of Philosophy*, Vol. 61, pp. 571–84.

—— (2005), *Nietzsche as Philosopher*, New York: Columbia University Press.

Darwin, C. (1999), *The Expression of the Emotions in Man and Animals*, London: Fontana.

—— (2004), *The Descent of Man*, Harmondsworth: Penguin.

Davies, S. (1994), *Musical Meaning and Expression*, Ithaca, NY and London: Cornell University Press.

—— (2001), *Musical Works and Performances*, Oxford: Clarendon Press.

—— (2003), 'What Is the Sound of One Piano Plummeting?' in his *Themes in the Philosophy of Music*, Oxford: Oxford University Press, pp. 108–18.

—— (forthcoming 2007), 'Perceiving Melodies and Perceiving Musical Colors', *European Review of Philosophy*, issue 7.

Davis, M. (1989), *Miles: The Autobiography*, New York: Simon & Schuster.

Deakin, A. (accessed 2003), 'Live Electronics and the Acousmatic Tradition', < http://www.cea.mdx.ac.uk > .

De Lorenzo, R. and Eilers, M. (1991), 'Lights and Sirens: A Review of Emergency Vehicle Warning Systems', *Annals of Emergency Medicine*, Vol. 20, pp. 1331–5.

Dewey, J. (1980), *Art as Experience*, New York: Perigree.

Dhomont, F. (accessed 2002), < http://www.sonicartsnetwork.org/ARTICLES/ARTICLE 1996D > .

Diliberto, J. (1986), 'Pierre Schaeffer and Pierre Henry: Pioneers in Sampling', *Electronic Musician*, December issue.

Dürr, W. (1966), 'Rhythm in Music: A Formal Scaffolding of Time', in Fraser (1966).

Dürr, W. and Gerstenberg, W. (1980), 'Rhythm', in Sadie (1980), Vol. XV, pp. 804–25.

Dutton, D. (2002), 'Aesthetic Universals', in B. Gaut and D. McIver Lopes eds, *The Routledge Companion to Aesthetics*, London: Routledge.

Dziemidok, B. (1993), 'Artistic Formalism: Its Achievements and Weakness', *Journal of Aesthetics and Art Criticism*, Vol. 51, No. 2, pp. 185–93.

Eiseman, F. (2004), *Bali: Sekala and Niskala. Vol. 2: Essays on Society, Tradition and Craft*, Singapore: Periplus.

Elias, N. (1993), *Mozart: Portrait of a Genius*, trans. E. Jephcott, Cambridge: Polity.

Emmerson, S., ed. (1986), *The Language of Electro-acoustic Music*, London: Macmillan.

—— (2000), *Music, Electronic Media and Culture*, Aldershot: Ashgate.

Evans, G. (1980), 'Things Without The Mind: A Commentary upon Chapter Two of Strawson's *Individuals*', in Z. Van Straaten (1980), pp. 76–117.

Eysteinsson, A. (1990), *The Concept of Modernism*, Ithaca, NY: Cornell University Press.

Feyerabend, P. (1993), *Against Method*, London: Verso.

Finkelstein, S. (1964), *Jazz: A People's Music*, London: Jazz Book Club, originally published New York: Citadel Press, 1948.

Fitterling, T. (1997), *Thelonious Monk: His Life and Music*, trans. R. Dobbin, Berkeley, CA: Berkeley Hills Books.

Frascina, F. et al (1993), *Modernity and Modernism: French Painting in the Nineteenth Century*, New Haven, CT: Yale University Press.

Fraser, J. ed. (1966), *The Voices of Time*, New York: George Braziller.

Fubini, E. (1991), *The History of Music Aesthetics*, trans. M. Hatwell, London: Macmillan.

Gardiner, P. (1963), *Schopenhauer*, Harmondsworth: Penguin.

Geuss, R. (1999), *Morality, Culture and History*, Cambridge: Cambridge University Press.

—— (2005), *Outside Ethics*, Princeton, NJ: Princeton University Press.

Gildea, R. (2003), *Barricades and Borders: Europe 1800–1914*, 3rd edition Oxford: Oxford University Press.

Gioia, E. (1988), *The Imperfect Art*, Oxford: Oxford University Press.

Godwin, J., ed. (1993), *Harmony of the Spheres: A Sourcebook of the Pythagorean Tradition in Music*, Rochester, VT: Inner Traditions International.

Goehr, L. (1992), *The Imaginary Museum of Musical Works*, Oxford: Clarendon Press.

Goffen, R. (2004), *Renaissance Rivals: Michelangelo, Leonardo, Raphael, Titian*, New Haven, CT: Yale University Press.

Gottlieb, R. (1997), *Reading Jazz*, London: Bloomsbury.

Gould, G. (1987), *The Glenn Gould Reader*, ed. T. Page, London: Faber & Faber.

Gracyk, T. (1992), 'Adorno, Jazz and the Aesthetics of Popular Music', *Musical Quarterly*, Vol. 76, No. 4: 526–42.

Grant, M. (2001), *Serial Music, Serial Aesthetics: Compositional Theory in Post-War Europe*, Cambridge: Cambridge University Press.

Greenberg, C. (1992), *Art and Culture: Critical Essays*, Boston, MA: Beacon Press.

Greene, T. (1940), *The Arts and the Art of Criticism*, Princeton, NJ: Princeton University Press.

Habermas, J. (1990), 'Modernity Versus Postmodernity', in Alexander and Seidman (1990), pp. 342–54.

—— (1992), 'A Generation Apart from Adorno', interview by J. Fruchtl, *Philosophy and Social Criticism*, Vol. 18, No. 2, pp. 119–24.

Hainge, G. (2004), 'Is Pop Music?', in Buchanan et al. (2004), pp. 36–53.

Hamilton, A. (1998), 'Thomas Adès: Sleaze Operas', *The Wire*, No. 176, p. 13.

—— (1999), 'The Aesthetics of Western Art Music' (Discussion of R. Scruton's *The Aesthetics of Music*), *Philosophical Books*, Vol. 40, No. 3, pp. 145–55.

—— (2000), 'Chancy Gardener: Christian Wolff', *The Wire*, No. 202, December.

—— (2002), 'The Music of Chance – Cage, Kagel, Zorn: Chance Operators, Musical Dice Men', in Young (2002), pp. 209–23.

—— (2003), 'Spectral Music', *The Wire*, No. 237, November, pp. 42–9.

—— (2006), 'Indeterminacy and Reciprocity: Contrasts and Connections between Natural and Artistic Beauty', forthcoming in *Journal of Visual Art Practice*.

—— (forthcoming 2007a), 'The Sound of Music', in Nudds and O'Callaghan (2007).

—— (forthcoming 2007b), *Lee Konitz: Conversations on the Art of the Improviser*, Ann Arbor, MI: University of Michigan Press.

—— (forthcoming 2007c), 'Music and the Aural Arts', *British Journal of Aesthetics*.

—— (forthcoming), *Memory and the Body: A Study of Self-Consciousness*.

—— (in preparation), *The Autonomy of Art*.

Handel, S. (1989), *Listening: An Introduction to the Perception of Auditory Events*, Cambridge, MA: MIT Press.

Hankins, T. and Silverman, R. (1995), *Instruments of the Imagination*, Princeton, NJ: Princeton University Press.

Hanslick, E. (1986), *On the Musically Beautiful*, trans. G. Payzant, IN: Indianapolis, Hackett.

Harding, J. (1992), 'Historical Dialectics and the Autonomy of Art in Adorno's *Aesthetische Theorie*', *Journal of Aesthetics and Art Criticism*, Vol. 50, No. 3, pp. 183–95.

Harrison, C. (1993), *Primitivism, Cubism, Abstraction*, New Haven, CT: Yale University Press.

Harrison, J. (1999), 'Imaginary Space – Spaces in the Imagination', Proceedings of Australasian Computer Music Conference, 1999.

Harrison, M. (1991), *A Jazz Retrospect*, London: Quartet.

Harvey, J. (1980), 'Rhythm (20th century)', in Sadie ed. (1980), Vol. XV, pp. 819–20.

—— (1999), *In Quest of Spirit*, Berkeley, CA: University of California Press.

—— (forthcoming 2007), 'Buddhism and Music', in Paddison and Deliege, eds (forthcoming 2007).

Hasty, C. (1997), *Meter As Rhythm*, New York: Oxford University Press.

Hayward Gallery (2000), *Sonic Boom: The Art of Sound*, London: Hayward Gallery Publishing.

Heathcote, A. (2004), 'Liberating Sounds: Philosophical Perspectives on the Music and Writings of Helmut Lachenmann', Durham: Durham University MA thesis.

—— (forthcoming 2007a), 'Interview with Helmut Lachenmann', in Paddison and Deliège, eds (forthcoming 2007).

—— (forthcoming 2007b) 'Sounds, Structures and Broken Magic: An Interview with Helmut Lachenmann', in Paddison and Deliège, eds (forthcoming 2007).

Hegel, G. (1975), *Hegel's Aesthetics: Lectures on Fine Art* , Vols I and II, trans. T. Knox, Oxford: Clarendon Press.

—— (1993), *Introductory Lectures on Aesthetics*, trans. B. Bosanquet, Harmondsworth: Penguin.

Hildesheimer, W. (1983), *Mozart*, trans. M. Faber, London: Dent.

Hobsbawn, E. (1962), *The Age of Revolution 1789–1848*, London: Weidenfeld & Nicolson.

Holmes, T. (2003), *Electronic and Experimental Music*, London: Routledge.

Hoppin, R. (1978), *Medieval Music*, New York: Norton.

Houlgate, S. (2004), *An Introduction to Hegel: Freedom, Truth and History*, Oxford: Blackwell.

Huhn, T. (2004), *The Cambridge Companion to Adorno*, Cambridge: Cambridge University Press.

Le Huray, P. and Day, J. (1988), *Music and Aesthetics in the Eighteenth and Early Nineteenth Centuries*, abridged edition. Cambridge: Cambridge University Press.

Hussey, E. (1997) 'Pythagoreans and Eleatics', in C. C. W. Taylor, ed. (1997), pp. 128–74.

Janaway, C. (1995), *Images of Excellence: Plato's Critique of the Arts*, Oxford: Clarendon Press.

Jarvis, S. (1998), *Adorno: A Critical Introduction*, Oxford: Polity.

—— (2004), 'Adorno, Marx, Materialism', in Huhn, ed. (2004).

Jay, M. (1984), *Adorno*, London: Fontana.

—— (1996), *The Dialectical Imagination: A History of the Frankfurt School and the Institute of Social Research 1923–50*, Berkeley, CA: University of California Press.

Johnson, J. (1991), 'Music in Hegel's Aesthetics: A Re-evaluation', *British Journal of Aesthetics*, Vol. 31, No. 2, pp. 152–62.

—— (2002), *Who Needs Classical Music?*, Oxford: Oxford University Press.

Kahn, D. (1999), *Noise Water Meat*, Cambridge, MA: MIT Press.

Kandinsky, W. (1982), *Complete Writings on Art*, ed. K. Lindsay and P. Vergo, Boston, MA: G. K. Hall.

Kant, I. (1987), *Critique of Judgment*, ed. W. Pluhar, Indianapolis, IN: Hackett.

Kelly, M., ed. (1998), *Encyclopedia of Aesthetics*, Oxford: Oxford University Press.

Kierkegaard, S. (1987), *Either/Or*, Part I, trans. H. Hong et al., Princeton, NJ: Princeton University Press.

Kirwan, J. (2004), *The Aesthetic in Kant*, London: Continuum.

Kramer, J. (1988), *The Time of Music: New Meanings, New Temporalities, New Listening Strategies*, New York: Schirmer.

Kristeller, P. (1990), 'The Modern System of the Arts', in his *Renaissance Thought and the Arts*, Princeton, NJ: Princeton University Press, pp. 163–227.

Kuhn, T. (1996), *The Structure of Scientific Revolutions*, Chicago, IL: University of Chicago Press.

LaBelle, B. (2006), *Background Noise: Perspectives on Sound Art*, London: Continuum.

Landels, J. (1999), *Music in Ancient Greece and Rome*, London: Routledge.

Larkin, P. (1985), *All What Jazz: A Record Diary*, London: Faber & Faber.

Ledbetter, D. (2002), *Bach's 'Well-Tempered Clavier': The 48 Preludes and Fugues*, New Haven, CT: Yale University Press.

Lee, R. K. (1988), 'Fu Ho U vs. Do Re Mi: the Technology of Notation Systems and Implications of Change in the Shakuhachi Tradition of Japan', *Asian Music*, Vol. 19, No. 2, pp. 71–81.

Lessing, G. (1962), *Laocoon: an Essay on the Limits of Poetry and Painting* (first published 1766), trans. E. A. McCormick, Baltimore, MD and London: Johns Hopkins University Press.

Levinson, J. (1991), 'The Concept of Music', in his *Music, Art and*

Metaphysics: Essays in Philosophical Aesthetics, Ithaca, NY: Cornell University Press.

—— (2002), 'Sound, Gesture, Spatial Imagination, and the Expression of Emotion in Music', *European Review of Philosophy*, Vol. 5, pp. 137–150.

—— (2006), *Contemplating Art: Essays in Aesthetics*, Oxford: Oxford University Press.

Levinson, J. and Alperson, P. (1991), 'What is a Temporal Art?', *Midwest Studies in Philosophy* Vol. 16, pp. 439–50.

Lewis, G. (1996), 'Improvised Music after 1950: Afrological and Eurological Perspectives', *Black Music Research Journal*, Vol. 16, No. 1, pp. 91–122.

Liébert, G. (2004), *Nietzsche and Music*, trans. D. Pellauer and G. Parker, Chicago, IL: Chicago University Press.

Lippman, E. (1964), *Musical Thought in Ancient Greece*, New York: Columbia University Press.

—— (1977), *A Humanistic Philosophy of Music*, New York: New York University Press.

—— (1994), *A History of Western Musical Aesthetics*, Lincoln, NE: University of Nebraska Press.

—— (1999), *The Philosophy and Aesthetics of Music*, Lincoln, NE: University of Nebraska Press.

London, J. (2004), *Hearing In Time: Psychological Aspects of Musical Meter*, New York: Oxford University Press.

López, F. (accessed 2004), interview at < http://www.franciscolopez.net >.

Lutoslawski, W. (1989), 'Witold Lutoslawski in Interview', *Tempo*, No. 170, pp. 4–12.

Mâche, F. (2001), 'The Necessity of and Problems with a Universal Musicology', in Wallin *et al.* (2001), pp. 473–9.

Maconie, R. (1990), *The Concept of Music*, Oxford: Clarendon Press.

Manning, P. (1993), *Electronic and Computer Music*, 2nd edition, Oxford: Oxford University Press.

Matravers, D. (2001), *Art and Emotion*, Oxford: Oxford University Press.

Mattick, P. (2003), *Art and Its Time: Theories and Practices of Modern Aesthetics*, London: Routledge.

McGurk, H., and MacDonald, J. (1976), 'Hearing Lips and Seeing Voices', *Nature*, No. 264, pp. 746–8.

McTaggart, J. M. (1927), *The Nature of Existence*, Cambridge: Cambridge University Press.

Moldenhauer, H. (1979), *Anton von Webern: A Chronicle of his Life and Work*, New York: Alfred A. Knopf.

Monro, G. (2000), 'An Acousmatic Experience: Thoughts, Reflections, and Comments on the 1999 Australasian Computer Music Association conference Imaginary Space', < http://cec.concordia.ca/econtact/ ACMA/AcousmaticExperience.html >.

Morgan, R. (1984), 'Secret Languages: the Roots of Musical Modernism', *Critical Inquiry*, Vol. 10, No. 3, pp. 442–61.

—— (1991), *Twentieth-Century Music*, New York: Norton.

Mothersill, M. (1984), *Beauty Restored*, Oxford: Oxford University Press.

Motion, A. (1982), *Philip Larkin*, London: Methuen.

Mueller, I. (1997), 'Greek Arithmetic, Geometry and Harmonics: Thales to Plato', in C. C. W. Taylor, ed. (1997), pp. 271–322.

Müller-Doohm, S. (2005), *Adorno: A Biography*, trans. R. Livingstone, Cambridge: Polity Press.

Murray, C. Shaar (2000), *Boogie Man: The Adventures of John Lee Hooker*, Harmondsworth: Penguin.

Nattiez, J.-J. (1990), *Music and Discourse: Toward a Semiology of Music*, Princeton, NJ: Princeton University Press.

Nettl, B. (1989), *Blackfoot Musical Thought: Comparative Perspectives*, Kent, Ohio: Kent State University Press.

—— (2001), 'An Ethnomusicologist Contemplates Universals in Musical Sound and Musical Culture', in Wallin *et al.*, eds (2001), pp. 462–72.

Nicholls, D., ed. (1998), *The Cambridge History of American Music*, Cambridge: Cambridge University Press.

Nietzsche, F. (1958), *Nietzsches Werke in Drei Bande*, Munich: Karl Hanser Verlag.

—— (1973), 'Über Musik und Wort', in *Sprache, Dichtung, Musik*, ed. J Knaus (1973), Tübingen: Niemeyer.

—— (1986), *Human, All Too Human*, trans. R. Hollingdale, Cambridge: University Press.

—— (1990), *Philosophy and Truth: Selections from Nietzsche's Notebooks of the Early 1870s*, location not given: Humanities Press.

—— (1999), *The Birth of Tragedy and Other Writings*, trans. R. Speirs, Cambridge: Cambridge University Press.

North, A., et al. (1999), 'The Influence of In-store Music on Wine Selections', *Journal of Applied Psychology*, Vol. 84, pp. 271–6.

Nudds, M. (2001), 'Experiencing the Production of Sounds', *European Journal of Philosophy*, Vol. 9, No. 2, pp. 210–29.

Nudds, M., and O'Callaghan, eds (forthcoming 2007), *Sounds and Perception: New Philosophical Essays*, Oxford: Oxford University Press.

Nussbaum, M. (1996), 'Classical Aesthetics', subsection of entry under 'Aesthetics', in Turner ed. (1996).

Ortega y Gasset, J. (1968), *The Dehumanization of Art and other Writings on Art and Culture*, Princeton, NJ: Princeton University Press.

Osborne, R. (1998), *Archaic and Classical Greek Art*, Oxford: Oxford University Press.

Packard, V. (1960), *The Hidden Persuaders*, Harmondsworth: Penguin.

Paddison, M. (1982), 'The Critique Criticised: Adorno and Popular Music', *Popular Music*, Vol. 2, pp. 201–18.

—— (1993), *Adorno's Aesthetics of Music*, Cambridge: Cambridge University Press.

—— (1996), *Adorno, Modernism and Mass Culture: Essays on Critical Theory and Music*, London: Kahn and Averill.

—— (2002), 'Music as Ideal: The Aesthetics of Autonomy', in Samson, ed. (2002).

—— (2004), 'Authenticity and Failure in Adorno's Aesthetics of Music', in Huhn, ed. (2004).

Paddison, M. and Deliège, I., eds (2007 forthcoming), *Contemporary Music: Theoretical and Philosophical Perspectives*, Aldershot: Ashgate.

Palombini, C. (accessed 2004), < http://www.rem.ufpr.br/REMv4/vol4/arti-palombini.htm >.

Pasnau, R. (1999), 'What Is Sound?', *Philosophical Quarterly*, Vol. 49, No. 196, pp. 309–24.

Pater, W. (1948), 'The School of Giorgione', in *Selected Works*, ed. R Aldington, London: Heinemann.

Pauly, H. (1959), 'The Autonomy of Art: Fact or Norm?', *Journal of Aesthetics and Art Criticism*, Vol. 18, No. 2, pp. 204–14.

Pettinger, P. (1998), *Bill Evans: How My Heart Sings*, New Haven, CT: Yale University Press.

Plato (1970), *The Laws*, trans. T. Saunders, Harmondsworth: Penguin.

—— (1974), *Timaeus and Critias*, trans. H. Lee, Harmondsworth: Penguin.

—— (1993), *The Republic*, trans. R. Waterfield, Oxford: Oxford University Press.

Pole, D. (1983), 'What Makes a Situation Aesthetic', in his *Aesthetics, Form and Emotion*, London: Duckworth, pp. 13–36.

Porter, L. (1986), *Lester Young*, London: Macmillan.

Pye, D. (1978), *The Nature and Aesthetics of Design*, Huntingdon: Herbert Press.

Read, H. (1960), *Art Nouveau*, London: Faber, first published 1933.

Repp, H. (1992), 'Probing the Cognitive Representation of Musical Time: Structural Constraints on the Perception of Timing Perturbations', *Cognition*, Vol. 44, pp. 241–81.

Rice, D. (1998), *A Guide to Plato's Republic*, Oxford: Oxford University Press.

Robertson-De Carbo, C. (1976), '*Tayil* as Category and Communication among the Argentine Mapuche: A Methodological Suggestion', *1976 Yearbook of the International Folk Music Council*, Vol. VIII, pp. 35–42.

Rosen, C. (1975), *Arnold Schoenberg*, Chicago, IL: Chicago University Press.

—— (1999), *The Romantic Generation*, London: Fontana.

—— (2002), *Piano Notes*, London: Penguin.

Rumph, S. (2004), *Beethoven after Napoleon: Political Romanticism in the Late Works*, Berkeley, CA: University of California Press.

Rushton, J. (2001), 'Music and the Poetic', in Samson, ed. (2001), pp. 151–77.

Sachs, C. (1953), *Rhythm and Tempo*, London: Dent.

Sadie, S., ed. (1980), *New Grove Dictionary of Music and Musicians*, London: Macmillan.

Sadie, S., and Tyrrell, J., eds (2004), *New Grove Dictionary of Music and Musicians*, New York: Oxford University Press.

Samson, J., ed. (2002), *The Cambridge History of Nineteenth Century Music*, Cambridge: Cambridge University Press.

Schaeffer, P. (1966), *Traité des Objets Musicaux*, Paris: Éditions du Seuil.

—— (1987), interview with Tim Hodgkinson, *Recommended Records Quarterly*, Vol. 2 No. 1, <http://www.cicv.fr/association/shaeffer>.

Schafer, R. Murray (1969), *The New Soundscape*, Scarborough, Ontario: Berandol Music Limited.

—— (1977), *The Tuning of the World*, Toronto: McClelland and Stewart.

Schaper, E. (1968), *Prelude to Aesthetics*, London: Allen & Unwin.

Schlegel, F. (1958–), *Kritische Friedrich–Schlegel–Ausgabe*, E. Behler, J.-J. Ansett and H. Eichner, eds, Paperborn: Schoenigh.

Schoenberg, A. (1984), *Style and Idea*, London: Faber & Faber.

Schopenhauer, A. (1969), *The World as Will and Representation*, 2 volumes, trans. E. Payne, New York: Dover.

—— (1970), *Essays and Aphorisms*, trans. R. Hollingdale, Harmondsworth: Penguin.

Schuller, G. (1986), 'The Future of Form in Jazz', in *Musings*, New York: Oxford University Press, pp. 18–25.

—— (1989), *The Swing Era*, New York: Oxford University Press.

Scruton, R. (1997), *The Aesthetics of Music*, Oxford: Clarendon Press.

—— (1999), 'Reply to Hamilton, "The Aesthetics of Western Art Music"', *Philosophical Books*, Vol. 40.

—— (forthcoming 2007a), 'Sounds as Secondary Objects and Pure Events', in Nudds and O'Callaghan, eds (forthcoming 2007).

—— (forthcoming 2007b), 'Thoughts on Rhythm', in Stock, ed. (forthcoming 2007).

Sethares, W. (1997), *Tuning, Timbre, Spectrum, Scale*, Berlin: Springer-Verlag.

Sharpe, R.A. (2000), *Music and Humanism: An Essay in the Aesthetics of Music*, Oxford: Oxford University Press.

Shiner, L. (2001), *The Invention of Art: A Cultural History*, Chicago, IL: University of Chicago Press.

Skvorecky, J. (1980), *The Bass Saxophone*, London: Picador.

Smalley, D. (1986), 'Spectro-morphology and Structuring Processes', in Emmerson, ed. (1986).

Smith, L. (1973), *Notes (8 Pieces) Source a new world music: creative music*, location unknown, Leo Smith.

Snow, C. P. (1993), *The Two Cultures*, Cambridge: Cambridge University Press.

Soll, I. (1988), 'Pessimism and the Tragic View of Life: Reconsiderations of Nietzsche's *Birth of Tragedy*', in Solomon and Higgins, eds, (1988).

Solomon, R. and Higgins. K., eds (1988), *Reading Nietzsche*, New York: Oxford University Press.

Spitzer, M. (2004), *Metaphor and Musical Thought*, Chicago, IL: University of Chicago Press.

Stein, J. (1960), *Richard Wagner and the Synthesis of the Arts*, Detroit, MI: Greenwood Press.

Stendhal (1970), *The Life of Rossini*, trans. R. Coe, London: Calder.

Stravinsky, I. (1970), *Poetics of Music, in the Form of Six Lessons*, Cambridge, MA: Harvard University Press.

Strawson, P. (1959), *Individuals: An Essay in Descriptive Metaphysics*, London: Methuen.

Stock, K., ed. (forthcoming 2007), *Philosophers on Music: Experience, Meaning and Work*, Oxford: Oxford University Press.

Stockhausen, K. (1989), *Stockhausen on Music: Lectures and Interviews*, compiled by Robin Maconie, London: Marion Boyars.

Stuckenschmidt, H. (1977), *Arnold Schoenberg: His Life, World and Work*, London: John Calder.

Subotnik, R. Rosengard (1991), *Developing Variations: Style and Ideology in Western Music*, Minneapolis, MN: University of Minnesota Press.

Swafford, J. (1998), *Johannes Brahms: A Biography*, London: Macmillan.

Szlavnics, C. (2006), 'Opening Ears: the Intimacy of the Detail of Sound', *Filigrane* No. 4: *Nouvelles sensibilités*, Paris: Éditions Delatour.

Taruskin, R. (1995), *Text and Act: Essays on Music and Performance*, New York: Oxford University Press.

Taylor, C. C. W., ed. (1997), *From the Beginning to Plato, Routledge History of Philosophy*, Vol. 1, London: Routledge.

Taylor, R., ed. (1977), *Aesthetics and Politics: The Key Texts of the Classic Debate within German Marxism*, London: Verso.

Tenzer, M. (1998), *Balinese Music*, Hong Kong: Periplus.

Thomson, W. (accessed 2004), entry under 'Musical Sound' in *Encyclopaedia Britannica*. < http://www.britannica.com > .

Toop, D. (2005), 'The Art of Noise', in *Tate Etc.* No. 3, spring, pp. 62–9.

Treitler, L. (1979), 'Regarding Meter and Rhythm in the *Ars Antiqua*', *Musical Quarterly*, Vol. 65, No. 4, pp. 524–58.

—— (1982), 'The Early History of Music Writing in the West', *Journal of the American Musicological Society*, Vol. 35, pp. 237–79.

—— (1989), 'Mozart and the Idea of Absolute Music', in his *Music and the Historical Imagination*, Harvard: Harvard University Press, pp. 176–214.

Trevelyan, H. (1981), *Goethe and the Greeks*, Cambridge: Cambridge University Press.

Turner, J., ed. (1996), *The Grove Dictionary of Art*, New York: Oxford University Press.

University of Melbourne (accessed 2006), *The Australian Sound Design Project*, < http://www.sounddesign.unimelb.edu.au/site/index1.html > .

van Straaten, Z., ed., (1980), *Philosophical Subjects: Essays Presented to P. F. Strawson*, Oxford: Clarendon Press.

van Leeuwen, T. (1999), *Speech, Music, Sound*, Basingstoke: Palgrave Macmillan.

Wallace, R. (1986), *Beethoven's Critics: Aesthetic Dilemmas and Resolutions During the Composer's Lifetime*, Cambridge: Cambridge University Press.

Wallin, N. et al., eds (2001), *The Origins of Music*, Cambridge, MA: MIT/ Bradford.

Walton, K. (1988), 'What Is Abstract About the Art of Music?', *Journal of Aesthetics and Art Criticism*, Vol. 46, No. 3, pp. 351–64.

Watson, B. (1995), *Frank Zappa: The Negative Dialectics of Poodle Play*, London: Quartet.

Watson, D. (1991), *Wordsworth Dictionary of Musical Quotations*, Edinburgh: Chambers.

Weber Nicholson, S. (1997), *Exact Imagination, Late Work: On Adorno's Aesthetics*, Cambridge, MA: MIT Press.

Webber, M. (1998), 'LaMonte Young meets Mark Webber', *The Wire*, No. 178.

Weiss, J., ed. (2006), *Steve Lacy: Conversations*, Durham, NC: Duke University Press.

West, M. (1992), *Ancient Greek Music*, Oxford: Clarendon Press.

West, S., ed. (1996), *Guide to Art*, London: Bloomsbury.

Whittall, A. (1999), 'review of Hasty, *Meter as Rhythm*', *Journal of Music Theory*, Vol. 43, No. 2, pp. 359–71.

Wicks, R. (1993), 'Hegel's Aesthetics: An Overview', in Beiser, ed. (1993).

Wilde, O. (1909), 'The Decay of Lying', in *The Complete Writings of Oscar Wilde*, Vol. VII, New York: The Nottingham Society.

—— (1994), *The Picture of Dorian Gray*, Harmondsworth: Penguin.

Wilder, A. (1972), *American Popular Song*, Oxford: Oxford University Press.

Windsor, L., (2000), 'Through and Around the Acousmatic: The Interpretation of Electroacoustic Sounds', in Emmerson (2000), pp. 7–35.

Wiora, M. (1965), *Les Quatre Âges de la musique*, Paris: Payot.

Wishart, T. (1986), 'Sound Symbols and Landscapes', in Emmerson, S., ed. (1986), pp. 41–60.

—— (1996), *On Sonic Art* revised edition, Amsterdam: Harwood Academic.

Withington, D. (1998), 'Siren Sounds: Do They Actually Contribute to Traffic Accidents?', *Impact*, spring < http://www.sound-alert.co.uk > .

Wittgenstein, L. (1953), *Philosophical Investigations*, Oxford: Blackwell.

Woideck, C. (1996), *Charlie Parker: His Music and Life*, Ann Arbor, MI: University of Michigan Press.

Wollheim, R. (1980), 'Seeing-as, Seeing-in', in his *Art and its Objects*, 2nd edn, Cambridge: Cambridge University Press, pp. 205–26.

Wolff, C. (2000), *Johann Sebastian Bach: the Learned Musician*, New York: W. W. Norton.

Wölfflin, H. (1986), *Principles of Art History: The Problem of the Development of Style in Later Art*, New York: Dover.

Worby, R. (2004), 'Loudspeakers Revolutionised the Way We Hear Music – But Not the Way We Talk about It', *Guardian*, 24 April, < http:// www.guardian.co.uk/arts/guesteditors/story/0,14481,1201741,00.html >

Yeston, M. (1976), *The Stratification of Musical Rhythm*, New Haven, CT: Yale University Press.

Young, R., ed. (2002), *Undercurrents: The Hidden Wiring of Modern Music*, London: Continuum/*The Wire*.

Young, J. (2005), 'The "Great Divide" in Music', *British Journal of Aesthetics*, Vol. 45, No. 2, pp. 175–84.

Young, Julian (1992), *Nietzsche's Philosophy of Art*, Cambridge: Cambridge University Press.

Zangwill, N. (2001), *The Metaphysics of Beauty*, Ithaca, NY and London: Cornell University Press.

—— (2004), 'Against Emotion: Hanslick Was Right about Music', *British Journal of Aesthetics*, Vol. 44, pp. 29–43.

Zuckerkandl, V. (1969), *Sound and Symbol: Music and the External World*, Princeton, NJ: Princeton University Press.

RECORDINGS

Aimard, Jean-Pierre (2003), *African Rhythms*, Multinational Corporation: Teldec.

Ayler, Albert (1998), *Live in Greenwich Village: the Complete Impulse Recordings*, EU: GRP/Universal.

Blackwood, Easley (1992), *Cello Sonatas* (with Sonata by Frank Bridge), Chicago, IL: Cedille Records.

Blamey, Peter and Denley, Jim (2006), *Findings*, Sydney: Split.

Blonk, Jaap (2004), *Blonk, Zach and Grydeland*, Amsterdam: Kontrans.

Davis, Miles (1959), *Kind of Blue*, New York: Columbia.

Evans, Bill (1962), *Moonbeams*, New York: Riverside.

Flynt, Henry (no date given), *Raga Electric: Experimental Music 1963–71*, Chicago, IL: Locust Music.

Harriott, Joe (1961), *Free Form*, London: Jazzland, reissued by PolyGram, 1998.

Hooker, John Lee (2002), *The Classic Early Years 1948–1951*, London: JSP.

Lewis, George and Masaoka, Miya (1998), *Duets*, Berkeley, CA: Music & Arts.

Lupu, Radu (1987), *Brahms: Two Rhapsodies, Op. 79 and other pieces*, London: Decca.

Ongaku Masters, the (2004), *An Anthology of Japanese Classical Music* (5 CDs), Tucson, AZ: Celestial Harmonies.

Parker, Charlie (1947), 'Embraceable You', Los Angeles, CA: Dial Records, reissued on *Charlie Parker Complete on Dial*, Sawbridgeworth: Spotlite, 1993.

Radigue, Elaine (2002), *Adnos I–III*, Milwaukee, WI: Table of the Elements.

Rihm, Wolfgang (2006), *String Quartets Vol. 4*, Bad Wiessee: Col Legno.

Russell, George (1982), *Live in an American Time Spiral*, Milan: Soul Note.

Rivers, Sam (1986), *Dimensions and Extensions*, New York: Blue Note.

Sachiko M; Rowe, Keith; Nakamura, Toshimaru and Yoshihide, Otomo (2005), *ErstLive 005*, Jersey City, NJ: Erstwhile.

Samartzis, Philip (2004), *Soft and Loud*, Melbourne: Microphonics.

Schaeffer, Pierre (1998), *L'Œuvre musicale*, Paris: Musidisc/INA.

Schwitters, Kurt (1995), *Ursonate*, Mainz: Wergo.

Tallis Scholars, the (1990), *Allegri: Miserere*, including Palestrina 'Missa Papae Marcelli', Oxford: Gimell.

Thibaudet, Jean-Yves (1997), *Conversations with Bill Evans*, London: Decca.

INDEX

absolute music, 34, 56, 62, 66,
67–9, 70, 76–8, 80, 81, 82–9, 90,
92, 114, 120, 148, 168, 178, 181,
184, 186
abstract conception of music/
abstractness, 6, 95–6, 111–16,
119–20, 142. *See also:*
mathematical conception of
music; humanistic conception of
music
accent, musical, definition of,
129–30, 137–41
acousmatic(s), 7, 20, 38, 40, 43, 45,
46, 57–8, 62, 89, 95–116, 117,
143, 214
acoustics, science of, 20–3, 48–49
Adès, Thomas, 164, 196
Adorno, Theodor, 1, 4, 5, 7, 30, 69,
71, 75, 82, 83, 84, 112, 114, 148,
153–4, 157, 158–86, 187, 189,
190–1, 197, 215; *Aesthetic
Theory*, 2, 159, 160, 168, 180;
Critique of Judgment, 162;
Dialectic of Enlightenment, 171;
'Farewell to Jazz', 173;
*Introduction to the Sociology of
Music*, 185; *Minima Moralia*,
180, 189; *Negative Dialectics*,
163, 177, 180, 190 (*See also:*

dialectics); 'On the Fetish
Character in Music and the
Regression of Listening', 172;
'On Jazz', 173; 'On Popular
music', 172; 'On the Social
Situation of Music', 190;
Philosophy of Modern Music,
159, 165, 176; Hektor
Rottweiler, 173; 'Surrealist
music', 164; culture industry,
171–4, 189, 203, 204. *See also:*
Frankfurt School of
contemporary Marxist
philosophy; Institute for Social
Research
Aeschylus, 12
aesthete, 1, 56, 86, 178
aesthetic, definition/concept of, 1,
2–3, 6, 31, 52–6
aesthetic conception of music, 5–6,
10–11, 31, 34, 40, 46–59
aestheticism, 30, 85–6, 158, 170
aesthetics of form and aesthetics of
expression, post-Romantic, 69–70,
77, 80, 82–99. *See also:* formalism;
emotion (expression of)
aesthetics of imperfection, 8, 113,
186, 192–9, 202, 204, 205, 206,
207, 212, 213, 214, 215

aesthetics of perfection, 7, 113, 186, 192–9, 204–7, 212, 213
Aimard, Pierre-Laurent, 150
alap, 135
aleatoric music, 204–5, 216
Alexander, 10
Allison, Mose, 107
Ambient, 54
ambient sound, 46, 61, 63
Anaxagoras, 20
animals, sounds of, 49–51
Antheil, George, 41
anthropology, 46–8
Apollonian (versus Dionysian), 78–80
Archytas, 24
Aristides, Quintilianus, 11, 12; *On Music (Perì musikes)*, 11
Aristophanes, 12
Aristotle, 3, 16, 18, 19, 20, 26–8, 37, 83, 121; Aristotelian, 27; *Metaphysics*, 27; *Poetics*, 37
Aristoxenus, 26–8, 38, 120–1; Aristoxenians, 25; *On Harmonics*, 27
Armstrong, Louis, 200, 215; 'Swing That Music', 105
Ars Nova, 149
art, autonomous. *See:* autonomous music/art
art, heteronomous. *See:* autonomous music/art
art for art's sake, 30, 69, 71, 85–6, 170–1, 177–9, 183, 187. *See also:* political art
Arts Council of England and Wales, 213
Attali, Jacques, 168
Auber, Daniel, 92
aulos (Greek musical instrument), 12, 21, 28, 79
autonomous music/art, 7, 28, 29–30, 31, 55, 56, 68–9, 71, 72, 81, 88, 90, 109, 114, 153, 160–2, 163, 167, 168–86, 191. *See also:* function, social, of music and art
Ayler, Albert, 133; 'Holy Ghost', 151

Babbitt, Milton, 176; 'Who cares if you listen?', 176
Babyshambles, 4
Bach, C. P. E., 70, 75
Bach, J. S., 23, 56, 84, 113, 114, 183, 184, 191, 194, 199, 202; *Art of Fugue*, 67; *The Well-Tempered Clavier (48 Preludes and Fugues)*, 23, 191
Bach, W. F., 199
Baggetta, Mike, 211
Bailey, Derek, 207
Balinese gamelan. *See:* gamelan
Barnes, Jonathan, 16
Bartók, Bela, 107, 133, 156, 175
Baudelaire, Charles, 86, 154
Bauhaus, 158
Baumgarten, Alexander Gottlieb, 2
Bayle, François, 116
BBC, 53
beat/groundbeat, definition/ concept of, 135–7, 145–6
beauty/beautiful, 1, 2, 3, 13, 18, 29–31, 73, 162–63; beauty, free (versus dependent beauty, Kant's distinction between), 71–2, 88, 191; beauty, musical, Hanslick on, 81–2. *See also:* kalon/kalos
Beckett, Samuel, 177; *Worstward Ho*, 177
Beecham, Sir Thomas, 95
Beethoven, Ludwig van, 4, 56, 66, 68, 75, 81, 90, 92, 107–8, 124, 133, 164, 166, 168, 170, 171, 176, 177, 185–6, 188, 194; op. 130 string quartet, 105; 5th

Symphony, 67, 170; 6th Symphony (The Pastoral), 67–8; 9th Symphony, 165
Bell, Clive, 88
Benjamin, Walter, 167, 172, 188–9
Bennink, Han, 136
Berg, Alban, 149, 157, 159, 162; *Wozzeck*, 157, 162, 163, 188. *See also:* Second Viennese School
Berger, Karol, 185
Bergson, Henri, 121
Berlioz, Hector, 81
Bernstein, Jay, 182
Beuys, Joseph, 164
Big Brother, 174
birdsong, 49, 51, 53, 103, 149
birth-of-tragedy thesis (that music originates in a union with poetry), 79–80. *See also:* Nietzsche
Birtwistle, Harrison, 133
Bizet, Georges: *Carmen*, 80
Blackwood, Easley: Cello Sonata, 188
Bley, Paul, 203
Bloch, Ernest, 190
Bloch, Ernst, 181
Blonk, Jaap, 63
blues, 108, 145, 201, 211
body, music's grounding in the, 6, 115–16, 144–6
Boethius, 32, 33
Boghossian, Paul, 147
Bordieu, Pierre, 184
Boretz, Benjamin, 87
Boulez, Pierre, 43, 135, 157, 159, 186–7, 204–5, 206
Brahms, Johannes, 81, 83, 92, 113, 197; 'Intermezzo', op. 117 no. 2, 83; 4th Symphony, 110
Brecht, Bertolt, 177, 189
Brendel, Alfred, 212
Bridge, Frank, 157

Britten, Benjamin, 157, 164
Broadbent, Alan, 125
Brown, James, 145
Bruce, Robert: *How To Write and Sell a Song Hit*, 172. *See also:* Abner Silver
Bruckner, Anton, 92, 108, 125, 164; Brucknerian, 164
Bryant, Ray, 201, 202, 203, 216; 'After Hours', 201
Budd, Malcolm, 94
Buddhist writings, 76
Budd, Malcolm, 143
Bujic, Bojan, 81
Bürger, Peter, 182
Burkert, Walter, 19–20, 21, 28; *Lore and Science in Ancient Pythagoreanism*, 19–20
Busoni, Ferruccio, 194, 195, 199, 212, 215

Cage, John, 44, 46, 61, 108, 115, 122, 137, 157, 159, 178, 181, 187, 203, 216; *4′ 33″*, 63; *I Ching*, 203; the 'number' pieces, 122, 144
Cardew, Cornelius, 137, 151, 178
Carney, Harry, 200
Caro, Anthony, 157
Carr, Ian, 213
Carry On films, 173
Carter, Elliott, 157, 204, 205, 206, 212
Cavell, Stanley, 201, 203
Cézanne, Paul, 154
Chaplin, Charlie, 180
Charisius, 151
China: Song Dynasty, 185; Ming Dynasty, 185
Chion, Michel, 117
Chopin, Frédéric, 56
Christie, Agatha, 165
Cicero, 26

Clark, Philip, 198; 'Composition's Finished?', 198; 'Jig Piano', 132; 'Thelonious Dreaming', 139
classical music, 3–4, 7, 35, 107, 124, 157, 164, 169, 170, 173, 176, 187, 193, 194, 202, 203, 205, 213. *See also:* Western art music
Coleman, Ornette, 207
Coltrane, John, 133, 145–6; *Ascension*, 145–6
Combarieu, Jules, 115
commodification (of art and music). *See:* autonomous art and music.
composition, 7, 13, 32, 34, 35, 42, 43, 60, 61, 62, 65, 98, 99, 101, 102, 104, 106, 107, 124, 135, 136, 137, 149, 150, 156, 159, 172, 181, 186, 191, 192–215, 216. *See also:* score, the; work-concept; Platonism, musical
conceptual holism. *See:* holism, conceptual
conceptual interdependence. *See:* holism, conceptual
Confucius, 26
Conrad, Joseph, 154, 165
Cooper, Grosvenor, 124–5, 141; *The Rhythmic Structure of Music*, 121. *See also:* Leonard B. Meyer
Corbusier, Le, 154
Couperin, Louis, 135
Coward, Noel, 215
Cubism, 186

Dack, John, 117
Dada, 63, 182
Dahlhaus, Carl, 34, 67, 69, 149
Damon of Athens, 26; ethos theory, 26
dance (especially music's origins in), 6–7, 13, 16, 25, 47, 52–3, 54,

55, 88, 95, 106, 111–12, 113, 119, 127, 140, 144–6, 169–70, 173, 183–84
Danto, Arthur, 2, 79
Darmstadt school, 159
Darwin, Charles, 84, 93, 166
Davies, Stephen, 47, 65, 115, 120, 192; *Musical Works and Performances*, 192
Davis, Miles: *Kind of Blue*, 197, 200
Debussy, Claude, 154, 155, 156; 'Prélude à l'apres-midi d'un faune', 154
'Deep in the Heart of Texas', 53
Dench, Chris, 152
Dewey, John, 121, 127, 150; *Art and Experience*, 128
Dhomont, Francis, 116
dialectics, 43, 75, 79, 112, 113, 114, 160, 163, 166, 168, 171, 174, 179–86, 193. *See also:* Theodor Adorno: *Negative Dialectics*
diffusion, sound, 99, 116
Dionysian (versus Apollonian), 78–80
Dittersdorf, Carl Ditters von, 200, 201, 203, 204
Downbeat, 201, 216
drum 'n' bass, 136, 151
Duchamp, Marcel, 137, 154
Dufay, Guillaume, 122, 133
Dunn, David, 44
Dvorak, Antonin: 'New World' Symphony, 183
Dylan, Bob, 107

Egan, Eric: 'Seed', 36
Eisler, Hanns, 177, 179
electronic music, 42, 43, 60, 95, 98, 99, 106, 112, 113, 116, 117, 124, 138, 174, 197. *See also:* musique concrète *and* sound synthesis

Eliot, T. S., 154, 157
elitism, 4, 63; Adorno's elitism, 159, 161–2, 163, 171–4.
Ellington, Duke, 200
emotion (expression of, in music/ ascription of, to music), 5, 6, 27, 67, 70, 73, 77–8, 80–2, 142, 145. *See also:* aesthetics of form and aesthetics of expression
Enlightenment, the, 17, 46, 47, 55, 66, 154, 167, 170
Epicureans, 28
equal temperament, 23
ethical conception of music, 26–7
ethics and aesthetics, relation of. *See:* separation of the value spheres (cognitive, ethical and aesthetic)
ethnomusicology, 46–8
Euclid, 24
Euripides, 12, 79
Eurocentrism, 5, 32, 182
Evans, Bill, 124, 199, 202, 203
Evans, Gil, 197, 200
evolutionary explanations of music, 83–4
expression, aesthetics of. *See:* aesthetics of form and aesthetics of expression
expression of emotion in music. *See:* emotion (expression of, in music)
eye music, 114. *See also:* Arnold Schoenberg: twelve-tone composition; serialism

fake book, 203
feeling, as content of music/music as language of feeling, 6, 69–70, 73, 75, 77–8, 80–2. *See also:* aesthetics of form and aesthetics of expression, emotion (expression of, in music)

Feldman, Morton, 60, 122, 129, 144, 151, 158
Ferneyhough, Brian, 152, 157
Fiat, 61
fine art, 3, 17–18, 29, 31, 46. *See also:* high art/culture; modern (Western) system of the (fine) arts
Finkelstein, Sidney, 213
Finnissy, Michael, 165
Fontana, Bill, 45
Forkel, Johann Nikolaus, 194
form. *See:* matter/material (as opposed to form)
formalism, 66, 70–2, 75, 78, 80–2, 85, 86–7, 88, 89, 94, 95, 112, 115, 147, 181, 184, 187. *See also:* matter/material (as opposed to form)
Foss, Lukas, 216
Frankfurt School of contemporary Marxist philosophy, 159, 166, 171, 173, 181. *See also:* Theodor Adorno; Institute for Social Research
free improvisation, 35, 135, 197, 207–15. *See also:* improvisation
free jazz, 108, 133, 145, 197, 200. *See also:* jazz
Freud, Sigmund, 166, 167
Frisius, Rudolf, 187
Fry, Roger, 88
Fubini, Enrico, 181
function, social, of music and art, 2, 55, 56, 182–5. *See also:* autonomous music/art
funk, 119, 138, 145
Furtwängler, Wilhelm, 212
Futurism/Futurist, 42, 155, 186

gagaku, 131, 135
gamelan, 4, 150
Gasset, Ortega y, 158

Gayle, Charles, 133
genius, concept of, 3, 71, 72, 76–7, 158–9, 162, 195
Gershwin, George, 195
Gillespie, Dizzy, 201
Gioia, Ted, 192, 193, 196
Glass, Philip, 149, 151
Goehr, Lydia, 193, 215
Goethe, Johann Wolfgang von, 18, 19, 79
Gould, Glenn, 113, 197, 199
graphic notation/score, 35, 36, 190
Greenberg, Clement, 89, 155, 187; *Avant-Garde and Kitsch*, 158; 'Problems of Art Criticism: Complaints of an Art Critic', 94
Gregorian chant, 122. *See also:* plainchant
Grocheo, Johannes de, 34
Gropius, Walter, 154
Group de Recherches Musicales (GRM), 61–2. *See also:* Pierre Schaeffer
Grove Dictionary of Music and Musicians, The New, 140

Habermas, Jürgen, 173
Halévy, Fromental, 92
Hanslick, Eduard, 4, 67, 72, 81–3, 84, 87, 88–9, 115, 120, 147, 149, 181; *Vom Musikalisch-Schonen*, 81
happenings, 44
harmonia, 16, 24, 27, 37. *See also:* modes (musical)
harmonics, 16, 20–3
harmony, 16, 23, 24–6, 61; inseparability of rhythm, harmony and melody, 124–7. *See also:* harmonia
Harry, Martyn; 134; 'Signal Failure', 134

Harvey, Jonathan, 109, 113, 117, 118, 124, 157
Hasty, Christopher, 121, 136–7; *Meter as Rhythm*, 121
Hawkins, Coleman: 'Wherever There's a Will, Baby', 200
Haydn, Joseph, 23, 66, 75, 107, 124, 194
hearing-in. *See:* twofoldness of musical experience.
Hegel, Georg Wilhelm Friedrich, 2, 66, 70, 72–5, 76, 82, 91, 159, 160, 161, 163, 165, 166, 179–80, 182, 187; Hegelian, 167; *Lectures on Fine Art*, 73; 'Positive Dialectics', 163, 190
Heine, Heinrich, 90
Hendrix, Jimi, 4, 5
Herder, Johann Gottfried von, 67
heteronomous music/art. *See:* autonomous music/art
high art/culture, 45–6, 157–8, 167–8, 173, 215; definition of, 45–6. *See also:* modern (Western) system of the (fine) arts
Hindemith, Paul, 157, 174, 175
Hindu Upanishads, 76
historicism, 73–4, 82, 161, 169–70
Hobsbawn, Eric, 85, 201, 202, 203; *The Jazz Scene*, 216
Hoffmann, E. T. A., 67, 90
Hölderlin, Friedrich, 18
Holiday, Billie, 107, 200, 215
holism, conceptual, (defined) 58–9; holism of art and the aesthetic, 5, 52; holism of dance, music and poetry, and rhythm, 119, 144; holism of rhythm, harmony, melody and music, 125, 127, 149; holism of rhythm, metre, stress and accent, 141; holism of tone and music, 58–9

Hollywood, 174
Homer: *Iliad*, 13; *Odyssey*, 13
Hooker, John Lee, 145; 'Stomp
 Boogie', 152
Horkheimer, Max, 171
Hughes, Langston, 85
humanistic conception of music,
 6–7, 32, 95–6, 111–16, 119–20,
 128, 136–7, 192–3. *See also:*
 abstract conception of music;
 mathematical conception of
 music
Hume, David, 2, 3
Husserl, Edmund, 121
Hutcheson, Francis, 2

Idealism, German, 66, 69, 190
Identity Thinking. *See:* dialectics
Ikeda, Ryoji, 44
Iliad, The, 13
Impressionism, 154
improvisation, 4, 5, 7, 8, 35, 106,
 107, 113, 115, 124, 135, 139, 173,
 181, 186, 189, 192–215, 216. *See
 also:* free improvisation
Indian classical music, 4, 149
installation (audio or audio-
 visual), 44
Institute for Social Research, 159.
 See also: Theodor Adorno;
 Frankfurt School of
 contemporary Marxist
 philosophy
instrumental puritanism, ideology
 of, 41–3, 45
Ives, Charles, 104, 154

James, William, 121
Janaway, Christopher, 29, 31
Jarrett, Keith, 213
Jarvis, Simon, 160
Jastrow, Joseph, 131
Jay, Martin, 178

jazz, 5, 30, 35, 39, 85, 104, 107, 125,
 136, 138, 139, 142, 145, 150, 157,
 173, 174, 188, 189, 193, 196, 197,
 200, 201, 204, 205, 213, 214, 215,
 216, 217. *See also:* free jazz
Johnson, Julian, 115
Jones, Elvin, 136
Josquin, Desprez, 122, 191
Jowett, Benjamin, 16
Joyce, James, 154, 157

Kafka, Franz, 154, 162, 163, 178;
 Metamorphosis, 161; *In the Penal
 Colony*, 161, 162
Kagel, Mauricio, 165
kalos/kalon, 13, 29, 38–9
Kandinsky, Wassily, 86, 87, 154,
 158; *Concerning the Spiritual In
 Art*, 94, 155
Kant, Immanuel, 1, 3, 5, 31, 65, 66,
 70, 71–2, 75, 76, 82, 158, 159,
 160–1, 162, 163, 166, 167, 169,
 187, 191; *The Critique of
 Judgment*, 66, 70, 73, 91; *The
 Critique of Pure Reason*, 159;
 Kantianism, 3, 7, 56, 73, 109;
 purposiveness without a
 purpose, 71, 73, 161, 169, 183
Kepler, Johannes, 34
Kierkegaard, Søren: 'Either/Or',
 92
kithara (Greek musical
 instrument), 12, 14, 30, 79
Koch, Heinrich, 90
Kocsis, Zoltán, 212
Kodak, 53
Konitz, Lee, 149, 202, 203, 206,
 207, 214, 216, 217
Kramer, Jonathan, 144
Krenek, Ernst, 163–4, 188; *Jonny
 Spielt Auf*, 188
Kristeller, Paul Oskar, 3, 17, 28,
 29

LaBelle, Brandon, 44
labour, physical, and music,
   connection of, 6, 119, 126, 144–5
Lachenmann, Helmut, 61, 111,
   118, 157, 187
Lacy, Steve, 5, 6, 205, 206, 211, 216
Lamb, Alan, 44
Landels, John G., 12
language above language thesis,
   67, 77
language-like character of music, 6,
   57, 70, 82, 83, 114–15, 165–6.
   See also: linguistic/rhetorical
   model of music
Larkin, Philip, 157
Ledbetter, David, 23, 191
Leitner, Bernhard, 44
Lieder, 68
Lessing, Gotthold Ephraim, 2, 16
Levinson, Jerrold, 52–3, 55, 56–7,
   58
Lévi-Straussian anthropology, 47
Lewis, George, 193, 212, 214
Ligeti, György, 42, 61, 131, 150,
   159, 164; 'Atmosphères', 61;
   'Clocks and Clouds', 61; Etudes,
   131; 'Lontano', 61; 'Requiem',
   61
linguistic/rhetorical models of
   music, 34, 67, 69, 84. See also:
   language-like character of music
Lipatti, Dinu, 212
Lippman, Edward, 23, 27, 49, 64,
   96–7, 117, 148
Liszt, Franz, 81, 105;
   Transcendental Studies, 105
Lloyd Webber, Andrew, 175
Lopez, Francisco, 44, 63, 65
Lucier, Alvin, 44
Lukács, György, 166, 167, 173
Lupu, Radu, 93

M, Sachiko, 122, 128, 148

Maconie, Robin, 46
Mahler, Gustav, 155, 156, 164,
   165; 5th Symphony, 140
Malevich, Kazimir, 156–7; 'From
   Cubism and Futurism to
   Suprematism', 186
Mallarmé, Stéphane, 154
Mantovani, (Annunzio Paolo), 173
Manuel and His Music of the
   Mountains (aka Geoff Love),
   173
Marx, Karl, 75, 159, 161, 163, 165,
   166–8, 190; Marxism, 69, 159,
   166, 167, 179, 181, 182, 188, 190
material, musical, 6–7, 31, 40–6,
   49, 53, 58, 60–2, 70, 82, 86, 87,
   88, 98–9, 100, 112, 163–65, 166,
   169–70, 204; historical nature of
   musical material, 6–7, 163–4,
   169–70
mathematical conception of music,
   11, 19–28, 32–4. See also:
   abstract conception of music/
   abstractness; humanistic
   conception of music
Matisse, Henri, 154
matter/material (as opposed to
   form), 49–50, 60–1, 87, 88–9,
   169–70. See also: formalism
Messiaen, Olivier, 124, 149
metaphorical perception of sounds
   as tones, 58, 64, 96–7, 107–8,
   111; movement in music as
   metaphorical rather than literal,
   83, 89, 142–8, 152
metaphysics of music, 2, 67–8,
   76–7, 79, 113, 120, 147. See also:
   Platonism, musical.
metre, 120–1, 128–9, 130–7, 142
Meyer, Leonard B., 124–5, 141;
   The Rhythmic Structure of
   Music, 121. See also: Grosvenor
   Cooper

Meyerbeer, Giacomo, 78, 92
Michelangelo, 185
Migone, Christof, 44
mimesis (imitation), 17–18, 165
minimalism, 42, 137, 149, 151
modern (Western) system of the
    (fine) arts, 3, 13, 16, 31, 46, *See
    also:* fine art; high art/culture;
    Kristeller
modernism/modernist, 4, 7, 40, 41,
    43, 49, 57, 62, 69, 74, 85, 86, 89,
    91, 97, 114, 148, 153–86, 187,
    189, 195, 203, 204, 205. *See also:*
    postmodernism/postmodernist
modes (musical), 16–17, 26, 27, 34.
    See also: harmonia
Monk, Thelonious, 124, 139, 211;
    'Misterioso', 211
Monteverdi, Claudio, 70, 84, 191
Moore, Michael: *Fahrenheit 9/11*,
    178
Morton, Jelly Roll, 216
Mothersill, Mary, 87
Mousikē, 11–18, 26, 28, 30
movement, 127–9; movement as
    fundamental conceptualisation
    of music, 141–8. *See also:*
    metaphorical perception
Mozart, Wolfgang Amadeus, 23,
    48, 52, 56, 66, 75, 164, 172, 185,
    194; *Don Giovanni*, 92, 113;
    Symphony no. 40, 147, 172;
    'Turkish Rondo', 164
Mueller, Ian, 24
'Music While You Work',
    53
music/harmony of the spheres, 16,
    19, 24–6, 34
musique concrète, 42–4, 61–2, 63,
    95, 98–100, 101–2, 103, 109, 112,
    116, 118. *See also:* electronic
    music; sound synthesis
muzak, 46, 48, 52, 53–5, 56, 119;

Muzak Corporation, 55. *See
    also:* Pavlovian

Nettl, Bruno, 47, 48, 56
Neuhaus, Max, 44, 65
New Age, 54
Newman, Barnett, 157
Newton, Isaac, 32
Nicomachus of Gerasa, 20, 33;
    Manual of Harmonics, 20
Niemetschek, Franz Xaver, 194
Nietzsche, Friedrich, 18, 66, 70,
    78–80, 81, 82, 86, 160, 180; the
    Apollonian and the Dionysian,
    37, 78–80; *The Birth of Tragedy
    Out of the Spirit of Music*, 18,
    78–80; *Human, All Too Human*,
    80; 'On Music and Words', 92;
    The Wagner Case, 80; birth-of-
    tragedy thesis, 79–80
noise, 41–4, 45, 46, 47, 48–9, 60–1,
    67, 95, 101, 104, 109, 128, 150
Noland, Kenneth, 157
Nono, Luigi, 157
notation (musical), 12, 13, 35, 36,
    96, 98, 99, 122, 123, 130–1, 133,
    136, 139, 148, 150, 151, 193, 195,
    200
Nussbaum, Martha, 29, 30

Odyssey, The, 13
ontology of music. *See:* score, the;
    work-concept; metaphysics of
    music

Packard, Vance, 54
Paddison, Max, 68, 69, 76, 78, 85,
    90, 158, 159, 160, 172, 176, 187,
    215
Paganini, Nicolo: *Caprices*, 105
painting, experience of compared
    to that of music, 110–11, 120;
    painting as autonomous art, 185

Palestrina, Giovanni Pierluigi da, 122, 124; *Missa Papae Marcelli*, 148
Palombini, Carlos, 64
Parker, Charlie, 4, 152, 157, 200, 207, 214, 216
Parker, Evan, 214; 'De Motu', 214, 217
Parmegiani, Bernard, 62
Parmenides, 20
Partch, Harry, 23
Pater, Walter, 87, 88
Pavlovian, 54. *See also:* muzak
Penderecki, Krzysztof, 164
performance, music as an art of, 106, 113–14, 192–9. *See also:* Platonism, musical
performance art, 44
Peterson, Oscar, 203
phenomenology, 121
Philodemus, 28
Picasso, Pablo, 154, 157
plainchant, 122, 129, 133, 135, 148, 150. *See also:* Gregorian chant
Plato, 2, 3, 11, 16, 17, 18, 19, 20, 23, 24, 25, 26, 27, 29–31, 33, 34, 37, 76, 127–8; *Gorgias*, 18; *Ion*, 18; *The Laws*, 26, 127; Platonism, 18, 19, 20, 24, 27, 32, 113, 129, 137, 143, 193; Platonism, musical, 7, 19, 24, 25–6, 30, 32, 34, 37, 76, 113, 127, 128, 129, 137, 141–2, 143, 192, 199; *The Republic*, 16, 25, 26, 30, 37; *Timaeus*, 25, 39; world-soul, 25
poetry, 3, 12, 13, 16, 17, 18, 24, 29–30, 31, 37, 41, 45, 57, 63, 74, 75, 80, 81, 119, 126, 144, 148, 156, 177; conceptual holism of dance, music and poetry, and rhythm, 119, 144. *See also:* birth-of-tragedy thesis (that music originates in a union with poetry)
Pole, David, 9
political art, Adorno's critique of, 177–9, 188. *See also:* truth in art/truth-content
Pollock, Jackson, 157
pop, 54, 119, 131, 150
Pop Idol, 173, 174
popular music/culture, 4, 13, 30, 53, 68, 78, 157–8, 171–5
postmodernism/postmodernist, 57, 134, 154, 157, 164. *See also:* modernism/modernist
Poulenc, Francis, 157
Pound, Ezra, 154, 157
Powell, Bud, 125
Praetorius, 34
Presley, Elvis Aaron, 30
programme music, 67–8, 69
Proust, Marcel, 154
Ptolemy, 24, 28
pulse, definition/concept of, 135–8, 149
punk, 30
Pythagoras, 19, 20, 33, 38, 98–100; *akousmatikoi*, 99–100; Pythagorean and Pythagoreans, 20–1, 23–4, 25, 26, 27, 28, 32, 99, 100, 101, 113, 119

qin music, 135

Radigue, Eliane, 122, 148
rap, 136
Raphael, 185
rationalism/rationalist, 11, 24–5, 28, 160
Ravel, Maurice: 'Bolero', 136
Read, Herbert, 155
recording, 40, 41–2, 98–100, 102, 105, 106, 116–17, 197–9, 200, 203, 213

'reduced listening'. *See:* acousmatic(s)

Reich, Steve, 149, 151

Rembrandt, 185

rhythm, 2, 16, 24–5, 26, 28, 35, 49, 57–8, 61, 83, 97, 102, 103, 113, 115–16, 119–52, 173, 211; divisive versus additive rhythm, definition of, 149

Rice, Daryl, 16

Richard, Cliff, 4

Richter, Jean Paul, 67

Riemann, Karl Wilhelm Julius Hugo, 124

Rihm, Wolfgang, 165, 187

Riley, Terry, 23, 149

Rimbaud, Arthur, 154

Roach, Max, 136

Robinson, Orphy, 198

Rochberg, George, 165

rock music, 42, 119, 150, 174

Rohe, Mies van der, 154

Rollins, Sonny, 201

Romanticism, 3, 69, 79; Romantic metaphysics of music, 67–8, 76–7; Hegel on Romantic art, 74–5

Rosen, Charles, 107; *The Classical Style*, 194

Rosenfeld, Marina, 60

Rossini, Gioachino Antonio, 78, 92, 175

Rothko, Mark, 158

rubato, definition of, 135

Russolo, Luigi, 42; *The Art of Noises*, 42

Saariaho, Kaija, 165

Sachs, Curt, 136, 150–1

Samartzis, Philip, 62, 63

Satie, Erik, 154

Schaeffer, Pierre, 42–3, 62–3, 95, 98, 100, 101–2, 103, 105, 109, 116–17. *See also:* Group de recherches musicale

Schafer, R. Murray, 44, 47

Schaper, Eva, 18

Schenker, Heinrich, 67

Schiller, (Johann Christoph) Friedrich von, 18

Schlegel, Friedrich von, 2, 160; *Kritische Fragmente*, 9

Schoenberg, Arnold, 64, 85, 86, 93, 113–14, 149, 154, 155, 156, 157, 159, 174, 175–6, 186, 194–6, 197, 212, 215; Chamber Symphony, 93; twelve-tone composition, 149, 156, 175 (*See also:* eye music; serialism); 'Erwartung', 175; *Verklaerte Nacht*, 93. *See also:* Second Viennese School

Schopenhauer, Arthur, 66, 70, 76–8, 80, 81, 82, 120; *The World as Will and Representation*, 76

Schuller, Gunther: 'The Future of Form in Jazz', 217

Schumann, Robert, 81, 87

Schwitters, Kurt, 63; *Ursonate*, 47

score, the, 7, 35, 36, 98, 113–14, 152, 193, 196, 198, 204–5, 212; work-concept, 35, 192–3, 205, 214. *See also:* aesthetics of perfection; composition; Platonism, musical;

Scruton, Roger, 2, 7, 45, 57, 58, 59, 69, 84, 89, 95, 96, 97, 98, 101–2, 109, 110, 111, 116, 117, 121, 135, 141, 142, 144, 152, 193, 213–14; *The Aesthetics of Music*, 7, 45, 96, 103, 193

'seeing-in'. *See:* twofoldness of musical experience; Wollheim

Second Viennese School, 159. *See also:* Alban Berg; Arnold Schoenberg; Anton Webern

separation of the value spheres

(cognitive, ethical and aesthetic), 18, 29–32, 56, 86, 89, 183
serialism, 42, 76, 114, 164, 175–6. *See:* eye music; Arnold Schoenberg: twelve-tone composition
Shaftesbury, Earl of, 2
shakuhachi music, 135, 151
Sharpe, R. A., 69
Shiner, Larry, 15, 29
Shostakovich, Dmitri, 164
Silver, Abner: *How To Write and Sell a Song Hit*, 172. *See also:* Robert Bruce
Simpson, Robert, 164
Skvorecky, Josef, 93; *The Bass Saxophone*, 85
Smalley, Denis, 42, 118
Smith, Leo, 207
Socialist Realist art, 184
Society for Private Musical Performances, 175
Socrates, 18, 19, 25, 26, 79
Solesmes, 122, 148
Sophocles, 12
sound-art, 7, 40–6, 57, 58, 59–62, 102, 103, 120, 122, 128, 144
sound-design, 53–4, 61
sound synthesis, 99. *See also:* electronic music; musique concrète
spectralism, 42
spheres, music of the. *See:* music of the spheres
Spice Girls, The, 173
Spitzer, Michael, 84
Squier, George Owen, 53
Stendhal: *Life of Rossini*, 175
Stitt, Sonny, 201
Stockhausen, Karlheinz, 42, 43, 60, 99, 99, 112, 124, 143, 157, 159, 204; *Carré*, 104; *Gesang der*

Jünglinge, 99; *Gruppen*, 104; *Hymnen*, 99
Stoics, 28
Strauss, Richard, 155, 156
Stravinsky, Igor, 120, 133, 149, 154, 156, 157, 159, 164, 175, 186; *The Rite of Spring*, 133; 'Three Pieces for String Quartet', 155
Subotnik, Rose Rosengard, 189, 196
Surrealism, 134, 164, 182
syncopation, definition of, 138–9
Szlavnics, Chiyoko, 42

Tafelmusik, 54, 65, 168
Tallis Scholars, The, 148
tango, 138
techne, 11–18
techno, 54
tempo, as related to rhythm, 142, 146–7
Tenney, James, 148; 'Koan', 124
Thales, 19
Theophrastus, 27
Thibaudet, Jean-Yves, 202
thinking in/with sound, music regarded as, 6, 115
Thomson, William E., 109
timbre, 16, 42, 64, 103–4, 111, 114, 117
Tiedemann, Rolf, 187
Tilbury, John, 151
Tinctoris, Johannes, 34
Tin Pan Alley, 214
Tippett, Michael, 149, 165
Titian, 185
tonality/tonal system, 22, 23, 27, 34, 38, 40, 41, 42, 45, 46, 48, 49, 52, 53, 59, 60, 61, 64, 82, 88, 96, 97, 98, 101, 103–4, 110, 115, 120, 124, 126, 133, 137–8, 147, 149, 156, 164, 175, 176, 202
tone (as opposed to non-musical

sound or noise), 25, 27, 34, 40, 42, 45, 48–50, 57–61, 64, 96–7, 98, 109; 'art of tones', music as an, 45, 57–8, 67, 95. *See also:* aesthetic conception of music; acousmatic(s); noise
Toop, David, 44
Tristano, Lennie, 125
truth in art/truth-content of art, 31, 73, 165–6, 170–1, 175–6. *See also:* political art
tuning, 16, 21, 23, 25, 30, 32, 104
Turnage, Mark-Anthony, 196
twofoldness of musical experience, 58, 62, 98, 108–11

universalism about music as an art of sound (music as the universal art of sound), 44–6, 59–60
'useless work', the aesthetic regarded as involving, 52

Valéry, Paul, 154
value spheres, separation of the. *See:* separation of the value spheres
Varèse, Edgard, 41, 42, 61, 105, 154, 155
Verve, 201
Vivaldi, Antonio, 55, 172; 'The Four Seasons', 172

Wagner, Richard, 67, 68, 76–8, 79, 80, 81, 86, 92, 154–5, 156, 157, 165; *The Flying Dutchman*, 76; *Parsifal*, 80; the *Ring* cycle, 78; *Tristan und Isolde*, 78, 140; music-drama, 78
Warner, Keith, 188
Waterfield, Robin, 16
Waters, Muddy: 'Hoochie Coochie Man', 145

Webber, Andrew Lloyd, 189
Webern, Anton, 135, 149, 187; Quartet op. 22, 122, 133, 150, 158, 159. *See also:* Second Viennese School
Weill, Kurt, 164
Westerkamp, Hildegard, 44
Western art music, 2, 3, 4, 5, 40, 41, 63, 66, 67, 108, 114, 119, 121, 133, 135, 159, 186, 192, 194, 196, 204, 215. *See also:* classical music
Whitmer, T. C.: *The Art of Improvisation*, 202
Wilde, Oscar, 86, 87, 88; *The Portrait of Dorian Gray*, 87
Williams, Vaughan, 164
Windsor, Luke, 102, 109–10
Wiora, Walter, 60
Wishart, Trevor, 117
Wittgenstein, Ludwig, 121, 131
Woideck, Carl, 207
Wolff, Christian, 115, 178–9
Wölfflin, Heinrich, 74
Wollheim, Richard, 2, 98, 110
work-concept. *See:* score, the
Wright, Frank Lloyd, 154

Xenakis, Iannis, 42, 44, 61

Yeats, William Butler, 154
Young, La Monte, 44, 137; 'X for Henry Flynt', 137–8, 178
Young, Lester, 125, 214, 215

Zangwill, Nick, 88
Zappa, Frank, 189
Zarlino, Gioseffo, 34
Zuckerkandl, Victor, 96, 120, 126, 151; *The External World*, 149